The first edition of witty, entertaining and memorable correspondence to *The Times* was greeted with great critical enthusiasm and went on to become a best-seller. Now Kenneth Gregory has brought up-to-date his selection of the most witty, amusing and memorable letters to *The Times* since 1900. Among the 'top people' whose eloquence fills these pages figure a host of writers, artists, sportsmen, statesmen and public personalities. There is Conan Doyle on a military invention, Neville Chamberlain on the grey wagtail, Winston Churchill on corporal punishment, Bernard Berenson on art forgeries, H. G. Wells on strike-breaking, T. S. Eliot and Malcolm Muggeridge on television, Vita Sackville-West on stamps as wallpaper, Field-Marshal Montgomery on skiing.

Among the letters he has chosen from the past five years are ones on toads, tea-boys, triremes, gnomes, postage stamps, British Rail, chamber-pots, knitting, foreigners and trade unions – from correspondents as diverse as Kenneth Clark, Beverley Nichols, Professor Hayek and Graham Greene – and of course more about the sighting of the first cuckoo in Spring.

THE FIRST
CUCKOO

Kenneth Gregory has contributed to *The Times*, *Guardian*, *Spectator* and many other publications. He claims to have helped educate some younger readers, his leading article in *The Times Everest Supplement* of May 1953 being included (along with extracts from Macaulay, Dickens, Boswell and Defoe) in the précis chapter of S. H. Burton's *A Comprehensive English Course*. *In Celebration of Cricket*, published in 1978, which he compiled and introduced, was described by Wisden as 'a classic'.

THE FIRST CUCKOO

A selection of the most witty, amusing and memorable letters to

THE TIMES

1900-1980

Chosen and introduced

by

KENNETH GREGORY

London
UNWIN PAPERBACKS
Boston   Sydney

in association with
TIMES BOOKS

First published in Great Britain by George Allen & Unwin
and Times Books 1976
Reprinted 1976, 1977, 1978, 1980
Second edition 1981

First published in Unwin Paperbacks 1978
Reprinted four times
Second edition 1983

UNWIN® PAPERBACKS
40 Museum Street, London WC1A 1LU

ISBN 0 04 808040 3

Set in 10 on 11 point Times by Grove Graphics, Tring
Printed and bound in the Channel Islands
by the Guernsey Press Co. Ltd.

ACKNOWLEDGEMENTS

The editor and publishers wish to thank all those who have so readily given permission for inclusion of the letters which appear in this volume. Among the many writers, literary agents and executors to whom thanks are owed, special mention should be made of Lady Beecham and Mrs T. S. Eliot for permission to reproduce their late husbands' letters; Mrs M. L. S. Bennett for the letter by H. A. L. Fisher; the present Lord Brabazon and the late Lord Buckmaster for letters by their late fathers; Mr Winston Churchill, MP, for the letter by Sir Winston Churchill; Mrs Dorothy Lloyd for the letter by Neville Chamberlain; Professor O. L. Zangwill for the letter by Israel Zangwill; Mr Nigel Nicolson for the letter by Vita Sackville-West; the Marquess of Salisbury for the letter by Lord Hugh Cecil (Lord Quickswood); Mr Raglan Squire for the letter by Sir John Squire; Mr Mark Bonham Carter for the letter by Lady Oxford; Mr Frank Magro for the letter by Sir Osbert Sitwell; Baron Cecil Anrep and the Agenzia Letteraria Internazionale for the letter by Bernhard Berenson; Baskerville Investments Ltd for the letter by Conan Doyle; Robson, McLean & Paterson, W. S., for the letter by Professor J. Dover Wilson; the Royal Society of Literature and Mr H. V. Stopes-Rowe for the letter by Marie Stopes; the National Westminster Bank for the letter by Sir Carleton Allen, QC; the trustees of the estate of Miss E. A. Dugdale for the letter by Thomas Hardy; the Society of Authors for letters by Galsworthy, Masefield and Shaw, as representatives of their literary estates; Curtis Brown for the letter by A. A. Milne; William Heinemann Ltd for the letter by Max Beerbohm; David Higham Associates for letters by Lord David Cecil, Captain B. H. Liddell Hart, Laurence Meynell and Malcolm Muggeridge; A. P. Watt & Son for letters by Robert Graves, A. P. Herbert, Field-Marshal Montgomery, Dame Margery Perham, H. G. Wells and P. G. Wodehouse.

Kenneth Gregory would also personally like to thank all those who have helped him during the course of his researches, including Mary S. Hodgson, Written Archives Officer, BBC;

R. C. Kenedy, Assistant Keeper of the Library, Victoria and Albert Museum; David Menhennet, Librarian, House of Commons; Gordon Phillips, Archivist of *The Times*; Geoffrey Langley, Avon County Reference Librarian; Dorking Public Library; the Foreign and Commonwealth Office; the International Wine and Food Society; Mr Silvino Trompetto Director of Food Services at the Savoy Hotel; the Ministry of Defence; the Musée du Louvre; and *Punch*.

Every effort has been made to trace the writers of the letters or their heirs and executors, including the publication of an appeal for current addresses in *The Times Literary Supplement*. Inevitably, we have not always met with success in tracking down the writers of letters in some cases published as many as seventy-five years ago. To those whom it has proved impossible to trace we would offer our sincerest apologies and express the earnest hope that they will find pleasure in the reproduction of their letters in these pages.

FOREWORD

by Bernard Levin

The first letter I ever wrote to *The Times* concerned the General Election of 1945, during which I was a schoolboy of marked left-wing sympathies. A rash of correspondence had broken out in the paper, doubtless started by a member of the Athenaeum with nothing better to do, offering Greek and Latin words and phrases that seemed to be comments on the political goings-on. Thus, someone found, say, a Greek word which sounded like 'Attlee' and meant, as it might be, 'to squeak like a mouse', whereupon someone else would find a Latin tag that looked like 'Churchill' and meant 'brave as a lion'. And so on.

Ho ho. But they had reckoned without Levin, the Zinoviev of the Upper Fifth. I sat down with a huge pile of dictionaries and lexicons and devilled away until I was rewarded by finding, in an immense German tome, a verb, 'Bracken', meaning 'to sort out refuse'. I could hardly believe my luck, and sent off my discovery, for favour of publication, to the Editor of *The Times*. Believe it or not, he didn't print it. Indeed, he never even acknowledged it. (He was Barrington-Ward, and if there is any justice in Heaven it must be drinks on him, in some celestial Printing House Square, every time the Heavenly Edition arrives with yet another couple of acres of my views embedded in it.)

My next attempt to get into those august columns was made a couple of years later, when I was a freshman undergraduate. There had been reports of a stormy Atlantic crossing by the *Queen Mary*, which had been badly delayed; our old friend A. Spokesman, on behalf of Cunard, had explained that the time would be made up by speeding up the process of 'turning the ship round'. This time they had reckoned without Levin the George Robey of the LSE. I wrote to *The Times* offering a permanent solution to this problem; provided Cunard did not mind their ship going backwards across the Atlantic, it would never be necessary to turn it round at all. True, I said,

9

the captain would not be able to see where he was going, but as some compensation for his loss, he would at any rate be able to take a last look at his native land, on each voyage, without being put to the trouble of turning his head.

They didn't print that one, either.

It was many years before I was prepared to bother with such a newspaper again. Apart from anything else, I won ten shillings, shortly after my second rebuff, in a *New Statesman* competition, and although my name was misspelt in the announcement of this epoch-making award, I felt that I had a foot in the door somewhere where they knew quality when they saw it. Moreover, I thought, perhaps I was not destined to contribute to the unpaid section of newspapers; that ten shillings certainly suggested that I might have a future in the more liberally rewarded columns. The rest you know.

Is there any difference between the impulse that drives a man to write letters to the newspapers and that which impels his neighbour to write for a living? I rather think not; we are all, gentlemen and players alike, engaged in the business (a very curious business indeed, when you come to think of it) of expressing our views to thousands, or even millions, of people who have not invited us to do so. 'No man but a blockhead ever wrote, except for money,' said Dr Johnson, but he was only half right; the ones who do it for money are blockheads, too. They have more gall than the others, of course, expecting strangers not only to read their opinions but to pay for doing so; the others are less self-assured, a huge proportion of letters submitted for publication containing some kind of (generally self-fulfilling) prophecy that it will be rejected ('the Editor regrets' is probably the greatest white lie in history), much as writers of fan letters almost invariably begin 'this is the first time I have ever written a fan letter'.

Mind you, if a man is going to write for nothing, there is no doubt that he would rather do so in *The Times* than anywhere else. Do letter-writers, I wonder, work their way up from the *Daily Thing* to the *Morning Whatsit*, and thence to the *Sunday Hoopla*, arriving finally, after years of striving, at *The Times*? There was an ancient *Punch* cartoon which showed a red-faced Englishman leaving a French hotel having had (as the caption explained at some length) a difference, regarding the bill, with the proprietor. 'Oui!' he was shouting, waving his English fist; 'cette fois je paye! Mais juste vous marquez mes mots, et juste vous regardez ici! Quand je retourne à England, je metterai ça dans le *Times*!' Somehow it would not have

10

sounded equally impressive if he had ended 'le *Brecon and Radnorshire Gazette*', or even 'le *News of the World*'.

Writers of round robins ('We, the undersigned, each in his or her personal capacity . . .') also choose *The Times* for preference, the second elevens being accommodated elsewhere. I am not sure what effect these multiple letters have, though close students of such matters can always tell whether it is a hopeless, and indeed ruinous, cause; there are two or three names which infallibly signal the fact that the enterprise commended is a waste of time, or the scandal they seek to expose already beyond human intervention. On the whole, the shorter the more telling; one of the most famous said only 'Are toastmasters really necessary?', and the ensuing correspondence went on for months; indeed, my own most striking contribution to the letters columns contained only twenty-one words, which were 'I have just got a crossed line on which I heard a man getting a wrong number; is this a record?'

There are no cuckoos, first or otherwise, where I live, so I can never hope to record the arrival of the creatures in the spring; in any case, it would now be felt, not without some justice, that for a man who occupies as much of the opposite page as I do to seep also into the letters would be over-egging the pudding a bit. Besides, I get in there anyway on the coat-tails of those who denounce me, by name, as a villain. These are not few, though I have never been able to tell in advance which are the subjects, or opinions, which will provoke uproar, and am still taken by surprise whenever the avalanche starts. As any journalist will tell you, bitterly, there is a fundamental distinction between letters written directly to him and those sent, for publication, to the Editor; the former are the ones which say what a splendid and gifted fellow he is, the latter those which ask wearily what on earth the paper imagines is the point of publishing such stuff. (I once, when I was writing for the *Mail*, got one, on my own behalf, beginning 'I must insist that you cease immediately to write the rubbish which appears under your name in my daily paper', and was about to throw it into the waste-paper basket when I thought I had better turn it over to make quite sure that it was not signed 'Rothermere'.) Apart from assaults on the Gas Board or television announcers' English, almost everything I write seems to provoke more disagreement than applause, but this (I like to think) is only because it is those who disagree who are moved to put pen to paper.

A correspondent suggested to me once that I should found a

magazine that would contain nothing but letters from readers, who could then ride hobby-horses and argue with one another without anybody interfering. If it comes to that, I once had a correspondent who said that he had the answer to all the world's problems, adding that in case I was inclined to doubt him, he wished to point out that he got his information direct from Hitler, to whom he spoke each night, before going to bed, on the telephone. But once I start on the lunatics who write letters to *The Times*, I shall never finish. (He wrote in green ink, another infallible sign.) Incidentally, I cannot remember how the toastmasters controversy ended: *are* they really necessary? I am sure the correspondence-columns of *The Times* are.

PREFACE

by Geoffrey Woolley
Letters Editor of *The Times*, 1953–1980

Those who have over the years been concerned in Printing House Square – and now in New Printing House Square – with the selection for publication of Letters to the Editor are always impressed by the courage of those who suggest anthologies drawn from the correspondence columns. Anyone embarking on such a task will, it is true, be concerned with only a fraction of the mountain of material dealt with by editors and their advisers and will also be free of those nightly pressures of timing, libel, space and make up.

But there are still daunting thousands to choose from, and tempting by-ways one has to avoid if the selection is not to become ill-balanced. There could indeed be separate anthologies for innumerable topics – sport, food, music, wild life, politics, conservation, church affairs, wars. But Kenneth Gregory has wisely made a selection varied enough to hold the interest of as many readers as possible – an aim always before those concerned with the preparation of each day's selection.

Also by limiting his period of choice to letters printed this century, he has been able to count on a wide measure of knowledge and understanding from generations personally involved in the great events and light-hearted moments with which they are concerned.

And to those of us who first saw so many of these letters in manuscript form, sometimes many years ago, it is heartening to see them now being given a new and more enduring prominence by Mr Gregory.

CONTENTS

INTRODUCTION

by Kenneth Gregory

Could not this outrage be averted? There sprang from my lips that fiery formula which has sprung from the lips of so many choleric old gentlemen in the course of the past hundred years and more: 'I shall write to *The Times*.' – Max Beerbohm, *A Letter That Was Not Written*, 1914

A myth may delight, and some of its perpetrators be especially dear to us, but that is no reason for accepting it. Only a few, however select, readers of *The Times* sit behind curtains and emphatic moustaches in Pall Mall. Indeed, of outrage-averting letters in this collection, scarcely more than a handful come from choleric old gentlemen of either sex. The formula inspiring most correspondents is not so much fiery as matter-of-fact, impish, or basely cynical. It jogs the courage, reminds a reader of his position as a former prime minister or active trade unionist, and compels him to reach for his pen. So moved, he proclaims what he holds to be self-evident truths. He rebukes sartorial unorthodoxy, admonishes heresies, ridicules pomposity and, as is the prerogative of P. G. Wodehouse, supplies esoteric intelligence concerning an heroic ancestor of Bertie Wooster. Sometimes when his memory is touched, he will pay tribute to a long forgotten figure like Gynes of Magdalen, sometimes he will release a theory explaining the universe. Meanwhile the elderly may muse, the diffident confide, the less diffident trumpet well-ordered visions. The letters which follow, bulletins on the temper of civilization, have all passed scrutiny in Printing House Square. It is to the credit of the resident deity that he encourages the sublimities of wits even when they are directed at himself.

There are further myths associated with a letter to *The Times*. One holds that not only is the subject important, and the writer's name and address equally so, but that all three must unite in majesty to ensure a letter's publication. In isolation, says myth, there will be a hint of incompleteness, perhaps a lack of gravitas. This is why a former postmaster-general, writing at inordinate length on bee-keeping in Tiverton, will be contacted by phone and politely asked to suggest cuts, why an unknown (missing from *Debrett* or *Who's Who*) correspondent in Tiverton who argues cogently for a revised monetary system must be content with 'The Editor has read your letter with interest'. But a perfect letter, and brevity adds to its impact, fulfils all the conditions imposed by myth. In spacious pre-war days, when the theme of the top letter was introduced first by the orchestra, and then in turn by brass and wind, it would have appeared thus:

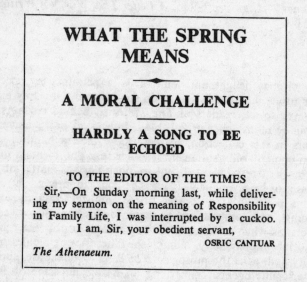

WHAT THE SPRING MEANS

—◆—

A MORAL CHALLENGE

HARDLY A SONG TO BE ECHOED

TO THE EDITOR OF THE TIMES

Sir,—On Sunday morning last, while delivering my sermon on the meaning of Responsibility in Family Life, I was interrupted by a cuckoo.

I am, Sir, your obedient servant,

OSRIC CANTUAR

The Athenaeum.

Anything resembling this, and the signature of a suffragan bishop would have sufficed, has proved untraceable. As compensation there are two myth-appeasing letters from a Fellow of the Royal Society and one from a senior member of the University of Oxford. They range over almost half a century yet deal with but a single cuckoo.

Ultimate myth identifies letters to *The Times* with that amorphous body, the Establishment. Ultimate myth is here destroyed. This book contains nothing from any Archbishop of Canterbury, Lord Chief Justice, Governor of the Bank of

England, Warden of All Souls, or Director-General of the BBC – and research has ruled out the possibility of an editor of *The Times* writing to himself disguised as a dowager duchess or as T. Kenelm Fortesque. But if the Establishment suffers a grievous blow, top people are revealed in all their glory. For those not conversant with the term, it was used in an advertising campaign during the mid–1950s: 'Top People Take The Times'. While it may now reflect a state of mind (a tory of mean intelligence has no objection to being called a top person, a socialist of outstanding intellect often has), in the context of this book it refers to a state of being. Top people are those who have achieved success and fame in their chosen occupations; they may reject everything written in *The Times* but they continue to read it. Of course the accolade is not conferred on a top person until he has submitted a letter found worthy of inclusion. Members of Parliament are here represented, though in decent proportion to their numbers, eminences already or soon to become members of the Order of Merit descend momentarily to earthly level. The actress and the architect, athlete and admiral of the fleet, connoisseur and field-marshal, mathematician and novelist, poet and scientist, all find surprised solace in one another's company. The nation's rogue elephants rampage, shattering complacency and compelling many to an agonizing reappraisal. Housewives, commuters, civil servants and parsons, hitherto unknown to the public at large, complete our assembly, delighted or resigned at having become top people. Should any feel there is nothing left to live for, they can follow the example of Bernard Shaw (and his letters to *The Times* spanned fifty-two years) who not only ranked as a very top person but who also formed an Establishment of one.

It must here be admitted that members of the Establishment are excluded not for their shortcomings as correspondents but on account of the book's scope. The great crises of the century are only occasionally touched on; had it been otherwise, high seriousness must have driven out wit and invective, innocence and nostalgia. 'Human kind cannot bear very much reality', wrote T. S. Eliot. Reminders of reality cannot but chasten the reader who, after all, may refer to history books for details of our unlovely century. What he will notice is the sometimes harsh intrusion of death into a seemingly never-land of absurdity and gay enlightenment. For the most part, however, this is a world which proves, in the words of a swain on St Valentine's Day 1975, that although some 'say *The Times* is snooty, you can see it's really quite cutey'. Such sentiments may be expressed by members of the Establishment when communicating with deans, recorders and favourite nieces, but not in their public pronouncements. However, if the reader believes he will encounter nothing in these pages to disturb his equanimity, he is greatly mistaken. Consider the man who dips as a prelude to sleep. If he is subject to stress of any kind, *The First Cuckoo* will surely lead to a restless night. True he may follow Mr Carter's advice and ensure his physical snugness, even if the next day erupts in marital discord, but mentally he who dips may be a ruin by midnight. Consider the reaction of a committed progressive who opens at an account of 'Socialist Jargon'. Will he subdue his rage, flick to the letter containing strictures upon the pre-nationalization South-Eastern Railway, and be restored? It is doubtful. Pity, too, the man who insists that all gyrations of the human body, most of all those conducted in high society, are inherently sinful, only to find himself reading 'Dancing and Manners'. In fact this book is a minefield for the casual reader. Should he survive the shock to his aesthetic sensibilities, he may succumb to a brutal unveiling of his ignorance. Perhaps a wrangler who thinks easily in octals, an orientalist proficient in the tongues of India, he may know the origins of the word 'googly', and have a ready explanation of luminous owls. But can he say offhand the size of *l'ancienne 'toise' de France*?

The more methodical and wary reader will choose to open at the beginning of the century when, incidentally, *The Times* was already more than 36,000 issues old. There is nothing in Conan Doyle's letter to turn him choleric unless he was on the War Office staff in 1900. But methodical reader has first to project himself backwards into a 'dear, delicate un-panic-stricken world'. This will not be easy. If he is young, he may suspect he is in the Middle Ages; even his elders, who not only handled sovereigns but were taught to calculate the value of farthings, may feel their heads whirling. (As a concession to both, the references to prices which follow have been converted into our own prosaic pence.) In 1900 *The Times* did not receive, or did not print, any letter suggesting our democratic institutions were in danger. A Cecil, the last prime minister to sit in the House of Lords, presided over the destinies of Britain and her Empire, and he was to be fortified at the 'khaki' election later in the year by a Unionist majority of 134. The Commons enjoyed the assorted talents of Balfour, Campbell-Bannerman and Asquith, and the young Lloyd George made a frequent nuisance of himself. Gladstone had been dead only eighteen months, Alfred Austin was not dead but poet laureate. If Cambridge had recently lost Rutherford to McGill University, Oxford welcomed as professor of music our most revered composer, Parry, whose personal profundities persuaded him that Mozart was superficial. Hardy had ceased to write novels, it was the age of *Stalky* and of *Love and Mr Lewisham*; Henry James had entered his last period. The world of fashionable art luxuriated in the *Pêche Melba* of Sargent ('the artist who exalted this dish to the rank of an ideal', later wrote Sir Osbert Sitwell) and the implied twelve-course dinners of Fildes. Far removed from *pêche* and kitchen was the theatrical sensation of 1900, Stephen Phillips's *Herod*:

> I dreamed last night of a dome of beaten gold
> To be a counter-glory to the Sun.
> There shall the eagle blindly dash himself,
> There the first beam shall strike, and there the moon
> Shall aim all night her argent archery.

Before long some critics were likening Phillips to Shakespeare, the more cautious to Milton or Racine.

It was an age of amateurism, Buller our most popular general. Members of Parliament, who recessed from August till February, were not paid, and neither were old age pensions. One and a half million women were engaged in domestic service, a good plain cook could earn £25 a year – less, or more, if she chanced to be bad and attractive. A farmboy worked a 75-hour week for forty-five pence, a kitchen maid even longer for twenty-seven pence. The housewife, whose duty it was to feed her kitchen maid, discovered that ¼ lb tea, ½ lb butter, ½ lb jam, and one pint of milk together cost seven pence, food subsidies being unheard of. It was the age of the lowly paid professional when the supreme amateur, Dr W. G. Grace, who had scored thousands of runs when he might have been delivering hundreds of babies, received £9,000 from testimonials as token of the public's esteem. But gradually, as letters to *The Times* testified, things changed. By 1904 retired colonels were arguing how to combat the infernal combustion machine; leave the garden hedge uncut, insisted one, and drivers will be compelled to slow down when rounding the corner. Yet change was not too drastic. As a man of taste, methodical reader will wish to be reminded that as late as the spring of 1914 his weekly expenditure on *The Times*, two

21

ounces of the best tobacco, and a seat at Queen's Hall to hear Arthur [sic] Rubenstein play Beethoven would have amounted to eleven pence. Or, to translate fantasy into fact, two shillings and twopence.

Fact shall henceforth prevail. If the editor of *The Times* should tire of selecting letters from his post bag and print the lot, then in a 32-page issue of today they would occupy the space currently given to home, west European and overseas news, women, the arts, books, sport and the leader page – *twice* over. Had such a policy been practised over three-quarters of a century, then this book must have been culled from seven or eight million letters. Fortunately the newspaper's policy of selection reduced this number to a mere 300,000 or so. Any bias in choice is disclaimed, eccentricity admitted. A passionate appeal for the relief of famine is more likely to compel notice if read just before lunch rather than after; by late in the day, having endured uninspired controversies relating to canon law and the price of beef, one is peculiarly susceptible to a display of wit or bad temper. The sole criterion for inclusion has been a letter's readability regardless of the opinions expressed. Some correspondents have agreed to publication with reluctance: 'Had I realized I would be immortalized in this fashion, I should most certainly have polished certain phrases.' (Time permitting, one ought always to hatch a letter to *The Times*.) Sad to relate, readers are deprived of a masterpiece of inanity because the writer's executor felt it must impress unfavourably as the outpourings of a 'foolish Blimp'; on the other hand, they are invited to spot the 'spoof' letter whose apparent erudition hoaxed the editor into printing it. The culprit chuckled long over this act of infamy but now admits to feeling pangs of guilt. Some letters were initially disowned: consider the violent response of a gentleman of distinction when told his dissertation on (let us say) Roast Pig was worthy of inclusion in this anthology. 'Sir, I did not write it. Only an idiot would write on such a subject.' On being shown a copy, he relented graciously: 'My dear sir, You must permit me to say this is admirable both in style and content. I have a hazy idea I wrote it after an excellent lunch at my club.'

Letters signed pseudonymously – generally Viator, Senex, Public School Man or Disgusted – continued to intrigue readers of *The Times* until the Second World War but have been excluded on account of their inherent modesty, an estimable quality quite out of place here. Chronological order is preserved save for transpositions within a year, introductions to the various sections of the book summarize the sentiments contained in some letters not included. The notes seek to set topics in perspective, to remind readers of the identity of now less familiar names or to pay passing tribute and indicate future activities. Keen students of *The Times* will observe that a few titles have been altered; what was starkly or artfully effective at the time of publication has become, at best, elusive. Readers to whom all ball games are anathema must forgive the recurrent theme of cricket. Formerly the national game, this has prompted more letters than all other sports and pastimes combined. Incidentally, cricket's 'Golden Age' encompassed the decade prior to 1906 when seven of our correspondents were playing with varying degrees of success either technical or conversational, and sometimes both: T. Beecham (Rossall), B. J. T. Bosanquet (England), A. Conan Doyle (MCC), C. B. Fry (England), A. A. Milne (Westminster), B. L. Montgomery (St Paul's) and P. G. Wodehouse (Dulwich). Ironically, and no doubt properly, their letters here presented deal only one of them with cricket, and that when the Empire's solidarity was threatened.

There remains the task of drawing attention to what was in some ways the most awesome letter published in *The Times* during the twentieth century. It appeared on March 16, 1914, the day on which the paper reduced its price to one penny:

> Sir, As a reader of *The Times* since early youth at Eton, may I congratulate you on the wisdom of the step you are taking and on the continued excellence of our national record?
> Yours faithfully,
> WEMYSS

The tenth Earl of Wemyss had, as Sir Francis Wemyss-Charteris-Douglas, entered the House of Commons in 1841 when Peel was Prime Minister. Born in the year of Jane Austen's *Persuasion*, when Beethoven was working on his *Missa Solemnis*, he lived to experience the impact of D. H. Lawrence and of *The Rite of Spring*. If a theatre-goer, Lord Wemyss must often have watched Irving, he might also have seen Edmund Kean and Noël Coward. Should any reader as venerable and faithful as Lord Wemyss exist today, he first scanned *The Times* in 1893 and probably applauded or regretted each of these letters at his breakfast table.

To him, or her, this book is dedicated.

As *The First Cuckoo* has been flitting round the world for over five years, it is time to flesh out the plumage. Toads and tea-boys, the National Front and chamber pots (no interconnection has been traced) are dealt with in the latest section, not to mention navigating the Greek trireme and garden gnomes in London's lusher suburbs. All letters are written with that 'magisterial self-assurance' reviewers discerned when commending the book's first edition in 1976. Since then *The First Cuckoo* has begun to propagate itself; in Canada and the United States as *Your Obedient Servant*, and now in France where *Le premier coucou* falls easily on the ear, though demanding the inclusion of the word *perfide*. If hosts of Japanese businessmen are seen decanting at Heathrow, noses in books and practising birdsong – to return home a week later with fat contracts signed – the cause should not be far to seek. Perhaps before long a Russian translation will enable Soviet citizens to conclude that letters in *The Times* continue to touch on the same social evils once so graphically described by C. Dickens.

Reviewers who asked questions, just wondered, or clicked their tongues, shall be acknowledged. Mr Benny Green read the letter of 15 June 1962, then complained he could not trace Mozart, W. A., in the Index. The omission has been rectified. *The New Yorker* begged for a follow-up to 'Luminous Owls' (9 January 1908) – surely there was some explanation? Alas, no, though someone did recall an incident at Hornby Hall (readers of *The Times* naturally knew where that was) in September 1900 when a keeper saw a nightjar emit a flash of light from under its wing as it flew past him. As the time was just after dusk, it seems unlikely the keeper had only recently emerged from some Goose and Grasshopper.

The severest criticism came from *The Times Literary Supplement*, which deplored the absence of Sir Almroth Wright's 'misogynous outpouring' mentioned on page 75. This editor's excuse was its inordinate length – two and a half columns of very small print. He may now admit to cowardice. Sir Almroth's comments on female suffrage were of a vigorous nature. 'Sexually embittered women in whom everything has turned into gall' was bad enough, but what of 'women must give a willing subordination to the husband or father'? Clearly, the inclusion of Sir Almroth Wright's letter must have encouraged hordes of liberated ladies to invade bookshops and tear out the offending pages. Incidentally, Wright was himself married, and inspired Sir Colenzo Ridgeon in Shaw's *The Doctor's Dilemma.*

Elsewhere light shone. Reviewers in the Republic of Ireland knocked off the most perfect prose, though one did add that he now knew why he so disliked English Top People. A South African was amazed that such a nation of eccentrics could ever have sustained the Empire. Washington, DC fell for the personality of J. W. Leaver who for so long contributed an annual letter on chosen names in the Births column of *The Times,* Boston for the J. R. B. Branson of 1940 – 'Not only were the British prepared to fight on the beaches and fight in the hills; when the last cartridge was expended, they would fight on a diet of grass-mowings.' Further north and west, editors-in-chief grabbed the book for themselves. The *Montreal Star* crooned over the way 'a group could handle a beautiful language with such taste and respect, such felicity and wit. . . If the English are, as many foreigners believe with some justice, an odd species, *Your Obedient Servant* will reinforce that judgment. But the English of course are not odd; the rest of the world is.'

In British Columbia the *Victoria Times* put its editorial foot down and insisted that in future those inflicting their views on the paper should first note how some English write. Deep in California's Reagan territory, an Anglophile applauded 'the evocative quality of distant cultivated voices speaking in clearly modulated, often self-conscious tones'. Letters arrived from readers. An Australian lady related how her husband made her read *The First Cuckoo* aloud to him in bed until four o'clock in the morning while he rocked with laughter and gasped 'Mad Poms!' A Canadian high-school teacher was so delighted by Shaw's operatic blockbuster that she swore she would instruct her senior pupils to compose in like style. After a couple of months she was obliged to admit defeat: 'They show interest but the result is more Runyon than Shaw.'

The *Jerusalem Post* reviewer wrote at least as well as Shaw, and rather more succinctly. '*The Times* correspondence page is the last resort of the piquant, the idiosyncratic, the nutty, the dotty and the potty.' Chamber pots, toads and tea-boys now present themselves for classification.

Faith, Obedience
or Humility

BERNARD SHAW was 'Yours truly' when writing to *The Times*, Thomas Hardy and Winston Churchill generally preferred to be obedient servants, H. G. Wells was content with 'Yours, &c.' – or nothing at all. Once, after being censured by Printing House Square, A. P. Herbert ended his broadside 'I am, Sir, your servant, but, regretfully, not so obedient as usual'.

On 9 January, 1930 'Victorian' discussed these grave matters; he also summarized the emotions of all who write to *The Times*: 'To have a letter in your columns is frequently felt to be the duty of the distinguished; it is ever the ambition of the obscure.'

From Mr Llewellyn Hutchinson   *11 January 1930*

Sir,

Like your correspondent 'Victorian,' I do not address you as 'Dear Sir,' because you are not dear to me, unless you print my letter. But I decline to accept 'Victorian's' dictum that I must sign myself 'always' (or even for a moment) 'your obedient servant.' I cannot tell a lie, with any chance of success, and I am *not* your obedient servant. I do not believe that 'Victorian' would remain your obedient servant if you told him not to write to you any more. 'Yours, &c.,' is horrible; 'yours sincerely' is insincere; 'yours truly' is untrue. 'Yours faithfully' seems to hit the mark. We obscure persons who write to you are full of Faith: so full, in fact, that there is no room for Hope.

Yours faithfully,
LLEWELLYN HUTCHINSON

Dear Sir,

   I cannot agree with 'Victorian' or Mr Hutchinson. To me the Editor of the journal which I read daily and from which I extract instruction and pleasure is indeed Dear. When I am abroad, does not the lack of your journal leave a real gap in my life? Is there anything I miss more than my *Times*? Why, Sir, it is one of my principal objections to living away from England. Therefore if I sign myself truthfully I write

Yours affectionately,
E. S. CAMPBELL

He Made Them High or Lowly
1900-1910

———◆———

EACH year had its representative topic in the correspondence
columns of *The Times*: housing the poor, crisis in industry,
the sale of obscene literature, a tough line with miners, tyranny
of the motor car, sensational advertising, women's rights,
picketing by strikers, terror in Ireland, Bath threatened by
demolition, the drain of works of art from Britain. A theme
common to most years was the inefficiency of our railways. To
emphasise the identity of the period, in January 1900 the Boer
War was going badly in spite of confidence expressed at Windsor ('We are not interested in the possibilities of defeat; they
do not exist'); Scotch whisky cost four shillings a bottle.

As 1901 became immersed in the treatment of habitual
crime and the ways of the home-migrant wood-pigeon, W. G.
Grace and Winston Churchill greeted May Day with letters,
brief and not so brief, on the leg before wicket law and
weapons for the army. Female hooliganism was deplored. The
artistic achievements of Cecil Rhodes and a need for tem-
perance enlightened 1902, the passion aroused by the latter
being somewhat offset the following year when a colonel
elaborated on the art of drinking excessively without becoming
intoxicated. In 1904 a speed trap on the road from Windsor
to Maidenhead caused resentment among those who had been
caught exceeding twenty miles per hour. A correspondent's
plea that all City dinners should be cancelled and the money
saved used to feed poor children was ignored; meanwhile the
Savoy Hotel offered a light four-course dinner for two, including a pint of Bordeaux, for eight shillings and tenpence.

The assertion that public schools were sadly under-educating
those destined to become army officers roused 1905 almost
as much as the news of bad manners in the House of Commons.
Even more unsettling was the how-de-doo which afflicted 1907
when *The Mikado* was withdrawn from public gaze lest it
offend the visiting heir to the throne of Japan. The award of
Honours bothered some ('no title could enhance the reputation
of a Gladstone, a Pasteur, or a Mommsen') as did seasonal

unrest in the Punjab and indecent novels written by women. A former member of the Argyllshire school board consoled 1908 with the thought that, if poor children walked shoeless to school, they would not only harden their feet but be prevented from catching colds. The death rate of babies under twelve months, 180 per 1,000 in Shoreditch compared with 138 in London as a whole, was discussed; misgivings were expressed concerning the modern habit of taking the trio of Beethoven's ninth symphony too fast. Apparently Hans von Bülow, long since dead, was to blame.

By 1909 the future loomed, one correspondent noting a marked deterioration of the British race. However a lady from W1 disagreed, suggesting that unmarried daughters from 'middle-class British families of the better sort' should be trained and then encouraged to emigrate to the colonies as wives for men of a similar background. The following year (after a proud glance at the past: 'my grandmother, who died in 1872, boasted that her grandfather was 12 years old when Charles I was executed') became aware of its predicament. Could an aeroplane be sued for trespass if it passed over one's garden? No one seemed certain. On 6 May 1910 King Edward VII died. In October a correspondent insisted that in the event of war we should need more horses. He therefore commanded the War Office to put its house in order and set up a government depot – twenty-five mares to each stallion.

But, as *The Times* noted in its review of the year, 1910 had been comparatively tranquil throughout the world.

The Twentieth Century

[During December 1899 correspondents had debated when the new century would begin]

From Mr John Sargeaunt   *2 January 1900*

Sir,

It is known that Julius Caesar was killed on 15 March, BC 44, that Augustus died on 19 August, AD 14, and that the period between these two dates was 57 years, five months, and some few days. It is obvious that there is no room for a year 0 – either BC or AD. Our century has yet a year to run.

Your obedient servant,

JOHN SARGEAUNT

[Boethius, Shakespeare, Goethe, Tacitus and Richard Brinsley Sheridan were called upon to bear witness]

From Mr Hastings Dent   *5 January 1900*

Sir,

In reply to L. Y. L. in your issue of 2nd inst., the twentieth century begins at 180 deg. E. latitude midnight 31 December 1900, which moment, travelling west from America, is then midnight 30 December Western time – midday 31 December at Greenwich.

Your most obedient servant,

HASTINGS C. DENT

[The future King George V – who as a sailor must certainly have raised an eyebrow at Mr Dent's 'latitude' – agreed with the above conclusions (see diary entry for 31 December 1900). Not so the correspondent who insisted that when he ceased to write 18 . . . at the head of his letters and substituted 19 . . . the twentieth century had begun. Hence the scope of this book]

War Office and Inventors

From Dr A. Conan Doyle   *22 February 1900*

[knighted in 1902; an ardent cricketer, Doyle was once bowled by a ball which rose to a height of thirty feet and fell on top of the bails. This incident inspired *The Story of Spedegue's Dropper*]

Sir,

In the coming reform of the War Office there is one department which will, I trust, undergo a complete reorganization – or rather I should say organization since it does not appear to exist at present. I mean the board which inquires into military inventions. I have heard before now of the curt treatment which inventors receive at the hands of the authorities. As I have myself had a similar experience I feel that it is a public duty to record it.

The problem which I was endeavouring to solve was how to attain accuracy – or approximate accuracy – for a dropping, or high angle, rifle fire. It appears to me to be certain that the actions of the future will be fought by men who are concealed either in trenches or behind cover. In the present war it has been quite unusual for our soldiers ever to see a Boer at all. Direct fire is under these circumstances almost useless. The most of your opponent which shows is only the edge of his face, and his two hands. When he is not firing he is entirely concealed. Under these conditions except at close quarters it appears to be a mere waste of ammunition to fire at all.

There is only one side upon which the man in the trench or behind the rock is vulnerable. That side is from above. Could a rain of bullets be dropped vertically all over the enemy's position your chance shot has the whole surface of his body to strike, while the direct chance shot has only a few square inches. There is no escape from this high angle fire. No trench or shield is of any avail. Human life can be made impossible within a given area.

In this system it is not the individual at whom you shoot, but at the position, the ridge, the kopje, whatever it is that the enemy holds. If you search this thoroughly enough you will find the individuals. For example, suppose that a kopje occupied is 1,000 yards long and 100 yards deep, 100,000 bullets falling within that area gives one bullet for every square yard. But 100,000 bullets are nothing – only the contents of the magazines of 10,000 men. It can be judged then how untenable

32

a position would be, if only fire of this sort could be made at all accurate.

But at present there is no means by which it can be regulated. If you were to say to the best marksman in the British Army 'Drop me a bullet on that kopje 500 yards off' he would be compelled to look helplessly at his rifle and confess that there was nothing to enable him to do this. He might hold his gun up at an angle and discharge it, but it would be pure guess work, and the probability is that he would be very far out, nor could he correct his error, since he would have no means of knowing where his bullet fell.

My experiments have been in the direction of affixing a small, simple, and economical apparatus to the rifle by which a man would know at what angle to hold his rifle in order to drop a bullet at any given range. It would weigh nothing, cost about a shilling, take up no space, and interfere in no way with the present sights, so that the rifle could be used either for direct or high-angle fire at the discretion of the officer. Having convinced myself that my idea was sound, I naturally wished to have it examined at once in order that, if it should be approved, the troops might have the use of it. I therefore communicated with the War Office, briefly stating what my idea was, and my letter was in due course forwarded to the Director-General of Ordnance. I have just received his reply:

'War Office, 16 February 1900
'Sir, With reference to your letter . . . concerning an appliance for adapting rifles to high-angle fire, I am directed by the Secretary of State for War to inform you that he will not trouble you in the matter.
'I am, Sir, your obedient servant,
(Signature illegible),
'Director-General of Ordnance.'

Now, Sir, my invention might be the greatest nonsense or it might be epoch-making, but I was given no opportunity either to explain or to illustrate it. It may be that the idea has been tried and failed, but, if that were so, why not inform me of it? I have shown it to practical soldiers – one of them with a Mauser bullet wound still open in his leg – and they have agreed that it is perfectly sound and practicable. And yet I can get no hearing. No wonder that we find the latest inventions in the hands of our enemies rather than of ourselves if those who try to improve our weapons meet with such encouragement as I have done.

Yours faithfully,
A. CONAN DOYLE

[Six days later Doyle sailed for South Africa as member of a hospital unit. Shortly after his return home in the summer he played for MCC against London Counties and dismissed W. G. Grace – not, alas, with a high-angle delivery but with 'one a foot off the wicket']

Wanted: Fauna and Flora

From Professor Ray Lankester   *14 August 1900*

[After holding chairs at the Universities of London and Oxford, Sir Ray Lankester had become Director of the Natural History Department of the British Museum]

Sir,

Now that our Army is guarding, for the most part peaceably, a line 1,000 miles long from Cape Town to Pretoria, and that many of its members may be in want of occupation to fill their time, may I suggest that the opportunity might be taken to help our National Museum to obtain series of specimens illustrating the fauna and flora of the country? Even of the larger animals many of the commonest are still *desiderata* to our collections, while of the smaller things, from meerkats to mosquitoes, from squirrels and stoats to snakes and snails, there are none, however common locally, of which sets would not be of value and interest to our scientific workers.

It should be remembered that for the study of variation, individual, seasonal and geographical, large series are wanted from as many different places as possible, so that no one, say, at Colesberg or De Aar, need think that his specimens will not be appreciated because someone else at Bloemfontein or Kroonstad is also sending specimens supposed to be of the same sort.

Especially all the 'game' animals are wanted, from antelopes to smaller buck of different sorts (steenbok, grysbok, &c.), hares, rock rabbits, and other things that our officers appear to be now frequently shooting. Also such 'vermin' as jackals, hyænas, monkeys, baboons, &c. Skins and skulls of all these, marked with locality, date, and a clear indication of which skull belongs to which skin, would be most acceptable. And the same with the smaller animals.

I shall be glad to hear from persons of natural history tastes in South Africa (and, indeed, in any other part of the world where our countrymen may be), and to give them fuller particulars about any special branch of natural history to which they may be attracted.

I am, Sir, &c.,
E. RAY LANKESTER

Ruination of Lord's—1

From Mr Harry Furniss   *7 July 1900*

[*Punch* caricaturist, book-illustrator and novelist]

Sir,

I am not surprised to read your cricket correspondent's complaint in today's issue regarding the unsportsmanlike treatment the Press has received at the hands of the officials at Lord's.

Your reader will recollect how the Empire was nearly shaken to its foundation when the members of Lord's had to decide who was to be the new secretary of the play-ground in St John's-wood! The Queen's-hall was filled with swelled heads, and, judging from your correspondent's note, the swelled heads elected one of their own body. After all, Lord's is to cricket what St Andrews is to golf; but at St Andrews golf is the one thing considered, at Lord's cricket is a mere detail. At St Andrews golfers, lovers of the game, and even mere sight-seers, and, may I add, members of the Press, are given every facility to enjoy the game. But, alas! Lord's is fast degenerating from a club of gentlemen cricketers into a show run for the sake of profit.

Under the old management, for many years, Lord's was an ideal retreat for the tired worker and the cricket lover. Then the stranger felt that by paying at the gate he was free to sit in peace, and with the aid of a good cigar it was the ideal place in which to spend a happy day. Not so now, to those seated on the paying stands. Boys, heavily laden with open baskets containing merchandise one sees on Hampstead Heath on Bank holiday or on a third-rate race course, but surely of little attraction to the frequenters of Lord's, trample continually on your toes and screech everlastingly into your ears 'Cigarettes, cigars, chocolates – Cigarettes, cigars, chocolates.' 'Correct card –

Correct card.' 'Cigarettes, cigars, chocolates.' 'Correct card.' 'Speshul 'dition – latest cricket scores.' 'Cigarettes, cigars, chocolates.' 'Speshul 'dition – latest cricket scores.' 'Correct card.' 'Cigarettes, cigars, chocolates.' And to offend the ear still further these calls of screeching boys are sandwiched by 'Any seat, Sir, but the first four rows.' 'Any seat, Sir, but the first four rows.'

Why, in the name of reason and peace, cannot the fact that, after paying extra, you can occupy certain seats be written on a placard, or, better still, on the tickets?

In fact, we may soon expect swings erected in the practice-ground, shooting booths under that atrocious erection, the big stand, and knock-me-downs in and out of the many drinking booths now disfiguring the club – a club, once a quiet gentle-manly retreat, now a huge conglomeration of various mon-strosities of masonry. In fact, I frankly confess, were I to see the buildings at Lord's, some winter's night, on fire, although I would not be guilty to incendiarism I would certainly not hurry to give the alarm, for, as an artist, I consider even the outside of Lord's Cricket Ground an outrage upon taste and an offence to the eye.

It is not enough that the committee of Lord's should offend the eye by having turned the pretty pitch of old into an ugly mass of sheds and patches of erratic architecture, but they must also offend the ear by turning it into a pandemonium as well.

Many use Lord's Club as a fashionable picnic ground for five days in the year – genuine cricket lovers are absent then and look to the Press to read in detail the doings of the colts – but now it appears that, during the paying-picnic days, the Press is turned out of the stand and relegated to the tool shed, or, perhaps, to the roller horse's stable.

Nearly every sport in this country is being ruined by 'the gate' question – can we not save cricket, and particularly Lord's, before it is too late?

I am, Sir, yours obediently,
HARRY FURNISS

West-End Imposter

From Oetzmann and Co.   *29 December 1900*
    [a leading London furnishers]

Sir,

We think the following facts would be appreciated as a warning to West-end tradesmen and others:

A tall, well-dressed, gentlemanly man, age about 40, with dark moustache, wearing frock-coat and silk hat, has favoured our establishment with a visit, representing himself to be Lord Wilmington, and eventually giving as his town address No. 98, Carlton-gardens.

He selected several thousands of pounds' worth of goods, including some of our finest modern and antique furniture, &c., and informed our representative that he wished to furnish a large mansion in Glamorganshire.

He also made an appointment to call again with her ladyship, and desired to have all the goods he had selected placed in position in one of our show-rooms; the next day, however, we received a communication postponing this appointment and signed 'Wilmington.'

Being doubtful about this gentleman, we made inquiries, and find he has been proceeding in a similar manner with other large West-end establishments, giving an infinite amount of trouble, and passing under *aliases* of Lord Raeburn, Lord Manners, Lord Radcliff, Lord Brereton, Lord Wilmington, Lord Rauben, at a variety of addresses in London and the provinces, also castles in Scotland and Wales – at one establishment we know he made daily visits of considerable length spread over a week.

We have communicated with the Marquis of Northampton, whose eldest son is Lord Compton (now an Eton boy), and who was during the late Marquis's lifetime Lord Wilmington.

His lordship says that any one using the title of Lord Wilmington is an impostor.

            We are, Sir, your obedient servants,

                    OETZMANN AND CO.

['Three addresses always inspire confidence, even in tradesmen,' said Wilde's Lady Bracknell. More than three apparently arouse suspicion]

Experiences of a New MP

From Mr Alfred Davies, MP   *17 August 1901*

[Radical, Carmarthen District, 1900–6]

Sir,

I have collated a few of the striking epithets and characteristics descriptive of myself that have appeared in the newspapers during this my first Parliamentary Session, and I venture to hope that, as the experiences of a one-year Parliamentary recruit, they will not be uninteresting to your readers.

More than one recent newspaper has contained the startling statement that Mr Pickwick has come to life again, and that I am that gentleman resuscitated under another name, *minus* the tights and gaiters, which indispensable accessories, however, two illustrated journals have been kind enough to supply in cartoons bearing a greater or lesser resemblance to myself. Other newspapers have been good enough to say that I combine the best features in the character of Mr Pickwick and the Brothers Cheeryble, whilst I am also informed that, 'like Oliver Twist, I am always asking for more.'

Probably no two characters in Shakespeare form a more striking contrast than Fluellen and Dogberry. Yet I have been compared to the former for 'pertinacity,' and to the latter for 'artless directness.'

Again, whilst one journal calls me 'an excited Welshman,' another speaks of me as 'imperturbable,' and a third styles me 'a comfortable Welshman.' One critic speaks of my 'magisterial air,' whilst according to another I am 'meek and deferential.'

It is satisfactory to read that though I am an 'incorrigible Welsh member,' I am 'no laggard in the cause of "my" country and the Carmarthen Boroughs.' May I hope that my constituents will note this last testimony, and bear it in mind at the next election?

It has fallen to my lot to be called, almost in the same breath, 'the charmer of the House,' 'the most polite of questioners,' 'a dogged Welsh member,' and 'an irreverent Philistine.'

My manner has been compared to 'the pompous air of a law Court usher,' and I have also been described as 'unctuous,' and 'the embodiment of the Welsh religious Radical,' as 'the indefatigable Mr Alfred Davies,' and, finally, as 'one of the most original characters and precious possessions of the House of Commons.'

A gentleman with a turn for poetical imagery styles me 'this son of the Red Dragon,' whilst a more prosaic contemporary states that I 'remind the old Parliamentary hands of Earl Granville.'

I fully appreciate the kindness of the genial journalist who writes that 'the House recognizes in "me" one of the quaintest and most delightful personalities that ever existed outside the pages of Dickens.'

Owing to the fact that I felt it my duty to put several questions to the Colonial Secretary in the House of Commons, I was on one occasion described as 'skimming to and fro in an absorbing and feverish desire to catch the Colonial weasel asleep, hoping that haply I may win a reputation by shaving the wily one's eyebrows.'

My personal appearance has also been noticed in such kindly terms as 'handsome,' 'dignified,' 'he looks grace, if not sweetness and light.'

Lastly, when I congratulated Mr Chamberlain on his recovery from his recent indisposition, it was humorously recorded that 'there was not a dry eye in the Strangers' Gallery.'*

As I am only a raw political recruit, I highly appreciate the encouragements and the warnings of the Press, both of which are equally useful to me; and when the newspapers raise a good-humoured laugh at my expense I gladly laugh, too, because I feel that a little bright cheerfulness varies the monotony of political life, and neutralizes the bitterness of party strife.

Whilst I cling tenaciously to my Radical principles, I feel that a national advantage is to be gained from my course of action. I try to rise above the pettiness of faction, and I regard my political opponents as my friends. Liberal members have told me 'my bland, courteous, and natural ways are new to the House, and they have urged me to continue them.' Tory members have informed me 'that there is not a member on their side of the House who would do me an unkindly act.' The Irish party, although they know I am neither a pro-Boer nor a Little Englander, have shown me great kindness, and have convinced me that, if genuine good feeling exists anywhere, it can be found in Irish hearts. One prominent Irish member said to me this week, 'If all members were as pleasant as you are the House would do much greater work.'

In conclusion, I may point out that I believe more ultimate good is effected in the world by courtesy and friendliness than by adopting the opposite course; and, whilst I have been told by a high authority I am acquiring a reputation by humour, I can truly say that I seek no reputation, but that I simply desire to do my duty to my constituents, and to strengthen the foundations of the Empire. If I have been at all humorous in the House of Commons, my reason is that I am of opinion that 'a merry heart doeth good like a medicine.'

I am, yours obediently,

ALFRED DAVIES

[* The Diary of Toby, MP, *Punch,* 3 July 1901. See letter for 17 September 1917]

Sandhurst Punishments

[After the latest instance of incendiarism at RMC Sandhurst, the Commander-in-Chief, Lord Roberts, decided in effect that all cadets in 'C' Company should be considered guilty unless able to prove their innocence. Some agreed with this procedure]

From Mr Winston Churchill, MP   *9 July 1902*

[Conservative Member for Oldham; Companion of Honour 1922; Order of Merit 1946; Nobel Prize for Literature 1953]

Sir,

The Headmaster of Sherborne writes you a truly remarkable letter. He says that a large part of the prosperity of the British Army depends upon the learning of lessons of general punishment. 'The innocent, doubtless, suffer with the guilty; but then they always do. The world has been so arranged.' Has it indeed? No doubt he has taken care that the little world over which he presides is arranged on that admirable plan, but it is necessary to tell him that elsewhere the punishment of innocent people is regarded as a crime or as a calamity to be prevented by unstinted exertion.

So long as the delinquencies of a schoolmaster are within the ordinary law the House of Commons has no right to intervene; but when a Commander-in-Chief and a Secretary of State are encouraged to imitate him, it is time to take notice.

Does Mr Westcott flog his boys in their corporate capacity?

Your obedient servant,

WINSTON S. CHURCHILL

[The Commander-in-Chief later promised that each individual case would be investigated again]

Art Forgeries

From Mr Bernhard Berenson   4 April 1903

[who in 1903 brought out his *Drawings of the Florentine Masters*. This immediately became a standard reference book and established Berenson as a major authority on Italian Renaissance painting. He died in 1959 aged 94]

Sir,

Whether the famous Tiara of Saitapharnes turns out to be a forgery or not the discussion will have done much good in bringing before the public the general question of forgeries. That there is nothing impossible in the Louvre authorities falling victims to fraud is proved by at least one of their recent purchases. The body that could buy the obviously cinquecent copy of Desiderio's famous Putto at San Lorenzo, believing this statue of forms at once mincing and puffy to be Desiderio's own handiwork, would seem to be the natural prey of the clever forger.

And if a responsible committee, living under the continuous menace of public reproach, is thus liable to error, how much more the irresponsible private buyer! Last spring at Christie's there was exposed for sale, and in fact actually sold for a relatively large price, a picture by a now well-known Sienese forger, a picture that several of us had seen brand-new on the painter's easel, before it underwent the process of staining and cracking and 'worm-holing.' To draw 'un po' di mistero' – a little mystery – over the face of a picture is a process well known in Italy; and even for those who live there and keep their eyes open the veil of mystery is not always easy to lift. For the Italians, from the Quattrocento on, have always been clever forgers, and the technical skill of the race that produced the greatest European school of painting is by no means dead. Taste is dead and honesty has not yet come to take its place; but extreme dexterity remains. And this dexterity is now more and more turned to account to satisfy the constantly increasing demand for old masters. Their facility enables these forgers, as soon as the public begins to get on the track of a certain kind of falsification, to change to another style so different that only the eye trained to know a painter's work as the expert knows handwriting, almost by the pulse-beat vibrating in the stroke, can follow the Protean metamorphoses. My Italian friends addicted to this practice are constantly bringing me fresh specimens of their skill, hoping to wring from me the confession

41

that this time, at last, I could not, left to myself, have followed their doublings.

It is by no means an unknown case in literature that a writer may possess great talent as a forger, while being incapable of doing even mediocre work on his own account. And so it is with these imitators in paint and bronze and marble. When left to themselves, without a classical model, they can produce nothing but vulgar and flashy specimens of the 'Art Nouveau,' which, in his heart, the average Italian greatly prefers to anything in his *patrimonio artistico* he is so eloquent about. But as imitators they are admirable, betraying their native bad taste only in the most subtle ways that may well escape even the best educated *dilettante*. There are, indeed, amateurs who take the ground that, if the work of art is beautiful, it makes no difference whether it is a modern forgery or a genuine production. These people forget that a large part of our enjoyment of art depends upon the good will which we bring to its contemplation. No considerable work of art but has its defects; but we forgive them, we even do not see them, if we are well disposed to the object as a whole. But the moment the fatal word 'forgery' is pronounced these defects start into prominence, and little by little our loss of associative pleasure reacts upon our vision, and we actually see the object as less and less beautiful.

The curious thing is that these Italian forgers, unless they chance to be dealers as well, which is often the case in Italy, make very little money by this work. A few hundred francs will satisfy their happy-go-lucky natures, for the adventurous, dare-devil spirit of the Renaissance is still alive in them. And for all born forgers (the born forger is scarcely less common than the born artist) forging is its own reward. A volume would scarcely suffice to develop this theme – and what a fascinating volume, by the way, it could be, if one did not confine oneself to art alone, but included literature and even scholarship! But to return to our subject – it is the dealers who make the enormous profits out of the credulous amateurs and ignorant gallery directors. A dealer who is also a forger has an undoubted advantage; and in this connexion I feel that the public ought to be especially warned against some of the cleverest dealer-forgers whose centre of operations is Florence. These 'artists' get hold of old ruined panels with just enough patches of the original paint left on them to enable them, if suspicion is aroused, to experiment on these carefully-chosen parts with solvents that would destroy modern work, and to point

42

triumphantly to their resistance as a 'scientific proof' of the picture's genuineness. The rest of the panel they fill in, with undeniable skill, in the style of Filippino Lippi, Ghirlandajo, Raphael – whom you will, according as they think they can spare their purchaser. Their productions are rarely to be found in such a vulgar place as a shop; they are 'discovered' in old palaces and castles, sometimes in the most out-of-the-way villages of Tuscany, and they boast an undisputed pedigree, sworn to by some spendthrift scamp bearing an historic name. What wonder if the unsuspecting American or English buyer is taken in, especially if the dealer has the cleverness to hypnotize them by dangling the picture before their eyes as an unheard-of bargain!

If my remarks have been followed to this point, it may pertinently be asked how the well-meaning collector is to escape the forger? Escape absolutely he never can. Even the expert buys his experience at the cost of his purse and his vanity. He can only hope to avoid being too grossly deceived if, having a definite passion as well as talent for the subject, he devotes himself seriously to training his eye to distinguish quality. Let him not imagine that a practical acquaintance with last year's forgeries will prevent his falling victim to this year's crop. Moreover, let him not pay the slightest attention to supposed pedigree or provenance, nor to the various papers and documents and alleged traditions that purport to guarantee the genuineness of a work of art, for these are much more easily forged than the work of art itself, nor is there anything to prevent a picture being painted or a marble carved to correspond with a description in a perfectly authentic document. Nothing but a fine sense of quality and a practised judgment can avail against the forger's skill. Technical, documentary, stylistic standards may all be satisfied, but the one thing the forger cannot do is to satisfy the standard of a specially trained taste, and to avoid betraying himself by some mannerism of his own which the experienced eye can learn to detect.

I am, Sir, your obedient servant,

BERNHARD BERENSON

[The Tiara of Saitapharnes, purchased by the Louvre in 1896 as a work of the third century BC, was made by Israel Rouchomowsky of Odessa (born 1860).

The marble tabernacle of Desiderio da Settignano (died 1464) is in S. Lorenzo at Florence. It is topped by a figure of the Christ Child which was considerably copied, perhaps because it was removed to the sacristy in the sixteenth century and was shown on the high altar only at Christmas. There are several sixteenth-century copies of the figure and that (of marble) in the Louvre is now usually recognized as such. It is so recorded and reproduced in L. Planiscig, *Desiderio da Settignano*, Vienna, 1942]

The French Pied

From Hachette et Cie   *2 May 1903*

Monsieur,

Dans une lettre publiée dans le *Times* du 15 Avril, un de vos correspondants fait remarquer que l'Almanach Hachette commet peut-être une erreur en attribuant à l'ancien 'pied de France' une longueur de 325 millimètres, alors que d'autres publications ne lui en donnent que 324.

Nous croyons cependant être dans le vrai. L'ancienne 'toise' de France était de 6 pieds et mesure exactement 1 mètre 949 millimètres ce qui donne pour le pied 0 mètre 32474, chiffre beaucoup plus rapproché de 325 que de 324. Votre correspondant dit en outre que Napoléon avait 5 pieds 7 pouces, c'est 5 pieds 2 pouces qu'il faut lire.

Veuillez agréer, Monsieur, l'expression de nos sentiments très distingués.

HACHETTE ET CIE

The Mosquito Plant

From Sir George Birdwood   *2 May 1903*

[a former professor of Anatomy and Physiology at Grant Medical College, Bombay]

Sir,

With reference to the letter in The *Times* of this morning from Captain H. D. Larymore on the so-called 'mosquito plant' (*Ocimum viride*), I may mention that allied basils have been known 'from time immemorial' to the Hindu throughout India as a defence against mosquitos, and a prophylactic in malarious districts. They recognize several species, such as *ran-tulsi*, or 'wild Tulsi'; *sufcid-tulsi*, or 'white Tulsi'; *kalo-tulsi*, or 'black Tulsi' (sweet basil); Ram-*tulsi* (*O. gratissimum*); Krishna-*tulsi*;

and *tulsi, par excellence*, called also *parnasa* (*O. sanctum*). One or other of those basils is found growing everywhere in India, especially about temples, and most of them are grown in gardens; in Farther India especially they are planted upon and about graves; and a decoction of the stalks and leaves is a universal remedy in cases of malarial fever. The last-named species is sacred to Vishnu, being called after the beautiful Tulsi, who excited the jealousy of his wife Lakshmi, who transformed the fair maiden into the plant which Vishnu at once consecrated to the service of his most distinguishing rites. The 'holy basil' is therefore planted before every Vaishnava house, and every Vaishnava wears necklaces, or armlets, and carries a rosary, made up of sections of its stalks or roots; and Hindus are sworn on the waters of the Ganges poured into the palm of the hand, crossed with a sprig of holy basil; and sprigs of the plant are borne by the Brahmans at all funeral ceremonies. One of the most charming sights in India – the India of the Hindus – is that of a fair Brahmini woman, in the villages of the Deccan ('right-hand' country), early every morning, after having ground the corn for the daily bread of the family, and performed her simple toilet, with the fearless frankness of the Athenian ladies at the fair-flowing fountains of Callirrhoe, walking, with stately steps and slow, round and round (*pradakshina*, 'turning to the right' – *i.e.*, with the sun's shadow), the Tulsi plant placed on the four-horned altar before the house of 'the father of her children,' invoking on him and them, with outstretched arms and uplifted eyes of supplication, the blessings of all-indulgent heaven – that is, praying for less and less carbonic acid and even more and more oxygen – a perfect object-lesson in sanitation, art, and religion. When the Victoria Gardens and Albert Museum were established in Bombay the men employed on these works were at first so pestered by mosquitos and suffered so much from malarious fever that, on the recommendation of the Hindu *karbari* ('manager'), the whole boundary of the gardens was planted with holy basil and any other basil at hand, on which the plague of mosquitos was at once abated, and fever altogether disappeared from among the resident gardeners and temporarily resident masons. The site of the gardens had before been one of the worst malaria-stricken spots on the island of Bombay. No one in those days knew anything of 'the mosquito-malaria theory' of today. I myself used myrrh as a protection against mosquitos. They never came near any bed in which a little myrrh was burnt or a little tincture of myrrh sprinkled when retiring for the night. I never knew natives who used much cinnamon or cloves, &c., in their daily diet ever take malarial fever or die of cholera.

I have the honour to be, Sir, your most obedient servant,

GEORGE BIRDWOOD

[Birdwood's writings included an article on Incense in the *Encyclopaedia Britannica* and a Report on the Cultivation of Carrots in India 1897–8]

The Lance in War

From Lieutenant-General D. Massy   *8 May 1903*

[who had fought in the Crimean War and the Afghan campaign of 1879–80]

Sir,

I am glad to see that Sir D. Drury-Lowe and Sir Henry Wilkinson, who have both served in and commanded lancer regiments, and have seen the lance used in war, have written strongly in favour of its retention.

I also, who have served for over 21 years in a lancer regiment, and held command of it for more than a third of that period, and have commanded a brigade on active service composed exclusively of British and Indian lancers, desire to add my testimony to theirs in favour of that 'queen of weapons.'

Both in moral and physical effect it is incomparably superior to the sword in all situations, except close *mêlée*, and it is difficult to understand why it is proposed to abolish it for all except ceremonial purposes.

It is strange how in our military arrangements we rush from one extreme to another. Only a few years ago not merely were the 21st Hussars made into 21st Lancers, but the front rank of the Household Cavalry, and of all Dragoon Guard and Dragoon regiments, was also armed with the lance, and now that weapon is to be taken away even from lancer regiments! Our system is apparently to be based on our experience in the South African war, but even there the charge of the 5th Royal Irish Lancers at the battle of Elandslaagte, at the commencement of the campaign, made such an impression upon the Boers that, although the war lasted for more than two years afterwards, they never gave any of the cavalry regiments which served in it another chance of charging home. The South African war, moreover, was quite of an exceptional nature, such as we have never been engaged in before, and probably never will again, and it seems unwise to base upon what happened there the organization or the arming of our Army, and to create a system which in many respects will not be applicable to our more probable future needs.

We have been of late years following German methods rather slavishly, and I think we are quite right to take every advantage of their military knowledge; but, as regards the lance, we propose to make a new departure which is quite contrary to German experience on the battlefield. They proved in the Franco-Prussian war that of the casualties found to have been inflicted by their cavalry upon the French, about 85 per cent were due to the lance and only 15 to the sword. I would urge, therefore, that, whatever may be done as regards taking away the lance from the front rank of the Household Cavalry, Dragoon Guards, and Dragoons, the arming of which with it has always seemed a somewhat fantastic proceeding, that weapon may be left to the lancer regiments, which have always, as their designation implies, been armed with it, and who have upon so many stricken fields used it with so much credit to themselves and advantage to their country.

I remain, Sir, your obedient servant,
DUNHAM MASSY, *Lieutenant-General*,
Colonel, 5th Royal Irish Lancers

[In September 1939, during the German invasion of Poland, General Guderian's tanks were counter-attacked by the Pomorska Brigade of cavalry using lances]

The Motor Problem

From Mr E. Reid-Matheson   24 June 1903

Sir,
There lie before me, as I write, newspaper clippings with these and similar headings: 'Motor accidents,' 'Mangled by a motor,' 'Motorists heavily fined,' 'Furious motoring,' 'Motor fiends,' &c.

These clippings were taken haphazard from two daily papers (one London, one local) for two following days last week; and nearly every clipping records, not one outrage, but several.

When one realizes that not one motorist in 20 is brought to book for his misdemeanours, these plain cut-and-dried newspaper reports are, perhaps, more eloquent than any comment. In spite of this it has needed the wholesale slaughter attending the Paris-Madrid race to arouse public feeling to the crying injustice which, even in our 'free' country, the majority has to suffer at the hands of the minority.

It can only be hoped that magistrates – county magistrates in particular – will realize how immensely that terrible tragedy has strengthened their hands.

The insidiousness of motoring lies in the fact that its potentialities for usefulness are no less great than its potentialities for misuse. Hence, partly, the reason why it has pursued its triumphant course relatively unchecked. Yet only partly. The motoring interest, like the brewing, is so largely represented in Parliament that it seems hopeless to expect unbiased, and, therefore, really effective, legislation on the subject.

Can one conceive any other form of 'sport' involving so much danger to the public which would for one instant be tolerated, except in enclosures or on tracks specially designed and reserved for the purpose?

It must remain a marvel to the open-minded that motorists who exercise (or claim that they exercise) moderation and considerateness in the pursuit of their sport can oppose any measure which may be promulgated in the interests of public safety and convenience, and to facilitate the identification of misdemeanants.

It is, in any case, so difficult to bring motorists to book; they have so disproportionately the advantage of speed and disguise, that one would fancy the right-thinking section of them would not only submit to, but initiate and further, any legislation designed for the protection of the public.

The psychological aspect of the motoring question seems to be little considered, and yet it is a fundamental factor to be reckoned with, viz:

Not every human being – probably not the majority – is qualified to bear the sudden acquisition of abnormal powers (whether political, social, or physical) without misusing them for their own profit or pleasure.

For such persons immunity from unpleasant personal consequences is, and will remain, the standard of permissibility; it is, therefore, upon recognition of this undoubted fact that any effective remedial legislation on the subject of motoring must be based.

Yours faithfully,
E. REID-MATHESON

[TANNER: I suppose you know that we have come from Hyde Park Corner to Richmond in twenty-one minutes.
THE CHAUFFEUR: I'd ha' done under fifteen if I'd had clear road all the way. – Bernard Shaw, *Man and Superman*, 1903]

Opera Seria

From Sir Charles Stanford   *28 December 1903*

[A composer now best remembered for his pupils who included Vaughan Williams, Holst, Ireland, Bridge (Britten's master), and Bliss]

Sir,

The recent issue of a Parliamentary White-paper in accordance with an address of the House of Commons, tabulating the financial support given to the musical, operatic, and dramatic arts in foreign countries, marks a distinct step forward in the ventilation of the question, and is at once an indictment and an example. From this record (incomplete in many respects though it be, especially with regard to the subsidized theatres of provincial Germany and France) it is obvious that music is recognized by the collective wisdom of Continental Europe as a supreme power in the education and cultivation of the people, and as such receives tangible encouragement from every country according to its means, and in some striking instances from the privy purse of the Ruler.

This country, then, stands alone in its apathy towards one of the noblest of the arts. It is, moreover, conspicuous for the topsy-turvydom of its methods; for, while it finances to a small extent the higher music schools, it provides no outlet and no career for the talent which it helps to foster, neither for composers, for singers, nor for orchestral players. Other nations first provide a career as an incentive to education, and afterwards the means for helping that education.

And this apathy is unfortunately confined to those who could, if they wished, found and preserve a home for National Opera and Drama. The masses of the public, who have not the means to initiate, would by an ample and growing enthusiasm thoroughly justify such a policy.

Is there no individual, or no body, who will step in and gain a unique position in the history of this, or indeed any other, nation by founding on a sure basis a permanent National

Opera? Why should London be worse off than Weimar or Toulouse? Does not everything which tends to elevate and cultivate the people raise the standard of the whole country? And what art comes nearer home to the heart of the people than that of music, the one art which cannot of itself utter a debasing word or fashion a degrading sight?

From this Parliamentary paper it is proved that nowhere can operatic art flourish without endowment, if the works given are to be of the best, irrespective of passing popularity, and if the prices are to be within the means of all classes. Such a National Institution, if it is to be of the highest educational and artistic value, must be unhampered by financial anxiety, must be on big broad lines, encouraging the artists and the public alike. It must be able to familiarize the ears of the now (alas!) necessarily ignorant with those masterpieces of the past and of the present which will eventually be their priceless possession, but which from enforced unfamiliarity will take time to become so.

Why should the small capital of Bavaria produce a complete cycle of the operas of Mozart or of Gluck, and England remain in crass ignorance even of the names of the majority of them?

It is not the entrance-money paid by the public which purchases Raphaels for the National Gallery; the State buys them, or the individual presents them, in order that the people may learn from and be refined by them.

Will Parliament be content with a glance at this White-paper, or will it legislate on its lines? Or will it be reserved for the foresight and public-spirited generosity of some private citizen to fill this void, to anticipate the delays of the Legislature, and thus wipe a reproach from the pages of the nation's history?

I remain, Sir, your obedient servant,
CHARLES V. STANFORD

[Between 1909 and 1920, four of them war years, Sir Thomas Beecham produced 120 operas at Covent Garden, sixty of them either new to this country or revived after a long period of neglect. In 1920 he was declared bankrupt. It was not until after the Second World War that the State began to subsidize a National Opera]

History of the Cinematograph

From Mr W. Friese-Greene   *6 April 1904*

Sir,

My attention has recently been called to the article on the cinematograph in the 'Encyclopædia Britannica,' volume 27, page 95. Certain statements in this article are likely to give a wrong impression to those not familiar with the facts; and therefore I request you as a matter of justice, which I am sure you would be the first to recognize, to allow me to state in brief the history of this invention.

I have been working on this invention for over 20 years – that is to say, over ten years prior to the time that it was brought out commercially in 1894. In 1885, at a meeting of the Photographic Society, Pall-mall, I showed an apparatus for taking pictures by merely turning a handle. This camera was made for glass plates, but I specifically mentioned that it would be used for films in the future. At that time no suitable film was obtainable, although they were being experimented with. (See report of the journal of the Photographic Society, December 1885.) From that date until 1889 I continued experimenting and perfecting my invention, and in 1889 brought out my first patent for a camera for taking pictures on a celluloid film at the rate of 600 per minute. This was made possible at that time by reason of the fact that celluloid films were then made for the first time in long lengths. One of these films which I took in 1889, a scene in Hyde Park, is now in possession of the Bath Photographic Society.

This camera and films were exhibited before various photographic societies in Great Britain in 1890, and also before a Friday meeting of the Royal Institution in 1892.

On 29 November 1893 I took out a further patent giving the improvements made up to that date, which patent not only covered the apparatus for taking the pictures, but also the apparatus for the projecting of the same upon a screen. This, in connexion with my patent of 1889, is the master patent on the cinematograph.

Yours respectfully,
W. FRIESE-GREENE

[At the time of his patent in 1889 Friese-Greene also had the idea of synchronizing motion pictures with Edison's phonograph, so anticipating the 'talkies' by almost forty years. He later worked on stereoscopic and colour films. He died in 1921, penniless]

Cows in St James's Park

From Mr E. W. Brabrook   *11 February 1905*

Sir,

It was with something like distress that, in coming here this morning through St James's Park, I missed the one piece of evidence of picturesque custom of which that park could boast.

Sixty or so years ago it was one of the 'delights of my youth,' passing through the park, to stop for a cup of milk and see it drawn from the cow; and I am sorry that it should now be 'the fallacious aspiration of my riper years.'

To us city boys it was almost our only chance of seeing a cow in the flesh. It is now, or was till yesterday, the only remaining evidence of the 'Spring Gardens' that once were so famous.

I hope that the authorities will restore the cows to their wonted place. To remove them is a tyrannous action to others than their proprietors, and it does not mend the matter that it has been necessary to call in the prerogative of his Majesty to justify the doing of an act that a private proprietor could not have lawfully done.

I have the honour to be, Sir, your most obedient humble servant.

E. W. BRABROOK

[This letter was sent from The Athenaeum]

Death from Overlaying of Children

[Christmas 1903 saw 1,600 infants put to death by overlaying, 'the slaughterer powerless under the weight of drink'. – Director, National Society for the Prevention of Cruelty to Children]

From Dr Henry Willson, JP   *3 January 1905*

Sir,

Having practised in a crowded London neighbourhood during 20 years, I can add my testimony to the truth of the statements of the Rev. Benjamin Waugh and the coroner for Nottingham.

My experience caused me to make quite different conclusions to those of the coroner for Westminster. Medical witnesses and juries have every desire to be true to their oaths, and, if any bias exists, it is generally in favour of the 'person in trouble'.

If Mr Troutbeck's opinion be correct, how is it that the great majority of these deaths are discovered on Sunday mornings? Healthy children do not as a rule die suddenly from natural causes, and delicate infants generally exhibit some signs of impending death, and do not die under the bedclothes with all the external and internal appearances of suffocation.

The term 'overlaid' may not always be absolutely correct, slow suffocation ensuing from the infant being buried under heavy bed-coverings between its parents or close to one of them.

I could relate many incidents and cases which prove my statements, but their recital would scarcely suit your columns.

I agree with the coroner for Nottingham that only a proportion of these cases is due to intemperance. 'Rest to the labouring man is sweet,' and his slumber is heavy, and I have known a case where the parents were undoubtedly total abstainers, but the great majority of these deaths occur among the drunken and degraded. As long as small children sleep in bed with their parents, a proportion will be suffocated.

I conclude with a suggestion. All who have influence with the poor should recommend the use of a cheap cot which can be made by any amateur from an egg-case. A box about 36in by 18in, and 12in in depth, is fitted with two outside legs, the inside being adjusted to the side of the parents' bedstead by iron or wooden angles, or by battens inserted under the bedding. These could be made and supplied at a trifling cost. I shall be glad to confer with any individual or society that will take an interest in lessening this terrible loss of infant life, a loss we can as a nation ill-afford in view of our lessening birthrate.

Yours,
HENRY WILLSON, MD, JP

Opera Buffa

From Mr Bernard Shaw   *3 July 1905*

Sir,

The Opera management at Covent Garden regulates the dress of its male patrons. When is it going to do the same to the women?

53

On Saturday night I went to the Opera. I wore the costume imposed on me by the regulations of the house. I fully recognize the advantage of those regulations. Evening dress is cheap, simple, durable, prevents rivalry and extravagance on the part of male leaders of fashion, annihilates class distinctions, and gives men who are poor and doubtful of their social position (that is, the great majority of men) a sense of security and satisfaction that no clothes of their own choosing could confer, besides saving a whole sex the trouble of considering what they should wear on state occasions. The objections to it are as dust in the balance in the eyes of the ordinary Briton. These objections are that it is colourless and characterless; that it involves a whitening process which makes the shirt troublesome, slightly uncomfortable, and seriously unclean; that it acts as a passport for undesirable persons; that it fails to guarantee sobriety, cleanliness, and order on the part of the wearer; and that it reduces to a formula a very vital human habit which should be the subject of constant experiment and active private enterprise. All such objections are thoroughly un-English. They appeal only to an eccentric few, and may be left out of account with the fantastic objections of men like Ruskin, Tennyson, Carlyle, and Morris to tall hats.

But I submit that what is sauce for the gander is sauce for the goose. Every argument that applies to the regulation of the man's dress applies equally to the regulation of the woman's. Now let me describe what actually happened to me at the Opera. Not only was I in evening dress by compulsion, but I voluntarily added many graces of conduct as to which the management made no stipulation whatever. I was in my seat in time for the first chord of the overture. I did not chatter during the music nor raise my voice when the Opera was too loud for normal conversation. I did not get up and go out when the statue music began. My language was fairly moderate considering the number and nature of the improvements on Mozart volunteered by Signor Caruso, and the respectful ignorance of the dramatic points of the score exhibited by the conductor and the stage manager – if there is such a functionary at Covent Garden. In short, my behaviour was exemplary.

At 9 o'clock (the Opera began at 8) a lady came in and sat down very conspicuously in my line of sight. She remained there until the beginning of the last act. I do not complain of her coming late and going early; on the contrary. I wish she had come later and gone earlier. For this lady, who had very black hair, had stuck over her right ear the pitiable corpse of a large white bird, which looked exactly as if someone had killed it by stamping on its breast, and then nailed it to the lady's temple, which was presumably of sufficient solidity to bear the operation. I am not, I hope, a morbidly squeamish person; but the spectacle sickened me. I presume that if I had presented myself at the doors with a dead snake round my neck, a collection of blackbeetles pinned to my shirtfront, and a grouse in my hair, I should have been refused admission. Why, then is a woman to be allowed to commit such a public outrage? Had the lady been refused admission, as she should have been, she would have soundly rated the tradesman who imposed the disgusting headdress on her under the false pretence that 'the best people' wear such things, and withdrawn her custom from him; and thus the root of the evil would be struck at; for your fashionable woman generally allows herself to be dressed according to the taste of a person whom she would not let sit down in her presence. I once, in Drury Lane Theatre, sat behind a *matinée* hat decorated with the two wings of a seagull, artificially reddened at the joints so as to produce an illusion of being freshly plucked from a live bird. But even that lady stopped short of the whole seagull. Both ladies were evidently regarded by their neighbours as ridiculous and vulgar; but that is hardly enough when the offence is one which produces a sensation of physical sickness in persons of normal humane sensibility.

I suggest to the Covent Garden authorities that, if they feel bound to protect their subscribers against the danger of my shocking them with a blue tie, they are at least equally bound to protect me against the danger of a woman shocking me with a dead bird.

Yours truly,
G. BERNARD SHAW

The English Boy

From Mr Henry A. Hall   *23 December 1905*

Sir,

I, as a former headmaster, have read with great interest the letter signed by Sir Dyce Duckworth and other eminent authorities, and dealing with the question of the importance of longer hours of sleep for growing boys. But the letter deals with but one aid to right physical development, and, I venture to think, it somewhat exaggerates the amount of the remedy, and omits to emphasize the wisdom of the old adage, 'Early to bed and early to rise.'

I suggest that the average boy of today is confronted with a larger proportion of special difficulties – difficulties which too often come in the specious guise of easements – than his unaided strength can fairly be expected to withstand. And I write as one who loves that finest of *matériel* – the English boy.

He not infrequently spends the most plastic period of his life in the surroundings of a home which is lacking in any element of true discipline; he is almost forced to be selfish and of softened fibre. And in choosing a school the parents – fond in more than one sense of the word – seek one where their boys will be most comfortable, and where in the terms to come they are likely to receive from their sons, who are to be the final arbiters, satisfactory assurances as to a more than adequate supply of food served up in lordly dishes. Questions of discipline, tone, culture are considered of primary importance only in a minority of cases.

The demand creates the supply; boys are allowed to 'go easy' at the cost of gathering bitter fruits by the man of whom the boy is father.

If this be so, what are the remedies? The reshaping of the home theories? Certainly, but that is not the point of discussion now. The establishing a high moral and definitely religious ideal? I believe so, but I do not seek to dwell upon that now. The strengthening a boy's physical nature? Yes. And I venture to press home a truth to which my experience year by year has made me hold more and more tenaciously. Let the average boy work harder, play harder. Let him know something of the elements of the physiology of his body. Let him get up at half-past 6 in the morning, plunge into a cold bath, rub himself briskly down, take a biscuit or two, do an hour's work, then sit down to a breakfast of porridge, meat, bread and butter, and coffee. Let him divide the day between hard work and hard exercise out of doors. Give him plenty of plain, wholesome food. Teach him military drill and the use of a rifle. Let him have daily gymnastic instruction from a qualified teacher. Point out to him the need of a non-smoking ordinance to assist in his physical development. Teach him from early days something of his duties as well as his rights as a son of this Empire. Let him go to bed at half-past 9. And a day wisely employed will send him to bed healthily tired to enjoy an equally healthy rest. He will get his full eight or eight and a half hours' sleep.

The results will be a healthy mind in a healthy body, an increase in self-discipline and true manliness, a gain in courage and self-respect, a higher standard of schoolboy morality, a not unreliable basis for the making of such a man of restraint and strength and chivalry as – to choose the most striking class example of today – the average British naval officer is known the whole world over to be.

I am,
HENRY A. HALL

[During the spring school term of 1973 almost one-fifth of 12-year-old English boys were watching television at 11 p.m. – *Children as Viewers and Listeners,* BBC Publications, 1974]

The Purity of English

From Professor J. Churton Collins   *29 March 1906*

[Professor of English Literature in the University of Birmingham 1904–8, once described by Alfred, Lord Tennyson as 'a louse on the locks of literature']

Sir,

As since its foundation *The Times* has always been distinguished among English journals by its regard for the purity of our language, and as therefore we feel that we have a sort of right to appeal to you on such a subject, may I venture in your columns to enter a protest against the latest hideous importation from American journalism? The monstrous word 'electrocute,' for kill by electricity, is now of regular occurrence, and bids fair to become part of our language. When we have the legitimately formed word 'electrocide' at our service why should it not be adopted and so detestable a solecism as the word referred to be repudiated?

I am, Sir, your obedient servant,
J. CHURTON COLLINS

['*To electrocute* appeared inevitably in the first public discussion of capital punishment by electricity.' – H. L. Mencken, *The American Language,* New York, 1919]

The Duty of Motherhood

From Mrs St Loe Strachey   *20 October 1906*

Sir,

May I suggest to Mr Sidney Webb as an educationist that in looking for remedies for the decline of the birth-rate he should consider the question whether the present education of girls does or does not teach them that the highest duty of women to the State is the duty of motherhood? Intelligent and successful motherhood is of all professions the most necessary to the well-being of the nation. It is also the most exacting of all professions (it may certainly be scheduled as a 'dangerous trade'), and it calls for infinite daily and hourly self-sacrifice. Yet, except in a few special schools, from the beginning to the end of their education, not one serious word is taught on the subject to the girls who are to be the mothers of the next generation. Even our schools of domestic economy, excellent though they are, do not consciously teach the ideal of motherhood. They aim at making the girls good housewives, but never teach plainly that the girl who wishes to do her duty as a 'citizen' must fit herself physically and mentally to be a good mother. There is no reason why the curriculum of girls' education should be altered, because there is no kind of mental training which will be wasted in the education of a person whose function in life is to be in her turn an educator. What should be changed are the ideals and objects of women's education. They should be clearly taught that the highest service which women can perform for the State is to help in the care and bringing up of children – either their own or those of their neighbour.

I am, Sir, your obedient servant,
AMY STRACHEY

A Glimpse of J. S. Mill

From Mr Thomas Hardy   *21 May 1906*

[Order of Merit 1910]

Sir,

This being the 100th anniversary of J. Stuart Mill's birth, and as writers like Carlyle, Leslie Stephen, and others have held that anything, however imperfect, which affords an idea of a human personage in his actual form and flesh, is of value in respect of him, the few following words on how one of the profoundest thinkers of the last century appeared 40 years ago to the man in the street may be worth recording as a footnote to Mr Morley's admirable estimate of Mill's life and philosophy in your impression of Friday.

It was a day in 1865, about 3 in the afternoon, during Mill's candidature for Westminster. The hustings had been erected in Covent-garden, near the front of St Paul's Church; and when I – a young man living in London – drew near to the spot, Mill was speaking. The appearance of the author of the treatise 'On Liberty' (which we students of that date knew almost by heart) was so different from the look of persons who usually address crowds in the open air that it held the attention of people for whom such a gathering in itself had little interest. Yet it was, primarily, that of a man out of place. The religious sincerity of his speech was jarred on by his environment – a group on the hustings who, with few exceptions, did not care to understand him fully, and a crowd below who could not. He stood bareheaded, and his vast pale brow, so thin-skinned as to show the blue veins, sloped back like a stretching upland, and conveyed to the observer a curious sense of perilous exposure. The picture of him as personified earnestness surrounded for the most part by careless curiosity derived an added piquancy – if it can be called such – from the fact that the cameo clearness of his face chanced to be in relief against the blue shadow of a church which, on its transcendental side, his doctrines antagonized. But it would not be right to say that the throng was absolutely unimpressed by his words; it felt that they were weighty, though it did not quite know why.

> Your obedient servant,
> THOMAS HARDY

[Mill, one of whose supporters was Bertrand Russell's father, began his campaign only nine days before the poll on 12 July 1865. Asked if he had written a passage stating that the English working classes were 'generally liars', he replied 'I did.' Grosvenor (Whig) and Mill (Radical) were elected, the defeated Liberal-Conservative being W. H. Smith, later Gilbert's 'Ruler of the Queen's Navee']

Women's Suffrage

From Mr Israel Zangwill　　　　　　　　　*29 October 1906*

[novelist and dramatist who also wrote and lectured on
Jewish political questions; an early supporter of Winston
Churchill]

Sir,

If it is permitted to a man of letters to address you on any
subject but a commercial squabble, I should like to protest
against the tone of your leader today on the female-suffrage
demonstration. 'They all declined to find surety and went to
prison. It is all excessively vulgar and silly.' Surely, in a silly
and vulgar age, to go to prison for an ideal is to escape the
scope of these capacious adjectives. You continue: 'But it
affords a very good object-lesson upon the unfitness of women
to enter public life.' What savage sarcasm at the expense of
public life! Is self-sacrifice, then, quite vanished from politics?
But if you mean merely that noisiness and hysteria are proofs
of unfitness for public life, then every Parliament in the world
should close, every election meeting be prohibited, every sex be
disfranchised. Did Englishmen ever get their voting rights save
by noisiness and hysteria? Have you forgotten the March of
the Blanketeers and the Manchester Massacre of 1819, or the
Bristol and other riots, with fire and slaughter, that followed
the Lords' rejection of the Reform Bill of 1831? And surely
you have somebody on your staff old enough to remember how
the voteless working men of 1867 pulled down the railings of
Hyde Park? One should rather say that only now are women
proving their fitness for public life, since only now have they
learnt how to make English politics. And if women are told
by male politicians that they must work out their own destinies,
they can scarcely be blamed for doing all they can to convert
the Prime Minister to his own opinion. We should rather be
grateful for the feminine mildness of their methods.

In another leader on the very same page you defend plural
voting on the ground of the necessity of 'the representation of
local interests.' Yet the enormous local interests of women –
even of propertied spinsters – are to go unrepresented by a
single vote. The objection to female franchise is, indeed, so
antiquated that it has been abandoned even by such an Oriental
people as the Jews, the Zionist Congress, which is the nearest
approach to a Jewish Parliament, permitting women deputies

equally with men. But Europe still persists in retaining this vestige of the harem stage of civilization.

I learned the other day, to my surprise, that some reviews in your always admirable *Literary Supplement*, which I had particularly admired for virile sanity, were the work of women. And have these wise and witty ladies less right than Tom, Dick, or 'Arry to a direct influence on the government of their country? Sir, if you dread the influence of women's thought upon our life, remove their works from your notorious Library, or at least circulate them only after six months.

Your obedient servant,
ISRAEL ZANGWILL

Violation of Stoke Poges

From Mr E. H. Parry   *29 July 1907*

Sir,

Can you find room for a complaint from one of the custodians of a well-known churchyard? On Wednesday, the 24th inst., among the many Americans who visited Stoke Poges Church was a party of three, two ladies and one boy of about 18. The last-named succeeded, in spite of the protests of an elderly lady who acts as caretaker of the church, in carrying off a notice to visitors, which hangs up in the churchyard, having first tried unsuccessfully to smuggle out a similar notice from the church. He said he wanted it as a souvenir, and, though hotly pursued by the caretaker, the party succeeded in reaching their motor and went off triumphantly with their booty. Even 'the chill penury' which prevents our having a policeman to guard our treasures cannot 'repress our noble rage' at this dastardly act of petty larceny, which will perhaps not be repeated if you could kindly record it in your columns.

Yours faithfully,
E. H. PARRY

Marriage with a Deceased Wife's Sister

From Lord Hugh Cecil   *30 August 1907*

[later Lord Quickswood; as Conservative MP for Greenwich in 1902 he had opposed a bill designed to permit a man to marry the sister of his deceased wife]

Sir,

I see with surprise that while it is thought at worst merely mistaken to speak of marriage with a deceased wife's sister as contrary to the law of God, to call it sexual vice is regarded as unreasonably violent. But what is the distinction? That which is contrary to the law of God is vice. Sexual vice might be defined as any sexual relation contrary to the law of God. I compared these marriages to concubinage. Concubinage is immoral only because it is against the law of God. If marriage with a wife's sister be also against the law of God, what is the difference between the two, and what is amiss with my language? I venture to deprecate that intellectual infirmity which supposes that there can be no moderation without a certain degree of mental obscurity.

Parliament meantime has achieved a very remarkable settlement of the position of the clergy in respect to these marriages. A clergyman may, if he pleases, solemnize the marriage of a man with his wife's sister after the form of service in the Prayer-book; that is, he may declare that they are man and wife in the name of the Trinity, and that God has joined them together, and may compare their union to that of Christ and His Church. In a word, he may officially and in the name of the Church pronounce their relation to be holy and divine. But if he venture himself to enter into this sacred relation which he has blessed for others on behalf of the Church, he may be prosecuted for incest (such is the classification of the Canons of 1603) and deprived of his benefice under the laws of the same Church. It would seem that if these marriages are not immoral, it is unjust to punish clergy who contract them; if they are immoral, it is blasphemous to use the marriage service to solemnize them. Surely it is a pity when legislation sinks to this depth of incoherence. Clearness of thought is always desirable, not least in respect to questions of morality.

It is to be hoped that the infection of this confusion of mind will not spread from State to Church. If the Church has been wrong in teaching that it is immoral for a man to marry his wife's sister, let the Bishops and clergy say so, and let the Canons and Table of Kindred and Affinity be amended accordingly. But if the authorities of the Church still hold that these unions are against the law of God, let us act as if we believed our Church's teaching to be true. Any attempt to treat what we maintain to be immoral as though it were, after all, not very reprehensible will justly deserve contempt. There is no half-way house between morality and immorality. Nor is a desire to make things work smoothly an adequate attitude for a Christian ministry towards a violation of the law of God. Firm loyalty to the teaching of the Church will earn us the respect even of those who differ from us; for the public conscience expects firmness on moral questions from every body of Christians. But if we seem to forget that the first duty of the Church is to witness to Christian morals, we shall be despised on all hands and earnest men will be tempted to doubt whether it is really possible for a Church to be both Established and Apostolic.

I am yours faithfully,
HUGH CECIL

[A year later Cecil was best man at the marriage of Mr Churchill and Miss Hozier]

The Isle of Wight as a Convict Settlement

From Admiral Sir Algernon de Horsey   15 August 1908

[Joint Deputy Governor of the Isle of Wight 1913–22]

Sir,

In *The Times* of the 10th inst. it is stated – apparently on authority – that the Home Secretary last week visited Parkhurst Prison and 'inspected the site of the proposed new prison for the treatment of habitual criminals.'

It appears scarcely credible that the Isle of Wight should be selected as a depot for the worst offenders of England. It is unfortunate enough for the island to be the home for the consumptives of England. It is foolish enough that for a petty economy we try to fill the island asylum with lunatics from other counties. It is bad enough that the Isle of Wight at Parkhurst should have been selected as a penal station for the convicts of other parts of England. And now, forsooth, another convict prison is to be erected in Parkhurst forest (one of the loveliest in England) for the internment of habitual criminals. What is the Isle of Wight County Council about? Is there a single member of that council who can patiently tolerate this proposed degradation of our island? What is the member for the island about that he does not attack the Home Secretary tooth and nail to induce him to stop this outrage – pointing out to him that there are plenty of bleak, desolate places in England suitable for such an establishment?

If these humble words should by chance meet the eye of our Royal Governor, will her Royal Highness not, with her usual loving solicitude for the island she governs, use her influence to induce the Government to select a site in some other part of England?

The Isle of Wight, as compared with other counties, is, I have reason to know, singularly free from serious crime. I feel confident that I am voicing the general feeling of the inhabitants in protesting in the strongest manner against our beautiful island being converted into a penal settlement for all England – an Ile du Diable.

The appropriation of Parkhurst forest as a home for the scoundrels of England strikes one with greater force now that the Board of Works has closed the forest gates, so that its beautiful drives, which have been open to us from time out of mind, are now no longer available for horse or motor traffic. It may be added that the forest is admirably adapted for the escape and concealment of these habitual criminals, who in such case will be a terror to our peaceable inhabitants.

Yours faithfully,
ALGERNON DE HORSEY

[Sir Algernon is now doubtless fretting over the implications of 'maximum security']

Luminous Owls

From Sir Digby Pigott   *9 January 1908*

[Controller of HM Stationery Office 1877–1905]

Sir,

The appearance of a luminous night-bird in North Norfolk, which you were good enough to allow me to chronicle in *The Times*, has attracted so much attention and given rise to so many questionings that, if you can, before finally dismissing the matter, find space to allow me to add a few words to what I have already written, I shall be much indebted to you.

I have this afternoon returned from a two days' visit to the gentleman on whose property the birds (there are two) have made themselves at home. Though not fortunate enough, as I had hoped, to see them myself, I have personally interviewed ten trustworthy witnesses of the many who have been more favoured, including, among others, the wife, daughter, and son of my host, the last an officer who served in the South African war, his bailiff, a policeman, the village schoolmaster, and the clerk and porter at the railway station.

I cannot expect you to spare room for the details of the stories they have to tell, interesting though they would be to every one who cares for natural history, and will only say that, unless evidence, one-half of which would be considered by any Court of law sufficient to hang a man, is to be entirely ignored, there can be no doubt that a pair of birds carrying a yellowish light, so strong as to have been when first noticed mistaken by two men at different places for bicycle lamps, have during the last few weeks been seen by some one (often by many people at once) almost every night hawking, like barn owls, along the hedge rows on brook side, resting for five or ten minutes at a time on a gate or trees, and every now and then swooping on to the ground.

A swoop a few nights ago was, the schoolmaster told me, in his hearing followed immediately by what he believed to be the squeal of a young rat.

Perhaps the most interesting story of all was that told by the farm bailiff, who assured me that when one of the birds, which he had been watching for some time as it hunted round a wheat stack on a very dark night, flew off and lit on a tree, which he pointed out to me, on the other side of the field, the light it gave out was so strong that he could see distinctly the outlines of the branches round it.

I confine myself to a repetition of the facts as told to me, and do not attempt to offer any explanation. But to no one who has puzzled over the phosphorescent trail of such small creatures as centipedes on a damp autumn evening, or read in the reports of the Challenger expedition or elsewhere of the wonderful light-carrying contrivances of many deep sea fishes, will the phenomenon appear either impossible or unnatural.

If the use or purpose is asked, none who as boys have caught sparrows with a bull's eye lantern or watched the startled amazement which for a moment paralyses a dormouse if a match is struck suddenly and held to the cage, will have any difficulty in finding a possible answer.

If, as your correspondent 'A Shropshire Teacher' believes, the light is brightest when the bird is in a poor condition, one might be tempted to fancy that nature, red in tooth and claw, may have her softer moments and be ready at times to step down from the iron pedestal from which she watches with

65

impartial eye the struggle for existence, to lend a hand to help the lame dog over the stile.

From stories which have reached me since 'luminous owls' became the talk of the neighbourhood I am inclined to think lights of the kind may be less rare than has been supposed, and that, but for the fear of ridicule, we might oftener hear of them.

I should like to repeat some of the strange tales told me, but have already, I am afraid, put a dangerous strain on your patience.

Your obedient servant,
T. DIGBY PIGOTT

Kissing the Book

From Colonel Henry Mapleson   *2 January 1909*

[who followed his father as Director of Italian Opera in London]

Sir,

A very eminent *prima donna* (who is at present under engagement to me, but whose name I purposely withhold for fear that this letter might be regarded as an advertisement) was recently subpoenaed as a witness in a law case. The Book which was handed her to kiss was dirty and ill-smelling. Some days after the lady in question was troubled with a rash on her mouth and chin, which finally affected her throat. The doctor pronounced it a malignant itch, and he felt no hesitancy in declaring it to have been transmitted to his patient through the foul Testament she had been compelled to kiss at the Court. It took two months to cure this ailment, and during this time the *prima donna* lost a considerable sum through inability to fulfil professional engagements. Ever since the science of preventing disease became a serious study attention has been drawn to the danger and risks which witnesses run in kissing Court Testaments. Even a casual inspection of these books is sufficient to reveal their horribly grimy condition and a microscopical examination would undoubtedly reveal a state of things too disgusting to contemplate. The late Judge Pitt-Taylor is reported to have stated that he considered the practice of kissing the Book as insanitary, repulsive, and absolutely unnecessary; and he advocated, in language not less emphatic, that the older ceremony of laying the hand on the Testament should be reverted to.

Not long ago it was proved that a witness suffering from a virulent contagious disease of the lips was allowed by a High Court Judge to kiss the Book; and although there was a talk of drawing the attention of Parliament to the matter, nothing has been done to remedy the evil.

Why not adopt in this country the Scottish system whereby the oath is administered by the witness holding up the right hand when taking the ordinary oath?

I remember about five years ago, during an epidemic of smallpox in London, that the High Court Judges had notices issued informing witnesses of their right to be sworn in the Scottish form in accordance with the provisions of the Oaths Act. 'Kissing the Book' is unknown in Continental countries, where the old English form is used of laying the hand upon an open Bible whilst repeating the words, 'I swear to tell the truth, the whole truth, and nothing but the truth,' excepting in France, where the same formula is used, but the witness holds up his right hand instead of touching the Bible.

Witnesses in English Courts should take the law in their own hands and refuse to kiss 'filthy and unclean' books, rather than run the risk of catching a cutaneous disease or something worse.

Your obedient servant,
HENRY MAPLESON

Colonial Players and County Cricket

From Mr C. E. Green   *24 August 1909*

[President of MCC in 1905]

Sir,

I have seen it reported in several of the newspapers that inducements have been offered by one or more of our first-class counties to Mr W. Bardsley, the brilliant batsman and cricketer now with the Australian team, to qualify to play in English county cricket.

In face of the very widely expressed condemnation some two years ago of this system of qualifying colonial players for our county cricket, I can hardly credit the rumour as being correct. But in case there is any foundation for the report, I would venture, as an old cricketer and one who has taken a very active interest in the welfare and maintenance of English cricket, and especially county cricket, to make a very strong protest against this action, which, in my opinion, and that of many other cricketers and supporters of our great English game, does so much to prejudice and do away with the real character and best traditions of county cricket and the *esprit de corps* which should exist in this class of cricket, for not only is it unfair to the Colonies that inducements should be made to deprive them of any of their players, but it is also most unfair and discouraging to our home-bred players that their places should be taken in county teams by those who have not learnt their cricket in England.

Real county cricket is the backbone of our English cricket, and every possible endeavour should be made to keep this as genuine and real as it is possible and to prevent it ever becoming merely a gate money business affair, which the engaging of outside 'star' players to strengthen a county side must ultimately cause it to be.

Should there be any truth in the report, I would venture to suggest that all the other counties should abstain from making fixtures with that county which induces a colonial player to qualify.

I would like to say that I have written this in no unfriendly spirit towards our colonial cousins, who have shown us splendid cricket during their tour in this country, and have played the game in the most thorough and sportsmanlike manner at all times. I have merely been prompted to write as I have done in the best interests of real and *bona fide* county cricket, and in the hopes of seeing its very best traditions maintained.

It is with hesitation that I have written this letter, but I feel very strongly upon this subject, and I know that my opinions and sentiments are shared by a very large number of influential supporters of the game.

I remain yours truly,
C. E. GREEN

[Bardsley did not qualify. But a representative side drawn from the counties today would include only two or three players born in this country]

The 'People's Budget'

From Lord Redesdale   *8 May 1909*

Sir,

As owner of a brickyard I am in touch with some of the principal builders of the Midlands.

One of these gentlemen told my agent three days ago that this spring he received invitations to tender for the erection of three country mansions. Then came the Budget – and the orders were at once withdrawn. Comment is superfluous.

Your obedient servant,

REDESDALE

The White Slave Trade

From Mr John Masefield   *29 April 1910*

[succeeded Bridges as Poet Laureate in 1930; appointed to the Order of Merit 1935]

Sir,

I read with interest the leading article on the White Slave Traffic in *The Times* for 20 April.

Will you allow me to point out some of the methods by which criminals engaged in this traffic contrive to carry on their business in spite of the law?

The procureurs (the cant name is 'ponce') at work in this country are mostly foreigners. They advertise in country newspapers for good-looking housemaids. Girls living in the country answer the advertisements, send references, and perhaps photographs. The procureurs promise them positions and ask them to come to London. In some cases they send money for the ticket. When a girl arrives at the house or office of a procureur, she is told that the lady who advertised has had to go abroad, to France, Turkey, or wherever it may be; but that she has left word for the new servant to follow her as soon as possible. Money has been left for the ticket. The procureur bids the girl think well before she decides to go abroad. He recommends that she should consult her parents and obtain their written consent. When this has been done he persuades her to sign a statement that she goes abroad of her own will.

To deceive the police officials who watch the Continental steamboats at their ports of sailing, the procureur dresses the girl in good clothes, and sends or takes her to the Continent as a first-class passenger. He can afford a lavish expenditure. A young English girl will fetch £50. On her arrival abroad the girl is taken to a brothel, and detained there as the slave of the keeper of the house. As the writer of your article shows, she is 'brought into debt to the house.' It is almost impossible for her to escape. It is said that after 12 months of existence in a brothel a girl exhibits no trace of a moral nature. In a few years she dies.

Many procureurs make their living by seducing women. Their victims are frequently deeply devoted to them. The procureurs, taking advantage of this devotion, persuade the girls to go into the streets to earn money for them. A clever procureur may have five or six women earning money for him in different parts of the town.

Sometimes the procureur, 'dressed like a foreign nobleman,' with a display of jewellery, goes to a seaside resort in the south of England. He contrives to scrape acquaintance with some good-looking girl. He invites her to come with him to Boulogne, or to some other French port, on one of the many all-day trips. When abroad with her he contrives that she shall miss the returning steamer. As a rule the girl is without money. She is in a foreign land in the care of a ruffian. It is easy for the procureur to dispose of her as he thinks fit.

There are three methods much in favour among procureurs in this country. It is extremely difficult to obtain convictions against the criminals who employ them. All three methods are practised continually and successfully on Englishwomen. As a member of the police force said to me only a few days ago, 'They may hold a dozen conferences, but they'd do more good if they hung a dozen ponces.'

It is pitiful that the *maximum* punishment for this class of offence of procuring the swift, certain, bodily and spiritual ruin of a human being (often a girl of tender years) should be set at two years' hard labour.

I am, Sir, yours faithfully,
JOHN MASEFIELD

The Problem of Flight

From Commander Wilson-Barker   *18 May 1910*

[known to snotties and boys for *Elementary Seamanship*
which, at the time of Captain Sir David Wilson Barker's
death in 1941, had reached its tenth edition]

Sir,

Being interested by Mr Gustav Lilienthal's article on 'Flying'
may I add thereto a few observations of my own? That the key
to the puzzle 'How to Fly' will be found ultimately, if at all, in
close study of the flight of birds is certain. The true soaring
birds – the albatrosses and the vultures – have distinctly different types of wings. The albatross is pre-eminently the gliding
soarer of the bird kingdom; its wings are long and narrow; the
body is comparatively small and short, and is thickly covered
with feathers which contain a great amount of air. The wings
of the vulture are broad and the body is less well provided
with feather covering. Both birds have short stiff tails, massive
heads, and powerful beaks. An albatross weighing 18lb. may
soar from a few feet above water level to 200 or 300 feet and
can glide hither and thither at will for quite a long time, without once flapping its wings. With the aid of binoculars, I have
followed a ten minutes' flight of an albatross without once
seeing it flap its wings. Albatrosses fly little in calm weather and
then only with difficulty, but even in a calm the aid of a wing
flap seems necessary only to raise the bird from the water. In
a breeze – and the stronger the better – the wing is not flapped
at all. The bird appears to run up a wave, patting the water
with its feet, and then launches off from the wave top into a
graceful glide in the air.

There is apparent, however, a movement in the primaries of
the wings and in the tail which appears to serve as a rudder or
steering gear. The bird's legs also move at intervals. The head
is in constant motion, probably for sighting purposes. Birds
are alive to their feather tips, and are extraordinarily sensitive
to changes of atmosphere; they feel the slightest shift of an air
current before it strikes them. It should be noted also in these
oceanic birds that there is a distinct though slight difference in
the 'shaping' of the wings according as the bird is flying with,
against, or at an angle with the direction of the wind.

Recently I took a stereoscopic photograph of flying gulls.
The propeller-like action of the wings of these birds was
distinctly shown on the plate owing to the shutter failing to act

instantaneously, and, though at times in strong winds at great heights they may 'soar' in circles through the air, it is certain that the flap of the wings is generally necessary to propel these birds through the air.

The 'flight' of an aeroplane resembles that of flying fishes buffeted and driven along by the wind and thrown about by air waves thrown up from the sea. The flight of the great oceanic birds is entirely different. It exhibits a complete control of air and wind. The serious study of the flight of birds and a series of cinematograph photographs taken with a telephoto lens could not fail to give instructive and illuminating results of immense value to those engaged in solving the problem 'How to Fly.'

Your obedient servant,
D. WILSON-BARKER

HMS Worcester, Greenhithe.

P.S. – The area of the wings of a 10-foot albatross weighing about 18lb. is five square feet.

['A bird is an instrument working according to mathematical law, which instrument it is in the capacity of man to reproduce with all its movements but not with as much strength, though it is deficient only in power of maintaining equilibrium.' – Leonardo da Vinci, *The Flight of Birds*, 1505]

The South-Eastern Railway

From Lady Edward Cecil   *14 October 1910*

Sir,

On Saturday, travelling from Dover to Hawkhurst with my maid, I had a new experience in exaction on the part of railway officials. My hand baggage, consisting of a small bundle of rugs, a handbag, and a cardboard box, was weighed along with my heavy luggage. Thinking that this was a vagary of the Dover porter, I wrote to the Managing Director of the South-Eastern Railway to inform him of what had occurred, and I have received the following letter in reply. The italics are mine:

'Madam. The General Manager has handed me your ladyship's letter of the 8th inst., and I have to inform you all luggage, *whether conveyed with the passenger in the compartment* or labelled and placed in the guard's van, *is weighed in order that the excess weight, if any, may be ascertained.* Trusting this explanation will be satisfactory to you.

'I am, Madam, your ladyship's obedient servant,

'—— THOMSON'

(The initials are illegible.)

This weighing of hand baggage is unique in my experience, although we who live in this part of England have learned to expect anything of the South-Eastern Railway Company, which seems to devise every possible means for keeping people from travelling.

I am, Sir, yours, &c.,

VIOLET CECIL

Epithets of War
1911-118

THE nocturnal noises made by chauffeurs disturbed 1911, so
did the allegation that a clergyman owned a box containing
the head of Oliver Cromwell. And what was the point of
voting £5,000 a year so that experts could forecast the weather
wrongly when farmers got it right by reading the sky? 1912
was dominated by the bacteriologist Sir Almroth Wright who
outlined the evils of women's suffrage in a letter occupying two
and a half columns. The next nineteen months considered the
social effects caused by the break-up of large estates and the
obstetrical ones made likely by foolish women who refused to
ride side-saddle. The telephone service grew worse, someone
suggested a phonographic *Hansard*, and the sight of children
with hoops in Rotten Row outraged an eminent KC. A bishop
was more than outraged when Shaw wrote 'the suggestion,
gratification and education of sexual emotions is one of the
main uses and glories of the theatre'. Equally definitive was the
letter which touched on certain districts of London: 'What
would be a "new-laid" egg in Bermondsey might not rise above
the "cooker" class in Bayswater. A "new-laid" in Hammersmith probably would be a "breakfast egg" in Hampstead.'
The impact of 4 August 1914 was delayed for almost a
month, women then being urged to scorn men caught playing
tennis. A correspondent insisted we were engaged in a 'Holy
War', sentiments of a similar nature being expressed by an
officer at the Front who emphasized the value to England of
fox-hunting. On 15 January 1915 the term 'Great War' appeared for the first time. Meanwhile the nation, or those members who kept rifles in the porch, received instructions on firing
at enemy aeroplanes – aim six feet ahead of the target. An
MP felt that a seven-weeks parliamentary recess was unbecom-
ing, a headmaster wondered if there was any truth in rumours
that profiteering was rife. The pacifist view roused readers less
than the suggestion that women were turning to drink. 'Racing
and the War' proved a topic of such overriding interest that

one issue of *The Times* excluded letters on other matters. Racing continued and so did the war. As the daily casualty lists lengthened, an occasional plea – noble in its dignified grief – urged that the swords of fallen officers be returned to those bereaved.

With France apparently as distant as South Africa had been some years previously, 1916 discussed the funeral of Henry James and the advisability of a Channel tunnel. The propriety of the kilt in modern warfare was also touched on. Many were irritated by the habit of whistling for cabs; a few bewailed the high rate of taxation. The Easter rising in Dublin was duly deplored; could it be that Ireland was the 'weak spot in the Empire'? And what, if anything, had we in mind for India? H. G. Wells explained the merits of proportional representation to 1917, a year when rare birds were glimpsed in London. The consumption of beer by miners promised to become a moral issue, the sale of Honours for political services did. Those seeking the origin of the Eton word 'rouge' were referred to Vigfussen's *Icelandic Dictionary*. By 1918, and bothered perhaps by assertions that Brahms had been anti-British, correspondents were feeling the strain. Some put their faith in a League of Nations, others in equal pay for equal work; at least Stonehenge could serve as a national war memorial.

A week after the Armistice of 11 November 1918 an army officer inserted an announcement in the Personal column of *The Times*: could anyone oblige him, while on leave, with some shooting?

Aeroplanes and War

From Mr John Galsworthy   *7 April 1911*

[Order of Merit 1929, Nobel Prize for Literature 1932]

Sir,

Of all the varying symptoms of madness in the life of modern nations the most dreadful is this prostitution of the conquest of the air to the ends of warfare.

If ever men presented a spectacle of sheer inanity it is now – when, having at long last triumphed in their struggle to subordinate to their welfare the unconquered element, they have straightway commenced to defile that element, so heroically mastered, by filling it with engines of destruction. If ever the gods were justified of their ironic smile – by the gods, it is now! Is there any thinker alive watching this still utterly preventible calamity without horror and despair? Horror at what must come of it, if not promptly stopped; despair that men can be so blind, so hopelessly and childishly the slaves of their own marvellous inventive powers. Was there ever so patent a case for scotching at birth a hideous development of the black arts of warfare; ever such an occasion for the Powers in conference to ban once and for all a new and ghastly menace?

A little reason, a grain of commonsense, a gleam of sanity before it is too late – before vested interests and the chains of a new habit have enslaved us too hopelessly. If this fresh devilry be not quenched within the next few years it will be too late. Water and earth are wide enough for men to kill each other on. For the love of the sun, and stars, and the blue sky, that have given us all our aspirations since the beginning of time, let us leave the air to innocence! Will not those who have eyes to see, good will towards men, and the power to put that good will into practice, bestir themselves while there is yet time, and save mankind from this last and worst of all its follies?

Yours truly,
JOHN GALSWORTHY

[Galsworthy died in 1933 before the names of Guernica, Warsaw, Rotterdam, Coventry and Dresden became synonymous with a new kind of horror]

'Anti-Cyclone'

From Mr Logan Pearsall Smith   *4 March 1911*

Sir,

The Times has won the gratitude of lovers of good English by its successful effort, not long ago, to supplant the uncouth word 'aviator' by the excellent and idiomatic compound 'airman.' May I suggest another verbal reform which no mere individual can effect, but which is not beyond the powers of your journal?

Every one will, I think, admit that another word, or at least an alternative name, for 'anti-cyclone' would be an addition to the language. Now that the facts of meteorology have become matters of common knowledge, it is surely regrettable that for so benign a phenomenon as the anti-cyclone, with its periods of windless calm, we should have no better name than this – a word which is somewhat pedantic in conversation, impossible in verse, whose end is stormy, while its prefix is loaded with suggestions of conflict, from anti-Christ to anti-vivisection.

Both 'cyclone' and 'anti-cyclone' are deliberate 19th century creations, and, although open perhaps to philological criticism, they have served their scientific purpose admirably, and will no doubt continue to do so in the future. But while popular speech has been able to adopt 'cyclone', it has found, as we might expect from its form, 'anti-cyclone' unsuited for its purposes. For a word to be popular must, as *The Times* recently stated, not only describe the thing itself, but also express our feelings about it. Such a word for anti-cyclone can probably be found: indeed, I should like to suggest that we already have one in English, the Greek word 'halcyon,' which was naturalized 500 years ago, and in the 17th century was used to describe periods of quietude and calm. It only survives now as an adjective: but the substantive might easily be revived as a description of those periods when

'Birds of calm sit brooding on the charmed wave.'

No doubt the word is at present somewhat too literary and poetic; but a little use would soon lower its flight to more prosaic levels; and we might before long read with no undue shock the statement in the morning paper that 'the Atlantic halcyon is approaching our shores, and is likely to extend its influence over the south of England.'

Very likely this suggestion can be improved upon. My main

object in writing this letter is to show that some word is
needed.

Your obedient servant,
L. PEARSALL SMITH

[Perhaps the rarest compliment ever paid a journalist
came from Pearsall Smith. Writing to Robert Gathorne-
Hardy on 13 May 1929, he referred to an account in *The
Times* of the sun's eclipse as seen in Manila:

' "The weather was cloudless, the conditions were perfect. Acacia trees closed their leaves as for the night; dew
fell, chickens roosted, and the peasants in outlying villages,
terrified by the awful phenomenon, supplicated the Saints."

'Could this sentence, which Flaubert might have written
with the help of Gibbon, be the chance product of a
journalist's pen? I cannot think so.'

The Times archivist attributes the sentence to Sir Willmott
Lewis, Washington correspondent from 1920 to 1948]

The Coal Strike

[In January 1912, after a year's deterioration in industrial
relations, the Miners' Federation officially demanded a
minimum national wage and announced its intention to
call a strike if necessary. The Government proposed a
scheme for district negotiations, but various coal owners
refused to take part]

From Mr H. G. Wells   *7 March 1912*

Sir,

In common with the rest of the world, I am deeply interested
in the possibilities of a settlement of the present coal strike,
and I shall be glad if you will permit me to point out two considerations that seem to me to be quite fundamentally important in this problem. The first of these is the extreme suspicion
of the men. They appear to be resolved not to return to work
until they have a completely specific agreement that will leave
nothing to subsequent discussions. I will not attempt to explain
the origin of this suspicion, whether it be the work of the in-
sidious 'agitators,' or the vicious fruit of previous disappoint-
ments, or the reflection of our sordid political prepossessions in

the popular mind; the fact remains that it is there to an extent quite unprecedented in British labour quarrels. The general deterioration of our political tone is manifesting itself in this struggle. The men behave no longer as though they believe that our political leaders are in the last resort gentlemen, but as though they considered them in the worst sense of the words lawyers and 'exploiters.' I do not, I say, wish to discuss the sources of this persuasion, much less would I justify it. It is so, and for the present problem it cannot be altered. The Government is dealing with a mass of men hopelessly shy of promises or subsequent adjustments, and the only conceivable way of getting to a settlement with such men is absolute frankness and explicitness to the utmost detail.

And that brings me to the second essential fact to which I would call attention – the ignorance of our rulers. The men have submitted a detailed demand for a specific *minimum* wage in every district. They seem, to an unbiassed observer like myself, to have prepared that demand with considerable care and moderation. We are told that what they ask is in several cases unreasonable. If that is so, why are our expensive Government officials and why are the owners unprepared with an alternative schedule that is reasonable and that will permit of a working profit? This strike has been coming visibly for a long time. Why haven't the 'experts' a detailed, lucid statement to make that could be put up against the men's specific claim? This struggle, I submit, is amazingly discreditable to the English governing class. It is a worse disillusionment than the South African War. Here are the men on the one hand, clear, informed, exact; here are the owners and the Government on the other, windy and vague, and standing on their dignity. In my small experience of business transactions I have always refused to deal with people who stood on their dignity when I wanted accounts and figures. The people we trust to govern us seem to have been taken by surprise after a full half-year's warning, to be inadequately informed and planless. They didn't know; they didn't even know they ought to know. I sit over my dwindling fire full of the apprehension of discomforts to come, and it is not against the miners that my resentment gathers. It is against the traditions and shams of party politics, against the organization of ignorance by the public schools, against the systematic exploitation of Parliament by lawyers that leaves us now with nothing but shifty politicians in a crisis that cries in vain for knowledge and statecraft.

The miners, and not only the miners but the workers

generally, are restless and out of hand. The situation is stupendously dangerous; we must go back 130 years to find a situation as dangerous. If this strike goes on it will go on to social revolution and something indistinguishable from civil war. Let the ruling and owning classes stop a resistance that is at once planless and extraordinarily exasperating, give in at once to demands that are still clear and finite, stop this struggle now at any price, and then, with such haste as they can, set about learning their business a little more thoroughly than they know it at the present time and recovering that confidence which has until recently been given them in such generous measure by the mass of British workers.

H. G. WELLS

Mob Law in the East End

From the Reverend Lionel Lewis   *14 June 1912*

Sir,

It is time that some one speaks out, and that the nation understands what is going on. In this free country, afraid to go home, are hiding in the docks thousands of men doing the work of the Port. I have seen it with my own eyes. In this free country gangs of men lie in wait in back streets for men who exercise their freedom to work and beat them and kick them for working, and often get away unobserved or undetained, leaving their victim senseless. It goes on in my own parish.

There is a quiet but regular reign of terror. The man who wants to work is not protected by the Government. The enormous majority of working men know that they have been misled in this strike. Were it not for fear of present or future illtreatment they would walk into the docks by thousands and start work. They know that they were called out to oppress non-unionists, and they know that they have failed, and they know that they are fighting now to save the face and dominance of Ben Tillett and others. And yet working man after working man (able-bodied, strong, and genuine) assures me that his one reason for letting his wife and children go short is fear of what would happen to him now, or in the future.

To stop this tyranny two things are needed – immediate protection in the streets of people exercising the right to earn their living, and strong legislation inflicting most severe penalties for their molestation.

The police are behaving splendidly, every man working over-time without a grumble, and being confined to his home or barracks when off duty. They are being overburdened. Ever since the strike began they have been virtual prisoners, and even the more fortunate are working half as long again as ordinarily. They can do no more. Troops and not police ought to have charge of the food convoys that continually pass through these streets. Troops and not police ought to hold the docks. Troops and not police ought to be outside the dock gates to protect the workers as they go in and out. The present police, with additional ones to help, are all needed to protect the workers in their homes and in the back streets.

It is all bunkum to talk 'tommy-rot' about shooting strikers. It is very hard to get lawfully shot in England. A man must be behaving villainously badly before this happens. It is sheer non-sense to say that troops exasperate the public. 'Tommy' is more popular than 'Bobby,' because the latter has to boss his own class and run them in occasionally. Let troops deal with large bodies of strikers and leave the police to do their own work – protect individuals in the streets.

Here are two cases that happened here yesterday. In the morning a husband and wife (two of our people) heard hurry-ing steps pass their door. They looked out in time to see three disappearing figures, and on the pavement lay a man beaten senseless and with an enormous lump on his head. He had gone to work the day before. He was molested in a back street on his way to work the next day. In the afternoon a mothers' meeting was being held in a mission room of ours. Suddenly screams of women were heard outside. Nine strikers had visited a foreman of small stables in another small back street. They began by singing 'Rule, Britannia!' three times. They then asked him why those stables were working. Then, by way of emphasizing the freedom of Britons, the nine set about him. He can fight, and they will remember it, but he slipped on a bit of seaweed and a horrible brute (today sentenced to two months' hard labour) kicked him full in the face while the others ran away. These wretched cowards go about in gangs, of threes and fours, and terrorize individual workers. Too often they get off scot-free. The police ought at once to be set free by the employment of troops to protect the workers in the mean streets. If this be a free country (and it is our business to make and keep it so) the scandal of men doing their duty by work-ing being afraid to go to their homes ought to cease at once. Otherwise we are under mob law, however veiled, and it is idle for persons holding high office to talk of the protection that they are affording to labour.

Faithfully yours,
LIONEL LEWIS

On Hearing the First Cuckoo

From Mr Lydekker, FRS   *6 February 1913*

Sir,

While gardening this afternoon I heard a faint note which led me to say to my under-gardener, who was working with me, 'Was that the cuckoo?' Almost immediately afterwards we both heard the full double note of a cuckoo, repeated either two or three times – I am not quite sure which. The time was 3.40; and the bird, which was to the westward – that is to say, to windward – appeared to be about a quarter of a mile away. There is not the slightest doubt that the song was that of a cuckoo.

The late Professor Newton, in the fourth edition of Yarrell's 'British Birds' (Vol. II., p. 389, note), stated that although the arrival of the cuckoo has frequently been reported in March, or even earlier, such records must be treated with suspicion, if not with incredulity. And Mr J. E. Harting ('Handbook of British Birds,' p. 112) goes even further than this, stating that there is no authentic record of the arrival of the cuckoo in this country earlier than 6 April.

R. LYDEKKER

[The above incident occurred in Hertfordshire]

12 February 1913

Sir,

I regret to say that, in common with many other persons, I have been completely deceived in the matter of the supposed cuckoo of February 4. The note was uttered by a bricklayer's labourer at work on a house in the neighbourhood of the spot whence the note appeared to come. I have interviewed the man, who tells me that he is able to draw cuckoos from considerable distances by the exactness of his imitation of their notes, which he produces without the aid of any instrument.

R. LYDEKKER

[*On Hearing The First Cuckoo In Spring* by Frederick Delius, received its first performance in Leipzig on 2 October 1913]

A Labourer's Weekly Budget

['Eight shillings a week!' said Mr St Lys, 'Can a labouring man with a family, perhaps of eight children, live on eight shillings a week?' – Benjamin Disraeli, *Sybil*, 1845]

From the Reverend W. Blissard   *18 April 1913*

Sir,

The question has been recently raised in your columns as to the wages of the country labourer. Can you find space to print the weekly budget for the food of a countryman, his wife, and four young children? Bread, 21 loaves, 5s 3d; tea or tea and cocoa, 1s 1½d; butter, 1lb. or margarine, 2lb, 1s; cheese, 4lb. at 8d, 2s 8d; sugar, 4lb. 8d; bacon, meat, and suet, 3s 6d; oddments, salt, pepper, matches. &c. 1½d; flour, 9d; currants, 4d; treacle or jam, 4d – total weekly cost, 15s. 9d. If each of the six persons has three meals a day this works out at 1½d per meal. This budget is given me by a countryman who has brought up a family on this scale, who knows therefore what he is talking about. No one can say that it is extravagant. Indeed life would be impossible upon it but for the vegetables which the man grows by labour outside that given in return for his wages.

Obediently yours,

W. BLISSARD

[During the next ten years the wages of country labourers increased so that by 1923 some were earning as much as £1 16s a week]

Dancing and Manners

From Lady Middleton   *3 June 1913*

Sir,

I cannot quote 'fools rush in where angels fear to tread,' because, judging from the complicated correspondence on above subject, both have alike rushed – and trodden!

But I was reckoned 'good on the floor' since the days when a distinguished teacher of the Opera in Paris caught me, a naughty damsel, amusing my fellow-pupils by making a 'moue' at his back, and gently suggested that 'Mademoiselle oublie que la salle est garnie de glaces!'

So, as he called me his 'meilleure élève' afterwards, he was forgiving; therefore I may have as much right as many to suggest opinions.

First, I think very few dancers understand expressing the musical rhythm of, say, the valse – dancing it in tune as well as in time. Some few of one's partners did understand this; and oh! the joy of floating with them, down and round a big ball-room; now gently restrained in action, as the band softened or slowed down, now swinging into pace and vigour as the instruments broke forth into loudness, sweeping with a rush (guarded) through or round obstacles, singing in your heart, flying with your feet – then, curbing enthusiasm for a temporary relax into rest as you would restrain a high-spirited horse carrying you over a good country. It is the next best thing to that! But you must have the sympathetic partner to whom tune and time expression both appeal.

I have seen 'the Boston' danced by American *gentlemen* (I underline this term), and thought it clever, graceful, needing excellent steering, but reversing elegantly required a space not often found in ordinary London rooms.

Owing to illness and mourning I have seen but little of these newly-brought dances; but at one country ball in recent times thought them dull and hideous, specially as danced by one man who appeared to be trying to tie himself into a knot, and who was called a South American.

They were made uglier by the sheathlike dresses of the ladies, revealing more of the 'human form' (rarely 'divine') than our grandmothers would have approved.

(N.B. – Our great-grandmothers did damp their India muslins to show theirs; one of mine received a shawl at the opera once from a Royal dame in kindly deprecation? But the said ancestress was the beauty of her day.)

The Times of 30 May quotes through a correspondent the *Spectator* of May 1710 in which is mentioned a dance called 'Hunt the Squirrel.'

It appears to resemble a charming Scotch dance of my early youth, whose name has evaded my memory for the moment. A couple stand out on the floor, 'setting' to each other, and it soon becomes the duty of other lads and lasses to sidle up and,

85

simply by adroit and nimble dancing, to oust the partner of either – girls turn away girls and men the men. A really good-at-the-game pair can show great sport trying to keep outsiders from separating them. The lady dancing backwards down the floor, now avoiding, now approaching her partner, can, if active and 'cannie,' keep the foe, whether male or female, at bay for a long time; while the gentleman can act with more persuasion towards one of his own sex by gently shouldering him aside while he himself dances gaily about.

I once in early days found myself *vis-à-vis* to a very great personage, who was quite resolved to keep the ground and chase away my cavalier. After flying round the room – a big one – at least twice – racing pace, despite much interference – at the bottom, I ventured, panting, to say, 'I am done, Sir!'

No lady being brave enough to come to my aid (though I glanced appeal at several friends looking on) and take possession of the future Monarch, his pitiless command, 'Go up to the top of the room again,' had to be obeyed. We both took a vast amount of exercise that evening.

I can imagine the above dance executed by roughs, when, of course, it could be made unsuitable for 'civil' society. One recalls with wrath the beautiful and coquettish Highland schottische, now romped off the floor, and the graceful visitant of a few years ago, 'The Washington Post,' vulgarized into obscurity; and now at one's servants' dances, when they and their friends mix with a young house party, as we frequently do for pleasant evenings, the so-called Kitchen Lancers, as pranced by the 'Salon,' scandalize kitchen, hall, and 'room' alike, and make the ladies'-maids next day spend all possible time in mending their ladies' rents and tatters. And the Lancers of old were such a pretty dance, showing graces and fine garments to all advantage. The old Scotch reel is rarely danced today, as the younger folk prefer eight-somes as more 'romping.' I hardly recall these in my child days in the North, I think they came from Perthshire. I would like to be informed on this point.

We know the cake-walk, which I have seen negroes dance, was the attempt of coloured folk to represent the grand and stately 'menuet de la cour'. The brilliant galop (how 'John Peel' cheered the most tired at the end of a good ball!) became feats of the 'bounding Bedouin'; the old polka with a sway and swing, was full of cheer and spirit; but all spoilt, as dances, by the dancers. The 'Tango' may be undesirable, the 'Turkey Trot' unsuited to polite society, but with all the afore-named wrecks of fine varieties on my mind, I query whether the *dancers* and

not the *dances* are to blame, and should be forbidden ball-
rooms as misinterpreting a high art, even used as expressing
religious joy, in those spirits that know worship. But we live
in a motor and irreverent age, rude and uncouth in many ways,
and 'gone from beauty.'

I am, Sir, yours, &c.,
E. Middleton

[Under the title of 'Tangomania' some Parisian picture
playwrights have evolved a story with a plot in which the
Tango figures prominently. – *The Times*, 26 January, 1914]

The Heartlessness of Parliament

From Mr John Galsworthy   *28 February 1914*

Sir,

I am moved to speak out what I and, I am sure, many others
are feeling. We are a so-called civilized country: we have a so-
called Christian religion: we profess humanity. We have a Parliament of chosen persons, to each of whom we pay £400 a
year, so that we have at last some right to say: 'Please do
our business, and that quickly.' And yet we sit and suffer such
barbarities and mean cruelties to go on amongst us as must
dry the heart of God. I cite a few only of the abhorrent things
done daily, daily left undone· done and left undone, without
shadow of doubt, against the conscience and general will of the
community:

Sweating of women workers.

Insufficient feeding of children.

Employment of boys on work that to all intents ruins their
chances in after-life – as mean a thing as can well be done.

Foul housing of those who have as much right as you and I
to the first decencies of life.

Consignment of paupers (that is of those without money or
friends) to lunatic asylums on the certificate of one doctor, the
certificate of two doctors being essential in the case of a person
who has money or friends.

Export of horses worn-out in work for Englishmen – save
the mark! Export that for a few pieces of blood-money delivers
up old and faithful servants to wretchedness.

Mutilation of horses by docking, so that they suffer, offend the eye, and are defenceless against the attacks of flies that would drive men, so treated, crazy.

Caging of wild things, especially wild song-birds, by those who themselves think liberty the breath of life, the jewel above price.

Slaughter for food of millions of creatures every year by obsolete methods that none but the interested defend.

Importation of the plumes of ruthlessly slain wild birds, mothers with young in the nest, to decorate our gentlewomen.

Such as these – shameful barbarities done to helpless creatures – we suffer amongst us year after year. They are admitted to be anathema; in favour of their abolition there would be found at any moment a round majority of unfettered Parliamentary and general opinion. One and all they are removable, and many of them by small expenditure of Parliamentary time, public money, and expert care. Almost any one of them is productive of more suffering to innocent and helpless creatures, human or not, and probably of more secret harm to our spiritual life, more damage to human nature, than for example, the admission or rejection of Tariff Reform, the Disestablishment or preservation of the Welsh Church. I would almost say than the granting or non-granting of Home Rule – questions that sop up *ad infinitum* the energies, the interest, the time of those we select and pay to manage our business. And I say it is rotten that, for mere want of Parliamentary interest and time, we cannot have manifest and stinking sores such as these treated and banished once for all from the nation's body. I say it is rotten that due time and machinery cannot be found to deal with these and other barbarities to man and beast, concerning which, in the main, no real controversy exists. Rotten that their removal should be left to the mercy of the ballot, to private members' Bills, liable to be obstructed; or to the hampered and inadequate efforts of societies unsupported by legislation.

Rome, I know, is not built in a day. Parliament works hard, it has worked harder during these last years than ever perhaps before – all honour to it for that. It is an august Assembly of which I wish to speak with all respect. But it works without sense of proportion, or sense of humour. Over and over again it turns things already talked into their graves; over and over again listens to the same partisan bickerings, to arguments which everybody knows by heart, to rolling periods which advance nothing but those who utter them. And all the time the fires of live misery that could, most of them, so easily be put out, are raging and the reek thereof is going up.

It is I, of course, who will be mocked at for lack of the senses of proportion and humour in daring to compare the Home Rule Bill with the caging of wild song birds. But if the tale of hours spent on the former *since the last new thing was said on both sides* be set against the tale of hours not yet spent on the latter, the mocker will yet be mocked.

I am not one of those who believe we can do without party, but I do see and I do say that party measures absorb far too much of the time that our common humanity demands for the redress of crying shames. And if, Sir, laymen see this with grief and anger, how much more poignant must be the feeling of members of Parliament themselves, to whom alone remedy has been entrusted!

Yours truly,
JOHN GALSWORTHY

The Ban on Marriage

From Dr Marie Stopes   *6 April 1914*

[who later made contraceptive devices respectable. 'For this she deserves to be remembered among the great benefactors of the age.' – A. J. P. Taylor, *English History 1914–1945*. 1965]

Sir,

I think it may serve a useful purpose to enunciate clearly three inevitable results of compelling professional women to give up their professions on marriage. (1) It prevents admirable women of a certain type of character from marrying at all, (2) it deprives the community of the work and the experience of another type of woman, who does not feel able to sacrifice her private life to her career, (3) it leads other women, of a more perfect balance, who demand the right to be both normal women as well as intelligences, to (a) wilfully and 'dishonestly' concealing the fact of their marriage from their employers; or (b) living in union with a man without the legal tie of marriage.

Regarding the last alternative, I may say that it is sure steadily to increase if interference with married women's work is persisted in. My own experience of three years of marriage, in which I have discovered the innumerable coercions, restrictions, legal injustices, and encroachments on her liberty imposed on a married woman by the community or sections of it, has brought me to the point of being ready to condone in any of my educated women friends a life lived (if in serious and binding union) with a man to whom she is not legally married. Three years ago such a course would have filled me with horror.

Only by treating married women properly, *i.e.*, by leaving them the freedom of choice allowed to all other individuals, can innumerable unexpected evils be avoided.

Yours faithfully,
MARIE C. STOPES

[Sixty years later 3(b) was helpful in everyman's, and woman's, conflict with the Inland Revenue]

An Effeminate Game?

From Mr B. J. T. Bosanquet   *4 June 1914*

[whose invention is discussed in the letter of 13 May 1963]

Sir,

The sooner it is realized that golf is merely a pleasant recreation and inducement to indolent people to take exercise the better. Golf has none of the essentials of a great game. It destroys rather than builds up character, and tends to selfishness and ill-temper. It calls for none of the essential qualities of a great game, such as pluck, endurance, physical fitness and agility, unselfishness and *esprit de corps*, or quickness of eye and judgement. Games which develop these qualities are of assistance for the more serious pursuits of life.

Golf is of the greatest value to thousands, and brings health and relief from the cares of business to many, but to contend that a game is great which is readily mastered by every youth who goes into a professional's shop as assistant (generally a scratch player within a year!) and by the majority of caddies is childish. No one is more grateful to golf for many a pleasant day's exercise than the writer, or more fully recognizes the difficulties and charm of the game, but there is charm and there are difficulties in (for instance) lawn tennis and croquet. It certainly seems to the writer that no game which does not demand a certain amount of pluck and physical courage from its exponents can be called great, or can be really beneficial to boys or men.

The present tendency is undoubtedly towards the more effeminate and less exacting pastimes, but the day that sees

the youth of England given up to lawn tennis and golf in preference to the old manly games (cricket, football, polo, &c.)
will be of sad omen for the future of the race.

I am, yours, &c.

B. J. T. BOSANQUET

[Golf sometimes demands physical courage from spectators, witness the occasion when Mr Spiro Agnew (once
Vice-President of the United States) aimed to the north
and wounded those standing to his east]

War

[On 4 August 1914 Britain entered the war against Ger-
many]

From Lord Knutsford   *12 August 1914*

Sir,

In the next few weeks many thousand grouse will be shot. I
suggest that they should be eaten instead of butcher's meat,
and not in addition to it. I suggest that it might be well to send
large quantities into cold storage to be used when needed. The
same applies to partridges and pheasants in due course, and to
ground game, and the hospitals would be very grateful for
some stags.

Yours truly,

KNUTSFORD

Leeches

From the Master of Christ's College, Cambridge
28 January 1915

Sir,

Our country has been for many months suffering from a
serious shortage of leeches. As long ago as last November
there were only a few dozen left in London, and *they* were
second-hand.

Whilst General Joffre, General von Kluck, General von
Hindenburg, and the Grand Duke Nicholas persist in fighting
over some of the best leech-areas in Europe, possibly un-

wittingly, this shortage will continue, for even in Wordsworth's time the native supply was diminishing, and since then we have for many years largely depended on importations from France and Central Europe. In November I made some efforts to alleviate the situation by applying to America and Canada, but without success. I then applied to India, and last week, owing to the kindness of Dr Annandale, Director of the Indian Museum at Calcutta, and to the officers of the P. and O. Company and to Colonel Alcock, MD, of the London School of Tropical Medicine, I have succeeded in landing a fine consignment of a leech which is used for blood-letting in India. It is true that the leech is not the *Hirudo medicinalis* of our pharmacopœias, but a different genus and species, *Limnatis granulosa.* Judging by its size, always a varying quantity in a leech, we may have to readjust our ideas as to a leech's cubic capacity, yet I believe, from seeing them a day or two ago, they are willing and even anxious to do their duty. They have stood the voyage from Bombay and the changed climatic conditions very satisfactorily, and are in a state of great activity and apparent hunger at 50, Wigmore-street, London, W.

It is true that leeches are not used to anything like the extent they were 80 years ago – Paris alone, about 1830, made use of some 52 millions a year – but still they are used, though in much smaller numbers.

It may be of some consolation to my fellow-countrymen to know that our deficiency in leeches is more than compensated by the appalling shortage of sausage-skins in Middle Europe. With true German thoroughness they are trying to make artificial ones!

I am yours faithfully,
A. E. SHIPLEY

[Sir Arthur Everett Shipley published nearly fifty papers on parasitic worms]

Oval or Intelligent?

From Mr B. Digby   *17 February 1915*

Sir,
A little light might be shed, with advantage, upon the high-handed methods of the Passports Department at the Foreign Office. On the form provided for the purpose I described my

face as 'intelligent.' Instead of finding this characterization entered, I have received a passport on which some official utterly unknown to me, has taken it upon himself to call my face 'oval'.

Yours very truly,
BASSETT DIGBY

Night Clubs

From the Dean of Lincoln   *30 September 1915*

Sir,

The stand you are making against London night clubs is sorely needed. The very words 'Freedom of the citizen' will stink in our nostrils if it is only to mean freedom to the prostitute, the harpy, the dissolute, and the shirker. By all means give power to the strong hands to put these nests of evil and temptation down. But do not confine your righteous purpose to London. These London night clubs, with profits and dividends based on corruption, spread their horrid tentacles out into the far suburbs, along the Thames and elsewhere, where local opposition is sometimes less easy to arouse and half-powerless when aroused. They must be driven out of their 'second line,' as their kith and kin, the Germans in Belgium, are now being driven out of theirs. The War Office will do it, given the powers.

Your obedient servant,
T. C. FRY

[Returning home on leave from France at this time, Robert Graves noted that 'London seemed unreally itself. Despite the number of uniforms in the streets, the general indifference to, and ignorance about, the war surprised me.' – *Goodbye to All That*, 1929]

Dirks for Trench Fighting

From Sir John H. A. Macdonald   *29 November 1915*

[Lord Justice-Clerk of Scotland from 1888 to 1915, and a former brigadier-general of the Forth Volunteer Brigade. Macdonald was possibly the most expert of all lawyers on military matters]

93

Sir,

As having for more than a year urged upon my military friends the need for some more close-acting weapon in the trenches than the rifle with bayonet attached, and observing that in France this matter is being attended to officially, I desire to call attention to one or two important points. When the soldier jumps down into a trench full of enemies – as he must do when charging, unless he remains above to be shot – he is no longer able to use rifle or bayonet to advantage. He is like a man in a close crowd, who cannot draw back his weapon so as to make it effective. Accordingly we read of men taking off the bayonet to use it by hands, and also of men resorting to their fists. Now it is plain: First, that the bayonet alone, being a long weapon, is not handy for use in a crowd; second, that the rifle and bayonet should be kept together, as proper bayonet work may become necessary at any moment.

Everything points to the advisability of a short knife or dirk being at instant command when the jump into the trench is made. And this is not for thrusting forward as in striking a blow, but for back-handed action, the arm being swung with the blade projecting – a dagger action in fact, which is much the quickest and most effective way of dealing with an enemy who is close up to you. I notice that in a weapon devised for use by the French, the idea of a thrust-blow instead of a swing-blow has been adopted, there being a loop-handle, and the point projecting from the back of the knuckles. This is not a good arrangement. I suggest that the soldier should have a short knife, ready to be whipped out in an instant by putting it in a small leather case sewed high up on the left breast, close to the armpit. The mode of use would be to have it out just before jumping into the trench, and to swing it into the face of the nearest man, and as rapidly as possible into the faces of as many men as can be reached, no stabbing at the body. The purpose should be to 'flabbergast' your man more than merely to wound. A 'job' in the face is the most effective way of getting in first, which is everything in a hand-to-hand struggle and the most disconcerting injury.

I am, &c.,
J. H. A. MACDONALD

94

The Cinematograph – a Protest

From the Dean of Durham   *1 September 1916*

[later, successively, Bishop of Hereford and Bishop of Durham]

Sir,

A few days since public opinion manifested so much disgust at the proposal to produce the British Cabinet on the cinematograph stage that the proposal was abandoned, to the satisfaction of all men. Yet crowds of Londoners feel no scruple at feasting their eyes on pictures which present the passion and death of British soldiers in the Battle of the Somme. A 'film' of a few statesmen sitting together in a chamber is held to be an insult to the self-respect of the nation, a 'film' of war's hideous tragedy is welcomed! I beg leave respectfully to enter a protest against an entertainment which wounds the heart and violates the very sanctities of bereavement. We are getting on. It will, perhaps, be thought decent to introduce the film-taker into the wards of the hospitals or into the operation theatre, or into the death-chamber of one's relatives. Arguments are superfluous on the question, because they are irrelevant. It is a question of right feeling and of self-respect.

I am, Sir, your obedient servant,
H. HENSLEY HENSON

Mr Bertrand Russell

From Mr H. W. Massingham   *5 September 1916*

[editor of *The Nation* 1907–23]

Sir,

Mr Bertrand Russell's view of pre-war diplomacy is not mine, and it is very far from yours; nevertheless, I hope *The Times* will allow me to protest against the military edict which forbids him to reside in any part of Scotland, in Manchester or Liverpool, or on the greater part of the English coast. Such an edict is obviously aimed at a man who may justly be suspected of communicating with the enemy, or of assisting his cause. Mr Russell is not only the most distinguished bearer of one of the greatest names in English political history, but he is a man so upright in thought and deed that such action is, in the view of every one who knows him, repugnant to his character. It is a gross libel, and an advertisement to the world that the administration of the Defence of the Realm Regulations is in the hands of men who do not understand their business. Incidentally, their action deprives Mr Russell, already debarred from entering the United States, of the power of earning his livelihood by arranged lectures on subjects unconnected with the war. *The Times* is the most active supporter of that war; but its support is intelligent, and it speaks as the mouthpiece of the country's intelligence as well as of its force. May I therefore appeal to it to use its great influence to discourage the persecution of an Englishman of whose accomplishments and character the nation may well be proud, even in the hour when his conscientious conclusions are not accepted by it?

Yours, &c.,

H. W. MASSINGHAM

[In June 1916 Russell was fined £100 for making, in a printed publication, 'statements likely to prejudice the recruiting discipline of His Majesty's forces'. Later he wrote an article for the No Conscription Fellowship Weekly, *The Tribunal*, in which he advocated acceptance of a peace offer made by Germany, and was sentenced to six months' imprisonment in Brixton gaol]

The Tyranny of Fashion

From Lady Grimston   *24 January 1917*

Sir,

I should like to voice a protest against the exploiting of any new fashion in the cut of women's clothes until the war is over. In today's issue of *The Times* I see one of our first-class costumiers beginning to advertise their 'new spring tailor-mades with peg-top skirts', advocating 'the straighter-hanging skirt' as being 'not in the least an extreme fashion, and therefore practical and becoming.' In 1914 the war found us women dressed in a way which prevented us from walking freely. It was only to be expected that when short wide skirts were offered to us we adopted them at once as giving great length of wear, being comfortable, practical, cleanly, and obviously suitable to the active independent life we were living. There is no need to change the fashion. More than that, there is every reason why we should not, for caprice, spend the thousands of pounds which the change would entail. We all know that there are still among us women who take not the slightest genuine interest in the war. Their interest is the same as before the war – the attraction of men. These are the women who will take up the new fashion if the chance is given to them. Others will follow suit because they happen to be genuinely in need of a new tailor-made, and they naturally will decide to choose one in the new fashion; others, because they cannot resist a pretty thing in a shop window, will buy clothes against their better judgment; some who may resist in the spring will fall into line in the summer, and before many months are out the rest of us, conscious that our appearance has become dowdy since last year, will, from lack of moral courage, try to make our appearance less eccentric. I should like to feel that I could look to our leading London houses to show their good taste in refusing to offer any goods which would involve a change of fashion. Their support would strengthen the hands of the many hundreds of women of position who are trying to give the right lead in these and similar matters.

I am, Sir, your obedient servant,
VIOLET GRIMSTON

[Less controversially, Marshall & Snelgrove offered a 'dainty new blouse in rich quality Crêpe de Chine, with fichu and collar of fine Brussels net, hem-stitched seams' for 21s 9d]

Flowers of the Front

From Sir Henry Lucy   *17 September 1917*

[the precursor of lobby correspondents who, as 'Toby, MP', wrote *Punch*'s 'Essence of Parliament' from 1881 to 1916]

Sir,
The subjoined letter has been received by the mother of a young officer in the Household Battalion, and was written from the fighting line in Flanders. It pleasantly varies the story of devastation daily transmitted from the front, and incidentally reveals the sort of young fellow who, in various degrees of rank, is captaining our gallant Armies. This one, impatiently awaiting the birthday that marked the minimum age for mili-

tary service, went from Eton straight to a training camp, and in due course had his heart's desire by obtaining a commission. He followed close in the footsteps of an elder brother, also an Etonian, killed in his first month's fighting.

'In England there seems to be a general belief that nothing but every imaginable hardship and horror is connected with the letters B.E.F., and, looking at these three letters, people see only bully beef, dug-outs, shell holes, mud, and such like as the eternal routine of life. True enough, these conditions do prevail very often, but in between whiles they are somewhat mitigated by most unexpected "corners." The other day we took over from a well-known Scottish regiment, whose reputation for making themselves comfortable was well known throughout the division, and when I went to examine my future abode I found everything up to the standard which I had anticipated. Standing on an oak table in the middle of the dug-out was a shell-case filled with flowers, and these not ordinary blossoms, but Madonna lilies, mignonette, and roses. This vase, if I may so term the receptacle, overshadowed all else and by its presence changed the whole atmosphere, the perfume reminding me of home, and what greater joy or luxury is there for any of us out here than such a memory?

'After having duly appreciated this most unexpected corner I inquired where the flowers had been gathered, and was told they had come from the utterly ruined village of Fampoux close by. At once I set out to explore and verify this information. Sure enough, between piles of bricks, shell holes, dirt, and every sort of *débris*, suddenly a rose in full bloom would smile at me, and a lily would waft its delicious scent and seem to say how it had defied the destroyer and all his frightfulness. In each corner where I saw a blossoming flower or even a ripening fruit, I seemed to realize a scene belonging to this unhappy village in peaceful days. Imagination might well lose her way in the paths of chivalry and romance perhaps quite unknown to the inhabitants of Fampoux. I meandered on through the village until I struck a trench leading up to the front line; this I followed for a while until quite suddenly I was confronted by a brilliancy which seemed to me one of the most perfect bits of colour I have ever seen. Amongst innumerable shell holes there was a small patch of ground absolutely carpeted with buttercups, over which blazed bright, red poppies intermixed with the bluest of cornflowers. Here was a really glorious corner, and how quickly came memories of home! No one, however hardened by the horrors of war, could pass that spot without a smile or a happy thought. Perhaps it is the contrast of the perfection of these corners with the sordidness of all around that makes them of such inestimable value. Some such corners exist throughout France, even in the front line trenches. It may not be flowers, it may be only the corner of a field or barn; it may be some spoken word or a chance meeting. No matter what it is if it brings back a happy memory or reminds one of home. It is like a jewel in a crown of thorns giving promise of another crown and of days to come wherein, under other circumstances, we may be more worthy of the wearing.'

Yours faithfully,
HENRY LUCY

The Nation's Young Lives

From Mrs H. B. Irving   *25 February 1918*

[daughter-in-law of Sir Henry Irving, mother of the designer and author Laurence Irving]

Sir,

Mr Galsworthy, in his article in today's *Times* on 'The Nation's Young Lives,' strongly advocates the adoption of widows' or mothers' pensions, and the proper protection and care of unmarried girl mothers and their illegitimate children. His words are opportune. No amount of Welfare Centres can do anything radical to help the children of widows or those born out of wedlock, until the State has awakened to its grave responsibility for their welfare.

I have, within the last two days, been present at a meeting of a committee of women Poor Law Guardians in one of our great provincial cities. They were engaged, no doubt unconsciously, in a game which, for want of a better name, I must call girl-baiting. I saw a young expectant mother cruelly handled, and tortured with bitter words and threats; an ordeal which she will have had to endure at the hands of four different sets of officials by the time her baby is three weeks old. These guardians told her, in my presence, that they hoped she would suffer severely for her wrong-doing, that they considered that her own mother, who had treated her kindly, had been too lenient, and that her sin was so great that she ought to be ashamed to be a cost to self-respecting ratepayers. They added that the man who was responsible for her condition was very good to have acknowledged his paternity, but expressed the belief, nay, rather the hope, that he would take an early opportunity of getting out of his obligation. Meanwhile, a pale, trembling girl, within a month of her confinement, stood, like a hunted animal, in the presence of such judges.

We pray constantly in our churches for 'all women labouring of child, sick persons, and young children, the fatherless, the widows, and all that are desolate and oppressed,' and yet we continue this oppression of the desolate.

Yours faithfully,
DOROTHEA IRVING

'How Shall We Rise to Greet the Dawn'
1919-1932

A WEEK after Armistice Day Osbert Sitwell's poem appeared in *The Nation*:

> We must create and fashion a new God –
> A God of power, of beauty, and of strength;
> Created painfully, cruelly,
> Labouring from the revulsion of men's minds.

Was Germany starving? Were our soldiers compelled to return home in cattle trucks? Did a Slough worker, unable to read or write, actually earn £4 11s 8d a week? There were differences of opinion in 1919 but all agreed the Post Office should be reformed. As the century entered its third decade, major discontents abounded: miners grossly overpaid, golf pricing itself out of existence, high buildings ruining the appearance of London, the railways still deteriorating, some major public schools raising their fees to £120 a year. Indeed, shortages were so marked that one correspondent asked if women's gloves might not be made from the skins of rats. After 1921 had been gratified by the appointment of a select committee to inquire into the inefficiency of the telephone service, the following year obliged with solutions to our problems: abolish betting, organize a postal delivery on Sundays, allow the Church of England to buttress itself with more bishops, command women barristers to wear toques in court. The fate of the woman medical student gave cause for concern: 'after a few months in a common room, she becomes coarse, immodest and vulgar.' However, democracy was not dead; when it was pointed out that a sixpenny entrance charge to museums would bear heavily on the poor, the scheme was dropped. Nevertheless, if any doubted the cause of the national malaise, it was the removal of 'degree'–the British did not wish to get mixed up. If the upper classes had their nursing homes, surely the middle classes could be permitted private hospital beds at five guineas a week?

The mid-twenties considered the fate of a motorist fined for doing 34 mph on the Brighton road. Some wished to know why, in spite of a 95 per cent wage increase between 1913 and 1924, the output of the 'coal-getting class' had dropped by 12 per cent. Wild flowers were not what they had been. A bishop denounced the playing of football on Good Friday, the response being somewhat muted when the annual attack on Jacob Epstein began. Advertising grew more vulgar, Labour politicians sang the *Red Flag* at too frequent intervals. Then in 1926 a change took place in the mood of correspondents. The general strike may have inconvenienced many, and certainly women's boxing was to be deplored. Undergraduates were criticized for acting – *The Times* was soon to applaud Mr R. W. Speaight's Falstaff for the OUDS while ignoring the Wart of Mr J. Betjeman – and Dr Julian Huxley was deemed subversive for mentioning birth control during a BBC debate. Yet sublime and, it seemed, omnipotent, were the Savoy Hill announcers whose perfect manners enchanted those with wireless sets.

But not even Sir John Reith could reconcile 1927 to the petrol pumps which began to disfigure the countryside. Trains became even more unpunctual. The wealthy socialist was told what to do with his money – finance a business to be controlled by the workers, then hand over the shares representing the total capital involved. The young professional man could not afford to marry. As the twenties lurched to a close, the plight of miners' families in South Wales was noted. Did they deserve sympathy? A horse knocked down by a motor car in London most certainly did. The depression settled. Postal delays defied rational explanation until someone remembered there had been eleven Postmasters-General during the past seventeen years. And surely at a time of economic difficulties MPs should set a good example by travelling third class to their constituencies? The member for East Aberdeenshire, Mr Boothby, saw fit to differ. 1932 gave itself briefly to a consideration of musical performers; though Mrs Beeton had been a very good pianist, should not foreigners (probably Toscanini and Furtwängler) be kept out of this country? Meanwhile there was unemployment in Durham.

Supply of Domestic Servants

From Mrs Morgan-Dockrell   *25 February 1919*

Sir,

   In answer to an advertisement in *The Times* newspaper for a cook and a house-parlourmaid I have had 42 applicants for the situations!

Yours, &c.,
EMILY MORGAN-DOCKRELL

   [Six years later unemployed ex-servicemen were urged to apply for such vacancies]

Bolshevism

From Admiral of the Fleet Lord Fisher, OM   12 January 1920

Sir,

   Newton saw an apple fall and deduced Gravitation. You and I might have seen millions of apples fall and only deduced pig-feeding. It's the same story about Bolshevism. We want some Newtonian Cromwell to enunciate that Bolshevism is the reaction from repressed Freedom. Armenian and Georgian Republics are going to be suppressed and thus Bolshevism propagated by perpetuating Turkish misrule in Asia. England herself is not free, so Bolshevism rears its head. A threat to dissolve Parliament makes its recalcitrant members feed out of the Prime Minister's hand. Did not some hundreds of them send a telegram to Paris? They can't save Armenia and Georgia if they wanted to. They don't represent the masses of this nation. It's the baldest, richest, effetest House of Commons we ever had. Look at the untrammelled, unparalleled, wanton waste everywhere in every department. And business men fettered by unbusiness fools. Innumerable tons of shipping now in our harbours waiting to be unloaded. Who loaded them?

Yours,
FISHER

Housing Problems

From the Reverend T. Thistle   *17 May 1920*

[remembered by the Reverend J. S. Boys Smith (a former Master of St John's College, Cambridge) as the 'kind of clergyman less often seen today – white tie, close-cut beard, cultured, critical and sometimes caustic in his opinions, but kindly']

Sir,

As a member of the council which is the housing authority of this district in Hampshire, and having therefore some interest in the question of housing, I asked a day or two ago a builder of my acquaintance, who is now building two or three smaller houses, if he could tell me what portion of the cost of a house was paid for labour and what portion for materials, and how these compared with the prices paid before the war. The information he gave me, though it is no doubt well known to all builders, is perhaps not known to most of your readers, and therefore it may be worth while to publish it for their benefit. The cost of labour, I find, is about 38 per cent of the whole cost; the remaining 62 per cent is the cost of materials. Bricklayers employed by my informant used to lay on an average 750 bricks a day, and when paid by piece-work from 1,000 to 1,200. They now lay on average 300. All other workers, carpenters, plumbers, painters, slaters, &c., have reduced their output in a similar degree. That is to say, men now do about two-fifths of the work they did before the war. Taking the cost of a cottage at £1,000, it follows that if men worked now as they used to work the £380 paid for labour would be reduced to about £150, a saving of £230 on the cost, and a similar proportionate saving would be effected on the labour required in the production of materials, which have advanced in price as follows: Bricks, 160 per cent; timber for scantlings and floorings and slates and tiles, 300 per cent; laths, 500 per cent; glass, 200 per cent; cement, 175 per cent; sand and ballast, 115 per cent; guttering and cast goods, 500 per cent; wages, 200 per cent. Time worked in August, 1914, was 56½ hours, and is now 44 hours a week.

Without entering into the question of the reasons why men now do much less work than they formerly did, and the further question whether they are themselves either the better or the happier for taking it so easy at their work, it seems clear that what housing authorities have to do is to build houses for working men who won't work.

T. THISTLE

[In January 1925 a correspondent acclaimed the superman who, under 'ideal conditions', had laid 879 bricks in one hour. 'Ideal conditions' consisted of an army of helpers who passed bricks and mortar to the hero]

The Anomalies of Divorce

From Lord Buckmaster   *11 October 1922*

[Lord Chancellor in Asquith's coalition cabinet 1915–16]

Sir,

During the last weeks of the Summer Term, at the request of the Lord Chancellor, I undertook the trial of undefended suits for divorce and heard about four hundred cases. They were taken in due order from the list, and included every class, but with a large preponderance of the poor, owing to their numbers, and also to the difficulty of their getting decent homes.

The experience was startling, and explains why it is that practically every Judge on whom a similar duty has devolved has urged an alteration of the law. I believe that the reason why this demand is not universal is that the facts are not known, and false modesty prevents their disclosure. Women's societies pass resolutions declaring that if any change be made, equality must be established between men and women, forgetting, or not knowing, that the present law produces the most insulting inequality, and that it is in the interests of women that reform is sought.

Plain facts need plain speech, and I beg, without apology, to ask attention to the following statement, based on the cases I tried, prefaced only by saying that I scrutinized the evidence with especial care, and that I am satisfied as to the truth of what I state.

A woman marries a man, and is at once infected by him with syphilis. She is an innocent woman, and knows nothing as to what is wrong until the disease has her fast in its grip. The doctor is satisfied that infection occurred immediately on marriage; consequently the law politely bows her out of Court and makes her pay the cost of her struggle for liberty. In the particular case to which I refer, the husband had deserted the woman, and it was possible to prove, though with difficulty, that he had also transferred his 'affections' to someone else; but for this his wife was bound for life.

Another woman had been made the victim of the unspeakable savagery of brutal and perverted lust. She also must have remained bound by the bonds of matrimony, enforced by violence, but that her husband went to satisfy his fury elsewhere, and was found out.

A third was deserted, after a week, by a soldier who went to the American continent, where he might have lived unmolested for ever in a life of peaceful adultery, but as he violated two children he also was discovered, and she was able to be free.

I could multiply the recital of individual cases, but lack of space forbids, and the general conditions need attention.

Bigamy was extremely common, but entirely confined to poor persons, for bigamy is not a vice of wealth; the rich can find other less illegal outlets for their emotions. The existing statute, however, provides that bigamy is not sufficient ground for divorce − it must be 'bigamy with adultery' − and, though it might be assumed, anywhere outside a law Court, that a man who has risked penal servitude to obtain possession of a woman was not prompted by platonic love, yet the law requires independent proof of the adultery. Further, by a decision now sixty-five years old, this adultery must be with the bigamous wife − adultery with any number of other people is quite inadequate.

On the wisdom and justice of this ancient judgment I will not comment, but it throws great difficulty in the way of a woman who can prove that her husband has been convicted of bigamy, but finds it difficult to trace and obtain evidence of adultery; *quoad hanc*, in one case before me, she almost failed.

Among the poorer people desertion was the commonest event: rich folk walk more delicately, and, being in a hurry, obtain a decree for restitution, to be obeyed in a fortnight, instead of waiting two years. It was, of course, only in the rare instances where the deserting husband could be traced and his undoubted adultery legally proved that any relief would be obtained. In one such case the husband, who had first insulted and then deserted his wife, left the country in a ship with the woman with his affection for whom he had often taunted his wife, but, of course, that did not constitute legal proof of adultery, but merely companionship.

In no case that I tried did there appear to me the faintest chance of reconciliation; the marriage tie had been broken beyond repair and its sanctity utterly defiled; nor, again, though I watched with extreme vigilance, was there any single case where collusion could be suggested. With regard to cruelty, there was no case which a competent lawyer, skilled in the knowledge of witnesses, could not have tried.

I was, of course, faced with the question as to what is cruelty, which, we are informed, is so difficult that you want the King's Proctor as an expert in cruelty to keep the law steady. I made my own rules. If a man who was sober kicked his wife in the stomach when she was pregnant, that seemed to me enough; if she were not pregnant, and he was drunk, he might have to do it again or else her complaint might be due to what the most persistent opponent of my Bill called 'nervous irritation.' So, also, with kicking her downstairs, or making her sleep on the doormat in winter – all of which cases I had to consider. But, however brutal and repeated the cruelty, no divorce must be granted for it, or we shall Americanize our institutions and soil the sanctity of English homes.

I had no case before me involving the question of lunacy or criminality, for these, as the law stands, are irrelevant considerations in connexion with divorce; but the evidence on that is near at hand. Within the last few months two women have been left eternally widowed, with their husbands fast immured in criminal lunatic asylums, and in this unnatural state they will remain while the shadow of the years lengthens and life's day grows dim. Surely the desire to help such people is not, as some appear to think, prompted by a Satan, but is a humble effort to carry out the principle of the supplication which asks that, while our own wants are satisfied, we should not be unmindful of the wants of others.

Parliament will shortly resume its work. Our divorce laws have been condemned by the most competent authority as immoral and unjust. The House of Lords has patiently heard every argument that can be advanced against further change from the lips of the most skilful advocates, and has repeatedly, and by emphatic majorities, demanded reform. Common sense – but for respect to my adversaries I should have added common decency – rejecting the existing law. Is it asking too much to entreat the Government to afford a chance to Parliament to cleanse our laws from this disgrace?

Yours faithfully,
BUCKMASTER

[A. P. Herbert's Marriage Bill, which passed into law as the Matrimonial Causes Act of 1937, provided that after three years a divorce might be sought by either partner on the grounds of adultery, desertion, cruelty or insanity, and certain vicious practices]

King Tutankhamen

From the Bishop of Chelmsford   *3 February 1923*

[the Rt Rev John Edwin Watts-Ditchfield]

Sir,

I wonder how many of us, born and brought up in the Victorian era, would like to think that in the year, say, 5923, the tomb of Queen Victoria would be invaded by a party of foreigners who rifled it of its contents, took the body of the great Queen from the mausoleum in which it had been placed amid the grief of the whole people, and exhibited it to all and sundry who might wish to see it?

The question arises whether such treatment as we should count unseemly in the case of the great English Queen is not equally unseemly in the case of King Tutankhamen. I am not unmindful of the great historical value which may accrue from the examination of the collection of jewelry, furniture, and, above all, of papyri discovered within the tomb, and I realize that wide interests may justify their thorough investigation and even, in special cases, their temporary removal. But, in any case, I protest strongly against the removal of the body of the King from the place where it has rested for thousands of years. Such a removal borders on indecency, and traverses all Christian sentiment concerning the sacredness of the burial places of the dead.

J. E. CHELMSFORD

[Queen Victoria once told Lord Melbourne (*Journal*, 2 January 1840), 'I should like to be burnt after I died']

The Ideal Wireless Announcer

From Mr A. Lloyd James   *28 May 1925*

[later linguistic adviser to the BBC, and Professor of Phonetics, School of Oriental and African Studies 1933–41]

Sir,

'Circuit's' letter on the subject of the 'Ideal Announcer' is interesting from many points of view, but possibly most interesting as representing an attempt, made by the committee at Regina, Saskatchewan, to lay down a standard of speech suitable for broadcasting. Such a standard must obviously be based upon a consideration of two factors – namely, the limitations of the present transmitting and receiving apparatus; and, secondly, the aesthetic element. The second factor may be dismissed, for the moment, with the reminder that in matters of taste there can be no agreement. Provided that the speech of the announcer is the speech of an educated Englishman, free from affectations, no more need be said. But much remains to be said, and much remains to be investigated, concerning the limitations of the apparatus and the constant effect of such limitations upon the type of speech most suitable for broadcasting.

The difference between broadcast speech and ordinary speech is briefly this: In the first case, the whole of the visual element is removed and the listener is left to rely for his understanding entirely upon the acoustic element of speech. How large a part the visual element plays in the understanding of speech has never been experimentally determined. We know that in the case of the deaf the visual element may be the only element, and it is a matter of common experience to most of us that we understand the speaker better when he is visible than when he is not visible.

It follows, then, that since the announcer is invisible, he must be sure that his hearers get the maximum of the acoustic element necessary for intelligibility. This would be easy if existing wireless apparatus transmitted all sounds equally well; but it does not. It automatically distorts every s, f and th (as in thin), as a recent test carried out at the London Station tended to show.

Since approximately 10 per cent of sounds are subject to distortion, it is obviously necessary to be particularly careful to make sure that listeners receive the remainder as purely as possible. But it has to be borne in mind, not only that the design of microphones is still far from having attained finality, but that conditions at the receiving end vary infinitely with the goodness according to the quality of loud speakers and the acoustic qualities of rooms.

Whether the Regina Committee arrived at its conclusion as the result of detailed research, or merely on empirical grounds, is not stated. The British Broadcasting Company are carrying out phonetic research before arriving at any conclusion, and possibly they are wise in postponing their decision until adequate research has been carried out. For the tests will be carried out shortly, and it is to be hoped that listeners will do their share in making them effective. Unless listeners cooperate in their experiments no real progress can be achieved, and criticism without cooperation cannot be justified.

Yours faithfuly,

A. LLOYD JAMES

A Recipe for Porridge

From Mr W. B. Hopkins   *17 August 1925*

Sir,

The recipe given last Saturday for porridge is not very helpful, nothing being said as to the quantity of water or of oatmeal a person.

The time for preparation given as $1\frac{1}{2}$ hour's boiling, during which stirring is to be frequent and therefore attendance constant, is enough to scare off anyone not cursed with too much leisure from attempting to supply an article of food which has no need to be so costly of one's time and for firing.

It is impossible to make good, appetizing porridge in a double saucepan, the only means of cooking it without stirring at frequent intervals, for the simple reason that it is not possible to bring the contents of the inner pan to the boil, and porridge that has not boiled for some time will not 'set' when poured out: and if it will not 'set' it is not nearly so palatable as if it does set. Porridge that is set will slide out of your plate a few minutes after being poured into it without leaving a smear behind. It is of a jelly-like consistency, not a viscous half-cooked mess. I repeat that it is impossible to attain this consistency with a double pan, and so far I agree with 'E. E. K.' I merely mention this to emphasize it. Having, then, a single unjacketed saucepan of a capacity equal to twice the amount of water to be put into it – so as to avoid boiling over, which porridge is very prone to do – put into it, overnight if porridge is wanted in the morning, or, say, for six hours before wanted, for every person or for each small soup-plateful of porridge required, 2 oz of best coarse Scotch oatmeal, and not any of the crushed and mangled or otherwise pre-treated substitutes. Add one pint of water, and leave to soak. About half an hour before it is required bring it to the boil and take care that it does not boil over, stirring nearly all the time. Then keep it gently boiling for 20 minutes, stirring often enough to prevent sticking and burning. Finally boil briskly for five minutes and pour into a tureen or direct into the soup plates from which it is to be eaten. As much salt as will stand on a sixpence may be added per portion when the oatmeal is put into soak, or not, as desired.

To enjoy porridge properly it should be 'set,' thoroughly swollen, and boiled, which the above treatment ensures, and eaten with plenty, say ½ pint per portion, of the best and freshest milk. There may be added salt, or sugar, or cream, or all three; or it may be eaten with treacle. Half an hour is ample for boiling, and I have cooked it satisfactorily in 20 minutes frequently. But it must boil, and not merely stew. Scattering the meal into the water is done to prevent it binding into lumps. It rarely does this if put into cold water for six hours before boiling begins, but it is just as well to see that there are no lumps before leaving to soak. I know of no reason why soaking beforehand should be objected to, and it saves firing and the cook's time and trouble.

W. B. HOPKINS

[Hominy porridge should boil for two to five hours over a very slow fire, at least in the opinion of George Augustus Sala, one-time special correspondent of the *Daily Telegraph*]

Modern Youth

From the Archdeacon of Chesterfield　　　　　*23 April 1926*

Sir,

The criticisms which have appeared in the correspondence on 'Modern Youth' have been on the severe side, though undoubtedly all that has been said must be acknowledged as embodying truth, but there is one aspect of the conduct of young people to which full justice has not been given, and that is the relationship between modern youth and old age. The graciousness of present-day youth to old age stands out as a remarkable contrast to the stilted respect of half a century ago. Affection was none the less true and sincere, no doubt, though we always addressed our fathers and grandsires as 'Sir,' and always rose when they entered the room where we were; but I do not recall my own relationship with the elders as being what I can speak of as quite natural and at ease.

Today it is much different. A while ago I happened to be present at a point-to-point hunt meeting, the first I had attended since my youth, but I could not help noticing the delightful and friendly way in which the young men and women came and chatted to me and to other old fogeys who were there, talking quite naturally about the events, the horses and the riders, and even confiding their 'backings.' It was very different half a century ago. The same kindliness runs through all classes. On a wild stormy night during the past winter I had occasion on a Sunday night to take the service in an outlying district church two miles from my house. Two young collier lads insisted on walking home with me a long distance out of their way 'because it was not fit for an old gentleman to go alone on a night like that,' and they came in the soaking rain, though one of them had to change and go to work that night.

I grant the young people often startle me, and I sometimes wonder! but their kindliness, their openness and their gracious consideration of age make me feel they are the most lovable youth of all time. It is the same with the young children. We are told they are independent and wilful and undisciplined, but there is a wonderful charm in their quite natural absence of 'awe' for the old people. In passing along one of the streets in our mining village, I was hailed and conducted into the backyard of a cottage home, a chair was brought from the cottage, and I witnessed a children's performance – 'Little Red Riding Hood,' a fairy dance, a recitation, and several songs. The dresses were made by the children of coloured crinkly paper and various homely devices which included old curtains and door-mats. The yard was full of children as spectators with a few collier lads. It was a priceless show, and had taken most of the Easter week holiday to prepare. There was no shyness and the stage manageress explained to me all details. The matter of note is that a lot of children should care to bring in an old gentleman and seemingly like to have him there just as one of themselves.

With all the difficulties which youth presents these days (and, my word, they are real difficulties) at least let it be chronicled there never was a time when the young were more gracious to the old.

Yours &c.
E. F. CROSSE

['I am convinced that the young of today are the kindest and most interesting adolescents that ever flourished in this green and pleasant, or indeed in any other, land.' – Sir Harold Nicolson in *The Observer*, 15th January 1961)

Socialist Jargon

From Mr A. P. Herbert   12 January 1927

[later Independent MP for Oxford University 1935–50; petty officer with two good conduct badges; knighted 1945; Companion of Honour 1970]

Sir,

Somewhere, it seems, a committee of simple working men is engaged in devising measures by which the youth of our race may be provided with a 'proletarian outlook' instead of a '*bourgeois* psychology' in the State schools of the future. For it is strange but true that in these days the simpler the man the longer the words he uses. And others, it seems, are gravely disturbed by this proposal. May I humbly suggest that opponents of the moth-eaten theory called Socialism make a great mistake when they treat this kind of thing with solemnity instead of with ridicule? The real defence against the fanatical Socialist is that he is extremely funny, and that the British voter, in spite of appearances, has a sense of humour. And the best way of defeating his 'propaganda' is not to suppress it but to publish it abroad, as humorous matter.

Especially his songs. I have been studying a 'proletarian' song-book, which contains, in lyrical form, many of these 'intellectual convictions' recently expressed by Mr Mosley in less effective prose. The proletarian outlook is, of course, nothing if not brotherly, and I have made a list of the fraternal epithets devoted to those who do not believe that the nationalization of the means of production, distribution, and exchange is the only cure for poverty, and are therefore enemies of the poor. They are called parasites, capitalists, idlers, drones, loafers, shirkers, tyrants, bullies, bosses, sweaters, exploiters, traitors, liars, despots, barons, spoilers, grafters, robbers, swindlers, plunderers, thieves and sneaks. Nor do the poor come off much better. The poor are addressed as slaves, serfs, serf-men, bond-men, cringers, crouchers, bone-heads, boobs, dolts, dupes, duffers, fools, tools, prisoners, catspaws, thralls, cowards, cravens, dogs, and beasts of burden. And there is a song about parasites to the tune of 'Annie Laurie.'

113

So much for verse. In prose, though it would seem impossible, the Socialists' words are growing longer and longer. And the most vocal reformers of England can write whole paragraphs without employing a single English word. It would be too much to expect a revolutionary to use the King's English, but they do not use anybody's English. 'The I.L.P.,' says Mr Maxton in your columns, 'aims at inspiring them with a revolutionary and not a gradualistic objective.' The honest milkman is not a milkman but a class-conscious proletarian; and I am not a struggling author but a spoiler and parasite infected with a *bourgeois* psychology and anxious to sabotage (!) the mass-enthusiasm of the international 'worker.'

Now, Sir, all this rubbish should be comic ammunition to be used against its creators. I flatter myself that I know as much about the poor as Mr Mosley. I live at Hammersmith, I meet them daily. I have served in the ranks of the infantry, I have worked in the East End, I am a 'toiler' myself; and though I do not believe in the nationalization of &c., &c., or in any other adamantine formula, I claim to be as much a friend of the poor as Comrade Mosley. And if I were to address one of my 'worker' friends as a class-conscious proletarian, or suggest that he was inspired with a gradualistic objective, he would hoot with laughter. Indeed, there are, thank Heaven, many millions of the proletariat who do not even know that they are proletarians. It is all unreal and ridiculous. And politicians should treat it as ridiculous, instead of answering it in terms as solemn and almost as long. They should fill their speeches with serfs and thralls, exploiters and parasites, and make the whole vocabulary such a stale joke that when at last the Socialist is able to introduce it into the schools the children will cackle with weary laughter. There should be comic songs about the class-conscious proletarian; there should be a comic dictionary of Socialist Jargon; there should be prizes for Essays in the Socialist Language, and polysyllabic Resolutions in Trade Unionese; the proletarian songs I have mentioned should be sung compulsorily in all the schools, and that would be the end of Communism and all the other 'isms. But so long as we treat this mongrel, Continental, lunatic drivel as if it were the utterance of reasonable Englishmen, no doubt it will continue to delude the poor.

I am, Sir, your obedient servant,

A. P. HERBERT

[James Maxton was ILP Member for Bridgeton. Oswald Mosley Labour Member for Smethwick]

From What a Depth Proceed Thy Honours

From Lord Rosebery   *16 February 1927*

[who became Prime Minister of Britain and won the Derby
in the same year, 1894]

Sir,

Will you assist an embarrassed old fogey to understand the
present position, for he hears that in the newspapers it is
reported that negotiations are going on with regard to a certain
electoral fund, in the possession of Mr Lloyd George, which
appears to be a main asset in the business.

Now the question, which is never asked, but which must
occur to us all, is: What is this sum, how was it obtained, and
what is its source? Certainly it is not from Mr Lloyd George's
private means; it comes from some other direction. What is
this! It surely cannot be the sale of the Royal Honours. If that
were so, there would be nothing in the worst times of Charles
II or Sir Robert Walpole to equal it. But what amazes me is
this: no one seems to think that there would be anything unusual in such a sale. If so, all the worse, for it would be the
prostitution of the Royal Prerogative, and so the ruin of the
British Constitution.

On such a matter there should be no possibility of doubt.
Scores, nay hundreds, of 'Honours' have been distributed. Have
any been sold and helped to produce the sum in question? An
authoritative statement should be furnished as to the source of
this fund.

                    I am, Sir, yours respectfully,
                                        ROSEBERY

[Some Honours had been sold, the proceeds going to Lloyd
George's £2m secret fund. Perhaps because the Honours
(Prevention of Abuses) Act had become law in August
1925, the British Constitution survived]

Police and Chewing Gum

From Millicent, Duchess of Sutherland   *3 July 1928*

Sir,

If I were to begin a letter on the subjects of the enforce-
ments and non-enforcements on the actions of the London

police, my pen might burn the paper. I will restrict myself to chewing gum!

Why in heaven's name are our police forbidden to chew gum? The steadying effect on the nerves, the calming of tiredness, the greater efficiency provoked by chewing gum is a question of common knowledge. I have proved this on long motor runs and exhausting journeys. I encourage my chauffeur to chew gum: he is always fresher at the end of a long excursion than if he smoked cigarettes. Think of the hours a policeman is standing on his beat.

This perpetual interference in England in minor details with the liberty of the subject, whether he be prince or policeman, seems pretty absurd abroad. The English people are indeed strong in their submission, but whenever I come over I find them tiresome in their complaints about it. Please give the Metropolitan policeman back his chewing gum, and merely ask him to be careful where he emits it.

MILLICENT SUTHERLAND

[Her Grace's concern with the spot where chewing gum could be emitted shows she was resident on the Continent and not in the United States. There, as Bertie Wooster had recently observed, policemen park their gum against a rainy day]

Sleeping Out of Doors

From Dr H. Wynne Thomas   *21 July 1928*

Sir,

I was much interested in your article 'Sleeping Out of Doors.' As I have myself slept out of doors every summer since 1912, perhaps some personal experience may be of use to others. My house is just ten miles from London Bridge, and, fortunately, my garden is not much overlooked, although I live in the centre of Bromley, in the High-street.

I first tried sleeping in a hammock, but found it draughty and difficult to turn over, so I soon took to sleeping on a canvas Army bed, which is easy to pack up if required. If the weather is fine, I always sleep under the stars, with no covering on my head, in a sleeping bag, with an extra rug if necessary. If the weather is cool or likely to rain, I sleep in a wooden shelter I had made facing south-east, just large enough to take the bed. I begin sleeping out when the night thermometer is about 47deg. to 50deg., that is, as a rule, early in May. This year I started on 20 April. Having once started, I go on through the summer till October, and have even slept out in my shelter on into November, when the temperature has fallen as low as 25deg. during the night. If it should be a wet night I stay indoors, but then usually feel the bedroom stuffy, although the windows are wide open, and not refreshed as I do outside. If it rains when I am in my bag, I do not mind, and have often slept out in a thunderstorm. This last week I slept six hours without waking and got up feeling fresh and keen like a school-boy, though I am well past 60.

Friends say, what about midges and insects? Well, all I can say is that in 16 years I have only been bitten once by a mosquito. As to midges, they are very busy up till 10, but evidently go to bed before I do. As to other animals and insects, they have never worried me, and the secret, I believe, is that my bed stands 1ft. from the ground. I hate the cold weather, and look forward to the spring that I may sleep out; and to hear the 'birds' chorus' in the early morning in May is worth waking up for; it only lasts about 20 minutes, but must be heard to be appreciated. In June it dies down, and few birds sing after Midsummer Day.

When sleeping outdoors I never get a cold. I do not require so much time in bed, and wake refreshed in a way I never do indoors, with such an appetite for breakfast as no tonic can give. I enjoy the best of health, and wonder more people do not try it. During this summer weather I have never had any difficulty in keeping my rooms cool. My study has never been higher than 70deg., while outside in the shade my thermometer is 84deg. and 88deg., simply because I shut my windows at 9 a.m. and pull down the blinds, and open them at 8 p.m. and leave them open all night. I bottle up the cool night air and shut out the air which is baked by the hot road and pavement. My study faces due west and has the sun streaming down nearly all day. Bedrooms may be kept cool in the same way.

Yours faithfully,
H. WYNNE THOMAS

[An ex-President of the British Homoeopathic Society, Dr Thomas had written on 'Nocturnal Emissions in Children' – Jl. Homoeop. Soc. 1899]

The Lenin Myth

From Lord Birkenhead   *26 February 1929*

[successively 1915–22 (first as Sir Frederick Smith) Solicitor-General, Attorney-General and Lord Chancellor; Secretary for India 1924–8]

Sir,

Mr Churchill's brilliant appreciation of Lenin in your columns will doubtless give fresh impetus to the myth of Lenin's greatness, and thus provide another heartache for the historians. Russia has always been to us a land of fable, and here is another in the making.

Lenin's claims to greatness appear to be four. First, he from the beginning of the Revolution enunciated the doctrine of 'All Power to the Soviets'; and the Soviets triumphed. Secondly, he headed the Bolshevist Government which for a few years menaced civilization. Thirdly, he repressed Trotsky's desire to break off the negotiations with Germany at Brest-Litovsk, and saved Soviet Russia from extinction. Fourthly, he courageously scrapped his own Bolshevist economic theories in 1921 and reinaugurated private trading.

The historian, however, will remember certain facts. First, had Kerensky possessed an ounce of statesmanship or courage the Soviets would never have acquired 'All Power,' nor would Lenin have lived to see their triumph. Secondly, the Bolshevist Government was no more a feat of constructive state-building than the supremacy of a typhus germ in a starving child's body is a proof of strong will and foresight in that germ; the Bolshevists followed the mob, they never led it. Thirdly, only a few hysterical fools imagined that the Bolshevists could fight Germany. Fourthly, Bolshevist economies having utterly failed to work, little courage was needed in Lenin to persuade the Soviet leaders to effect a change, which, to be sure, quickly broke down in its turn.

Furthermore, the historians will note that every prophecy Lenin ever made on any subject proved false. Whether he envisaged world revolution, a Bolshevised England, or even local changes in Russia, he was invariably wrong. Every one of his measures produced the opposite result from what he intended. Within 10 years of his rise to power, Bolshevism proved the most egregious failure of all political enterprises.

One grows weary of the modern cult of success. On the strength of 10 years' chaos in Russia, we are now asked to accept Lenin as a creature of demoniac energy, with a mind which 'revealed the whole world' and a will 'not less exceptional.' It is dangerous to gauge triumph by a time standard. Ten years in Revolutionary Russia do not represent 10 months in a healthier country. With more reason, Mr Churchill might magnify Mr A. J. Cook for paralysing Britain for a year!

Yours, &c.,

BIRKENHEAD

[A. J. Cook was secretary of the Miners' Federation of Great Britain during the general strike of 1926]

From the Warden of New College, Oxford   *1 March 1929*

Sir,

'Historians,' writes Lord Birkenhead, 'will note that every prophecy Lenin ever made on any subject proved false.' There is at least one notable instance to the contrary. Years before the Great War Lenin predicted his own destiny. He was confident that he would be master of the Russian State. M. Branting the well-known Swedish statesman, found him unshakable in that opinion. So, too, in 1909, when Mr Berendsen, of Copenhagen, met him at Vevey, he found his confidence unbroken and the programme of the Communist tyranny already developed in detail. Not even Louis Bonaparte was more certain of his star.

I asked M. Branting whether he thought Lenin intelligent. He replied in the negative, saying that the young man struck him as being enslaved by the theories of Marx, impenetrable to argument, and possessed by a mad conviction of destiny.

Yours, &c.,

H. A. L. FISHER

'To Caddie'

From Sir Berkeley Moynihan   *6 February 1929*

[later the first Baron Moynihan who, when not playing golf badly, was numbered among the greatest of surgeons]

Sir,

This will never do! For five days in the week we avail ourselves of *The Times* as it so competently deals with the less important affairs of life: politics, domestic or foreign; the imminence, hopes, fears of a General Election; the arrivals or departures of great people; the steady depreciation of our scanty investments; another century or two by Hobbs; or a stupendous break by Smith. But on the sixth day *The Times* is exalted in our eyes; for then your 'Golf Correspondent,' in a column of wisdom, humour, and unmatched literary charm, deals with the one real thing in life.

This week for the first time he has deeply shocked and disappointed us all. I am but a 'rabbit.' I confess to a handicap of 24 (at times) and a compassionate heart (always). I cannot bear to see a fellow creature suffer, and it is for this reason among others that I rarely find myself able to inflict upon an opponent the anguish of defeat. Today I suffer for a whole world of caddies, wounded in the house of their friend. They learn in a message almost sounding a note of disdain that the verb which signifies their full activity is 'to carry.'

By what restriction of mind can anyone suppose that this is adequate? Does not a caddy in truth take charge of our lives and control all our thoughts and actions while we are in his august company? He it is who comforts us in our time of sorrow, encourages us in moments of doubt, inspires us to that little added effort which, when crowned with rare success, brings a joy that nothing else can offer. It is he who with majestic gravity and indisputable authority hands to us the club that he thinks most fitted to our meagre power, as though it were not a rude mattock but indeed a royal sceptre. It is he who counsels us in time of crisis, urging that we should 'run her up' or 'loft her,' or 'take a line a wee bit to the left, with a shade of slice.' Does he not enjoin us with magisterial right not to raise our head? Are we not most properly rebuked when our left knee sags, or our right elbow soars; or our body is too rigid while our eye goes roaming? Does he not count our strokes with remorseless and unpardonable accuracy, keeping all the while a watchful eye upon our opponent's score? Does he not speak of 'our' honour, and is not his exhortation that 'we' must win this hole? Does he not make us feel that some share of happiness, or of misery, will be his in our moment of victory or defeat? Does he not with most subtle but delicious flattery coax us to a belief that if only we had time to play a 'bit oftener' we should reach the dignity of a single-figure handicap? Does he not hold aloft the flag as though it were indeed our standard, inspiring a reluctant ball at last to gain the hole?

Does such a man do nothing but 'carry' for us? Of course, he does infinitely more. He 'caddies' for us, bless him.

Yours,

BERKELEY MOYNIHAN

[Of the three great stylists referred to, Bernard Darwin served *The Times* for forty-six years and was the most illustrious of writers on golf. The Smith in question, Willie from Darlington, later had the sad privilege (with Joe Davis) of ringing down the curtain at Thurston's before that billiards hall was knocked down in 1955 to make way for some motoring organization's offices]

A Matter of Haberdashery

From Sir Frederick Ponsonby   **9 August 1929**

[Treasurer to King George V; later the first Baron Sysonby]

Sir,

Whether it is from a lack of imagination on the part of the college authorities, or a paucity of ideas on the part of the haberdashers, the fact remains that the Old Wykehamist tie, which to the best of my belief only sprang into existence of late years, resembles the Guards' tie so closely that expert students of haberdashery unaided by microscopes are unable to detect the difference, especially when it is somewhat faded. The Guards' tie is composed of the Royal colours, and this privilege was no doubt given to them as the Sovereign's Household troops, but it is difficult to understand what justification there is for the Old Wykehamists wearing the Royal colours in a faded condition.

Many years ago it was said that the tie of the Upper Tooting Bicycle Club was practically the same as the Guards' tie. If that club is still in existence the position must indeed be confusing, but perhaps a super-tie might be devised to denote those who, having been educated at Winchester, joined the Household Brigade and have not been subsequently black-balled for the Upper Tooting Bicycle Club.

I am, Sir, your obedient servant,

F. E. G. PONSONBY

[Sir Frederick had spent *his* school days at Eton]

The New Era in Russia

From Sir Bernard Pares   *5 February 1930*

[Professor of Russian Language, Literature and History
in the University of London]

Sir,

Apart from all questions of diplomatic relations, may I call
attention to the critical importance of the present moment for
the fate of the Russian peasantry? Stalin, on his 50th birthday
in December, wrote that 1930 is to be the year of the great
change and of that there is no doubt, whichever way the
change may go. On the anniversary of Lenin's death, he
denounced Lenin's last political act, the so-called New Economic Policy. We are already well on in an entirely new period.

The change, for all careful students of Russia, is fully
explained by the evolution of the preceding period. From the
Communist point of view the New Economic Policy, except in
one very important respect, failed. It was being eviscerated
by the trend of life in the country. The whole period was full
of glaring ironies. A mathematical demonstration was given
to the population that in practice Communism – that is, the
elimination of personal initiative – meant decay; that economic
recovery was proportionate to the abandonment of Communism. Every instinct suppressed by the Communists, the
religious, the academic, the economic, received a new vitality
from the repression. There was only one big success, a negative
one it is true – namely, that a number of hard young hooligans
have been brought up in blinkers and in complete ignorance
of the outside world and its laws.

All this has been very intelligible for many years past. It has
been emphasized with monotony in all serious evidence; but at
last its effects became manifest within the Communist Party
itself, and, though this small party has a complete monopoly of
power and of the Press, the cracks appeared only too visibly
on the surface, and the party has been torn by all sorts of dis-
sensions. In the main the trend of policy has for long been an
alternation between big drifts to the right and vehement tugs
to the left, and it is the latest of these that we are now
witnessing.

Stalin, whose violence was always feared by Lenin, has now
expelled or subdued all his colleagues, and is determined by
violence to force through at all costs the whole programme of
militant Communism. It was the peasants who defeated Lenin,

122

as Lenin himself admitted. He recognized, as all of us do who have spent long periods among them, that the peasants were the worst material for Communism, that they were essentially small-property men. This essential character is what Stalin is out to alter by force. As is known, the Bolsheviks hoped to win in an industrial country, and had no real agricultural policy till they found themselves the rulers of Russia. A more or less mechanical attempt to apply Communism off-hand to the Russian peasantry broke down in 1921 – because the peasant, when told that, except for the allowance assigned to him for his own needs, he was to grow grain, not for the market, but for the State, stopped growing what he was not allowed to keep, and the result was a colossal famine which is still a nightmare to those who survived it. Stalin is now going through at all costs. He will mechanize agriculture; and he hopes that the difference in output created by State-owned tractors on military farms will cancel the inevitable loss caused by the simultaneous elimination of thrift. At the best he seems in for another great famine, and as likely as not for assassination.

That is the position; and, as one who has lived long among the Russian peasantry, I want to call attention to their plight under this grisly experiment; for the peasants are the mass of the Russian people, the raw material of the Army and the main producers of the country. The bulk of their long and dreary history was the story of serfdom, abolished in 1861, and it is really serfdom that Stalin is trying to restore. Then, as now, it was instituted for State purposes – recruitment and taxation; and the Russian gentry were not squires in our sense but local officials; the peasants, not without reason, looked at them as intruders, and took comfort in the fact that at least the land remained with them. After Napoleon's Moscow campaign, when promises of emancipation had been issued, there was instead of this an actual militarization of agriculture in many districts, which produced peasant risings, and has always been regarded as one of the worst blots on the rule of the Tsars. Now we are back at that again.

In the name of a ridiculous and fantastic theory, which has already gone bankrupt once under the Bolshevists, the peasant is to be deprived of all interest in the produce of his toil, and that by a Government which has the effrontery to style itself the 'Government of the Workers and Peasants,' but is, of course, in spite of its complicated system of castrated elections, nothing else but the present master of the inner ring of the

Communist Party. The peasants are naturally divided into those who are laborious and produce and those who do not; but the label of 'kulak', earlier applied to the three or four hard-fisted and avaricious peasants in a village, has now been made to cover all the former section; so Rykov himself was saying a few months ago. Of course the peasants will resist, for even the poorer peasant generally owed his means of living to his more prosperous neighbour. But all the machinery of the State has been turned against them, and executions and wholesale confiscations are going on every day.

What will be the issue? Who can say, except that in any case it will be terrible? There are still arm-chair theorists who regard it all as an interesting experiment, perhaps worth the sacrifice of a generation of peasants, and there are capitalists who, if payment is secured, will be glad to supply the tractors. But, though its name has been eliminated from the State title, there is still Russia, a country with only 3,000,000 industrial workers and close on 120,000,000 peasants, and there is still enough of the love of liberty in this country for voices to be raised against this new slavery.

Yours faithfully,
BERNARD PARES

['The Party has succeeded in routing the kulaks as a class . . .' – J. Stalin, 7 January 1933]

The Ideal Waiter

From Mr W. Mumford   5 *April 1930*

Sir,

That the true waiter should receive his accolade, if not a step in the peerage, has long been my conviction. Consequently, although I have not the honour to be a waiter myself, I read your appreciation in *The Times* this morning with profound satisfaction, even while deprecating somewhat a touch here and there of the frivolous in treating a subject so inherently serious. Permit me, Sir, to assert, and I do so without hesitation, that the true waiter, in order to live up to the high standard of his calling, must be possessed of a greater variety of gifts and acquirements than the representative of any other profession. There are unquestionably today more good lawyers in Great Britain than there are good waiters – due to no other cause than the less exacting requirements of the Bar.

The waiter, as he should be and as he is expected to be, must have outward details such as the setting of the table or the pouring of the wine – matters of form as distinct from those of content – so completely mastered that at no time can there appear any flaw in his technique. He should have such knowledge of the viands and wines he has to offer as will command the respect of the most fastidious gourmet. He should be able to command at least two languages besides his own. He should be able so to control his temper as to receive even insults in accordance with the high and honourable traditions of his class rather than to attempt to compete with the lower standards of other classes.

But there are qualities, less self-evident, which he is expected to display. He must have infinite tact, so as to enable him to handle appropriately any human situation or disposition, a knowledge of character such as to give him to read promptly that of the guest of the moment and shape his course accordingly, as well as a sixth sense, which I shall call 'anticipatory,' informing him what the guest wants before the guest knows himself, that he may supply it unobtrusively. He should have true, not assumed, kindliness and sympathy, but with an insight that will enable him to display it in the manner most acceptable to the case in hand. In fine he should have the will, education, and natural gifts to produce in each patron, however trying and diverse the circumstances, a pleasant feeling of well-being, which alone can give food the final touch of the delectable that makes a perfect meal.

These qualities are rare. The combination of them is so unheard of that it is expected from no other calling. We do expect it from a waiter, thus rendering him an unconscious tribute.

I am, &c.,
WILLIAM MUMFORD

The Trade Disputes Bill

['Acts of Parliament are not passed to make illegal specific acts that either you or I think are legal. They are passed to define what illegality is, i.e. a political strike . . .' – Ramsay MacDonald to Neville Chamberlain]

Sir,

The Prime Minister, in his last letter to Mr Neville Chamberlain, has burst, somewhat unexpectedly, into humour. Perhaps, therefore, I may trespass into politics.

Is there not a simple solution to this rather childish controversy? I suggest that the Trade Disputes Bill be withdrawn and a two-clause measure be substituted as follows:

REVOLUTION (ENABLING) BILL

(1) A revolution shall be lawful if it be conducted by the manual workers in two or more basic industries.

(2) It shall be lawful for the income-tax payers to combine together to refuse payment of income-tax, provided that the primary purpose of such refusal be to further a financial dispute and not to embarrass the Government.

This, unlike most modern legislation, would be not only lucid but just. I cannot hope that even this measure would goad the Parliamentary Liberal Party to unanimity, but almost every other citizen would be satisfied.

I am, Sir, your obedient servant,

A. P. HERBERT

A New Style for Bishops

From the Bishop of Swansea and Brecon   *7 March 1931*
  [the Rt Rev. Edwin Bevan]

Sir,

I have grown quite accustomed to being addressed as the 'Bishop of Swansea, Esq.' That, indeed, appears to be almost a common usage on the part of the GPO and other of the Civil Service establishments in London. I hope the practice is not confined to Bishops, but that the holders of official titles in the Army and Navy and in other directions are equally favoured. In these sad days we must be grateful for anything which adds thus to the gaiety of the nation.

Today, however, the office of a Chief Inspector of Taxes in the Metropolis has introduced a delightful variation, and I find myself for the first time addressed as 'Messrs. Swansea and Brecon.'

Your obedient servant,

E. L. SWANSEA AND BRECON

The Musical Glasses

[While I'd gladly waft a *Vale*
To the fife and ukulele,
And the saxophone to me is simply chronic – Ah!
  Words would fail to paint my passion
  If this nightmare proved the fashion,
            Viz.,
            The
      Hydrolaktulopsychicharmonica
                  – *Punch*, 20 January 1932]

From Mr W. McG. Eagar   *31 January 1932*

Sir,
    Some neat verses in *Punch* have now raised to notoriety the
lady of Twyford who recently figured in the news as entertaining a Women's Institute with a performance on the 'Hydrodactulopsychicharmonica.' Thus was the portentous instrument
spelt in the daily papers, and thus in *Punch*. Can it be, Sir, that
a misprint even in dog-Greek can now pass undetected, and
that the strolling players who in late Victorian times awed
villages with the Hydrodactulopsychicharmonica can no longer
protest that their little Greek is strictly descriptive? Have the
Rural Community Councils and the cinemas, making fashionable topics everywhere of 'pictures, taste, and Shakespeare,'
destroyed the very memory of 'the musical glasses?'
    For fear that this is so will you, Sir, record in your im-
perishable pages one memory of a Cornish village in the
nineties? My brother and I, being of less than preparatory
school age and still innocent of the classics, reported home to
the vicarage that a Professor and his Talented Family were
going to give a refined music entertainment in the school.
There were bills posted up all over the place, on the door of
Mr Tripp's shop, on gate-posts, and even on the churchyard
gate, promising that the entertainment would include the
Hydrodaktulopsychicharmonica. I remember that the name
ran right across the bill, and that we pronounced the 'ps' as in
Topsy and the 'ch' as in cheese. Surviving the shock the vicar
first gave us a brief lesson in the pronunciation of Greek, and
then went to find the bold invader of his local monopoly of the
learned languages. Happily the Professor stood fire. His interpretation 'music of the soul drawn out by fingers dipped in
water' made the vicar wince, but it passed and, sitting in the

front row that evening, we heard strange harmonies produced from batteries of wine-glasses, red, blue, and green. We thought it very beautiful and the Talented Family, supping at the vicarage after the show, not only demonstrated their skill on our poor stock of wine-glasses, but taught us boys how to strike a note. . . . May the lady of Twyford continue for many years to delight women's institutes, but for the sake of the humour which lies in little pedantries let her not corrupt the 'Professor's' unsophisticated Greek.

I am, Sir, yours, &c.,

W. McG. Eagar

Shop Shyness

From Mr W. Hodgson Burnet   *19 May 1932*

Sir,

I wonder if any of your male readers suffer as I do from what I can only describe as 'Shop-shyness'? When I go into a shop I never seem to be able to get what I want, and I certainly never want what I eventually get. Take hats. When I want a grey soft hat which I have seen in the window priced at 17s. 6d. I come out with a *brown* hat (which doesn't suit me) costing 35s. All because I have not the pluck to insist upon having what I want. I have got into the habit of saying weakly, 'Yes, I'll have that one,' just because the shop assistant assures me that it suits me, fits me, and is a far, far better article than the one I originally asked for.

It is the same with shoes. In a shoe shop I am like clay in the hands of a potter. 'I want a pair of black shoes,' I say, 'about twenty-five shillings – like those in the window.' The man kneels down, measures my foot, produces a cardboard box, shoves on a shoe, and assures me it is 'a nice fit.' I get up and walk about. 'How much are these?' I ask. 'These are fifty-two and six, Sir,' he says, 'a very superior shoe, Sir.' After that I simply *dare* not ask to see the inferior shoes at 25s., which is all I had meant to pay. 'Very well,' I say in my weak way, 'I'll take these.' And I do. I also take a bottle of cream polish, a pair of 'gent's half-hose,' and some aluminium shoe-trees which the fellow persuades me to let him pack up with the shoes. I have made a mess of my shopping as usual.

Is there any cure for 'shop-shyness'? Is there any 'Course of Shopping Lessons' during which I could as it were 'Buy while I Learned?' If so I should like to hear of it. For I have just received a price list of 'Very Attractive Gent's Spring Suitings,' and I am afraid – yes I am afraid . . . !

I am, Sir, your obedient servant,

W. HODGSON BURNET

St James's Park and Beyond
1933-1945

———————◆———————

EVENTS in Germany dominated 1933; sundry academics, men of science and retired generals expressed their anxiety, the odd bishop dissenting. More parochial, or so it seemed, were complaints about RAF night flying. No matter, one way of curing insomnia was to sleep in a pair of shorts. A wave of handbag snatching found men unsympathetic; women should keep their money in pockets. The news that 1,700 Jewish students had been expelled from Germany bothered 1934, a year which sought unsuccessfully to define a 'pork sausage'. King George V's Jubilee celebrations offended Sir Stafford Cripps and his supporters as so much 'bally-hoo'. When the King died in 1936, the BBC misjudged the mood of many by playing extracts from operas instead of from Handel's *Messiah*. H. G. Wells looked at the League of Nations and felt pessimistic, others asked if concessions should be made to Germany. In South Wales 36 per cent of the insured population was still without work. On December 1 the Bishop of Bradford addressed a Diocesan Conference and referred to the private life of King Edward VIII. The ensuing abdication doubtless produced some letters to *The Times* but they were not printed. 1937 was greatly put out when it heard that peers' coaches would have to approach Westminster Abbey for the Coronation of King George VI through meagre back streets; the following year deplored the bombing of cities and condemned crooners. The appointment of bishops by a Unitarian prime minister convinced some that the Church of England was being undermined. After Munich the Unitarian Neville Chamberlain was so revered that a grateful nation might at least strike a medal in his honour.

War brought a heightened sense of awareness. Should children be obliged to carry gas-masks when blackberrying? An army officer protested that, on his return from France, the Customs had confiscated a book by P. G. Wodehouse. The matter was raised in the House of Lords, their lordships feeling much easier when reminded that Sherlock Holmes had once come across a cypher in the pages of *Whitaker's Almanack*. Charges of waste were directed at the army which had used a lorry to convey two bugles a distance of one hundred miles. As Britain approached its 'Finest Hour', the BBC was criticized for giving the racing results. Was not the whole nation obsessed by gambling? Air Ministry style did not meet with approval; an all too familiar sentence in the *communiqués* – 'one of our aircraft failed to return' – implied shortcomings on part of the crews. Rephrasing was necessary. On 28 September 1940 a bishop declared we were engaged in a 'Crusade for Civilization'.

The future of London and the rebuilding of its social life gripped 1941. For every complaint, there was a master plan. The nation naturally took Post Office delays for granted. But if there were food shortages, why not breed geese which exist on grass? Slipshod English was to be deplored, yet after the war when the two great English-speaking nations would walk together in unity all promised to be well. Someone reported having seen an inverted rainbow; a squadron-leader described how his pigeon had laid an egg when over the Rühr. If doubts scudded across 1942 (one MP was sure a declining birth-rate would reduce the country's population to four and a half million within a century), permanent waving was seen as good for hair hygiene. It was regrettable that coloured American soldiers were not welcomed in cafés by their white compatriots, clearly the latter were ignorant of the British way of life. 1943 remarked on the cost of cauliflowers, then hoped that land used by the military would be returned to its owners after the war. A plan for London was discussed: flats or houses? A tide of divorce threatened to swamp 1944, when a daring cook demanded £2 a week for a five-hour day. Less than a month after the end of war in Europe, C. R. Attlee was denounced for having referred to 'ruthless property owners'. When the Allied leaders met at Potsdam, a public relations man gave details of the menus. Readers of *The Times* were not amused.

A Grey Wagtail

From the Chancellor of the Exchequer   *24 January 1933*

Sir,

It may be of interest to record that, in walking through St James's Park today, I noticed a grey wagtail running about on the now temporarily dry bed of the lake, near the dam below the bridge, and occasionally picking small insects out of the cracks in the dam.

Probably the occurrence of this bird in the heart of London has been recorded before, but I have not myself previously noted it in the Park.

I am your obedient servant,
NEVILLE CHAMBERLAIN

P.S. For the purpose of removing doubts, as we say in the House of Commons, I should perhaps add that I mean a grey wagtail and not a pied.

[On 30 January Adolf Hitler became Chancellor of Germany]

'Body-Line Bowling'

[D. G. Bradman was the cause; in 26 innings for Australia prior to 1932–3 he had averaged 112. England's captain, D. R. Jardine (who invariably wore a Harlequin cap), ordered Larwood and Voce to direct their very fast and often short-pitched deliveries at the leg stump, so making self-protection the batsman's main concern]

From Mr A. A. Milne   *20 January 1933*

Sir,

Now that it is officially announced that the bitter feeling already aroused by the colour of Mr Jardine's cap has been so intensified by the direction of Mr Larwood's bowling as to impair friendly relations between England and Australia, it is necessary that this new 'leg theory,' as it is called, should be considered, not only without heat, but also, if possible, with whatever of a sense of humour Test Matches can leave to a cricketer.

It seems funny, then, to one who did not serve his apprenticeshop as a writer by playing for Australia that a few years ago we were all agreed that cricket was being 'killed' by 'mammoth scores' and 'Marathon matches,' and that as soon as a means is devised of keeping scores down to a reasonable size cricket is 'killed' again. It seems comic to such a one that, after years of outcry against over-prepared wickets, a scream of horror should go up when a bowler proves that even such a wicket has no terrors for him. It is definitely the laugh of the year that, season after season, batsmen should break the hearts of bowlers by protecting their wickets with their persons, and that, when at last the bowler accepts the challenge and bowls at their persons, the outraged batsmen and ex-batsmen should shriek in chorus that he is not playing cricket.

These things seem funny: but there is, of course, a serious side to the Australian Board of Control's protest. This says that the English bowling has made 'protection of the body by the batsman the main consideration,' and if this were so there would be legitimate cause of complaint. But let us not forget that Mr McCabe, in his spare moments during the first Test Match, managed to collect 180 runs, and Mr Bradman, in the second, 100; each of them scoring (even though scoring was necessarily a minor consideration) four times as quickly as Mr Jardine, whose body (up to the cap) was held as sacred. Let us not forget that, if this new form of bowling is really as startingly new as is implied, lesser batsmen than these two should at least be given a chance of adapting themselves to it before the white flag is waved. But if modern batsmanship is really so unadventurous and unflexible that after three failures it announces itself beaten and calls for the laws to be altered, why, then, let the laws be altered; let everybody go on making runs, the artisan no less easily than the master, and let us admit frankly that the game is made for the batsmen only, and that it ceases to be cricket as soon as it can no longer be called 'a batsman's paradise.'

Yours, &c.,
A. A. MILNE

[Mr Bradman's concern for his head showed he had not read Milne. When Eeyore lost his tail, it was recovered and nailed on]

From Mr Leonard Crawley   *27 January 1933*

[who played for Cambridge University, Essex and the Gentlemen]

Sir,

May I trespass on your valuable space to discuss the article which appeared in your pages on 19 January with regard to the protest recently received by the MCC from the Australian Board of Control against the employment of a 'leg-theory' in cricket?

In the first place, though Macdonald and Gregory did undoubtedly send down an occasional ball at the batsman's body, they cannot be said, anyway while playing for Australia, to have employed a 'leg-theory,' in that such balls were exceptional and were bowled to a field with only two men on the leg-side. It is surely unfair to compare these tactics with the policy of delivering six such balls per over to a field so set as to penalize a batsman who is defending not his wicket, but his head.

Your correspondent further suggests that 'so long as a "shock" bowler is not deliberately bumping down short-pitched balls or purposely aiming at the batsman, his bowling is perfectly fair.' Granted: but when six such balls are bowled in each over, either the action is a deliberate one, or else, if the bowler is continuously doing it accidentally, he is a rank bad bowler. You cannot have it both ways. The last thing I wish to do is to bring a charge of malice-aforethought towards the batsman against either our captain or the bowlers he employs. But that our 'shock' bowlers bowl deliberately at the batsman's body cannot honestly be denied.

The real objection of the Australians, your correspondent alleges, is to the 'array of leg-fielders.' I submit that it is to this, in conjunction with body-line bowling, that the Australians, very rightly, in my view, take exception. As long as these tactics are allowed, the batsman will be frightened into giving up his wicket, and if Bradman cannot survive them, I am satisfied that not one of the great players of the past could have fared any better.

It would obviously be impossible for even so august a body as the MCC to dictate to a captain as to how he should place his field. But a short-pitched ball is a bad ball, and one which, without the remotest chance of striking the wicket, stands a considerable chance of doing the batsman bodily harm. And it seems to me that the very least that can be done in the best

135

interests of the game is to empower the umpire to 'no-ball' a bowler for pitching his deliveries short. But to my mind the whole question demands consideration from an entirely different angle. Your correspondent urges the point that 'Cricket is not played with a soft ball, and that a fast ball which hits a batsman on the body is bound to hurt.' Rugby football is also considered by some a fair training ground for manly and courageous virtues. And yet in the event of a player wilfully hacking, tripping, or striking another player, instead of going for the ball, the referee is required by the Laws of Rugby Football to order the offender off the field on the second offence. It seems to me that the analogy between this and the policy of deliberately bowling at a portion of the batsman's body which is not obscuring the wicket is a fairly close one; and the penalty is as well deserved in the one case as the other. In either game enough knocks are given and received in the ordinary course of events to satisfy the most bloodthirsty fire-eater among the spectators. But I would like to see some of the most eloquent supporters of the 'leg-theory' step into the arena against a bowler of Larwood's pace and face it for themselves.

Yours, &c.,
LEONARD CRAWLEY

[England won the series, during which no one was killed, Bradman averaging only 56. Eventually intimidatory bowling was prohibited under Law 46. The side led by Jardine, an Old Wykehamist, included a third and highly successful fast bowler, G. O. Allen, who refused to employ 'body-line'. Allen was an Old Etonian. After playing a further 46 innings for Australia with an average of 100, Bradman was knighted]

Nazis and Jews

From Lord Horder   *31 March 1933*

[a great clinician who included among his patients King George V, King George VI, and Queen Elizabeth II]

Sir,
The eyes of the civilized world are focused upon events that have been taking place in Germany since 5 March last. Amid the confusion of the various accounts that are presented from day to day one thing seems clear – that the effects of the

counter-revolution must inevitably have their repercussion upon culture and upon thought in all countries.

It is not my intention in this letter to express a view concerning the political implications, or the ethics, of recent developments in Germany, but there is one aspect which my conscience impels me to bring to the notice of your readers. I find it difficult to believe that, as has been reported, men and women of the highest attainments and standing in medicine are being compelled to vacate their positions at the dictation of a prejudice that is narrow, racial, and, in this twentieth century, hardly conceivable. If report be true, the world is to be deprived, at the least for a time, of the humanitarian and scientific services of pre-eminent medical authorities in Germany on the ground that they are Jews.

We doctors are naturally dependent for any usefulness we may possess upon the labours of a brotherhood of medical science the world over; a brotherhood which knows neither race nor creed; and we needs must lose enormously by the sterilization of so fertile a source of knowledge as our German colleagues have for a very long time provided.

I would respectfully appeal to the learned medical societies of the country to keep in touch with the march of events in Germany, with a view, should the necessity arise – but I trust it may not – of registering in no ambiguous terms a sense of apprehension of the inevitable consequences of any action of this nature. Medical science can ill afford a sacrifice of so far-reaching a character.

I am, Sir, yours faithfully,

HORDER

The MacNess

From Sir John Squire   *22 December 1933*

[poet and parodist, first literary editor of the *New Statesman* and an expert on Stilton, Squire was immortalized as Mr Hodge in A. G. Macdonell's *England Their England*]

Sir,

Like myriads of your readers I have been following with the keenest interest, and (candidly) an intense wish to be finally convinced of this particular illustration of the celebrated remark to Horatio, the correspondence engendered in your columns by the article contributed by my friend Commander

Gould. But why should the unfortunate animal be universally, in your pages as elsewhere, called 'a monster'? Why not, as the saying goes, 'Give it a name'?

My zoological friends, quite properly and scientifically, refuse to give it a name until they have seen it. One of them, when I earnestly sought conjectures of its species, replied bluntly: 'There is always plenty of evidence for miracles.' Another, when I played the 'there are more things in heaven and earth' card, remarked: 'If you really believe in it you had better start a public subscription to get us the money for a tank large enough to hold a creature of such vast, if varied, dimensions: we haven't one, either at Regent's Park or Whipsnade.' But for the rest of us, some name, not necessarily of the 'gigantosaurus' type, is needed. It would be dreadful if the populace, taking matters into its own hands, were to begin calling it 'Jock,' 'Ernie,' or 'Alf'; and it is extremely unkind, in view of the monstrous associations of the word 'monster,' to hammer away daily with that prejudicial and, question-begging appellation.

The 'Wee' sleekit, timorous, cowering beastie of Burns scarcely, perhaps, applies in its entirety: our friend, though doubtlessly (and there is evidence for this) many things, is described by no witness as 'wee' – and it takes a lot to prevent the Scotch people from calling anything 'wee.' But we have Commander Gould's authority for the view that creatures of this kind, capillary or otherwise, are extremely 'timid'; and the rumour that the denizen (as I will provisionally term him) of Loch Ness was once seen returning to the loch with a lamb in his mouth (though that might be a proper reprisal for the onslaughts on fish by cats) finds no confirmation in Commander Gould's story. Surely the question of the creature's nature should, at worst, be regarded as in abeyance; and pending a final decision on that, and his existence, a provisional and noncommittal name for him should be agreed upon.

It is with the utmost diffidence that I embark upon suggestions. We all know how difficult and heated may be debates upon the naming of new things. There was proof of this in your pages only a few days ago: all the Fellows of the Royal Society failing to reach agrement about the title of something called 'heavy hydrogen,' which is mysteriously implicated with something called 'heavy water.' But somebody must begin: and I take the plunge.

My first thought was that, if this enchanting mammal or fish must be called a monster, the word might at least be spelt in a Scotch (or Scots) way. There are alternatives: it might be spelt 'Monstuhar' (*cf.* Farquhar) or 'Monstquhar' (*cf.* Colquhoun). My next thought was that that would only put the offence at one remove for English people and at no remove for Scotch (or Scots) people. 'MacKraken?' thought I: near enough to an actual Scotch name and a persistent legend. Then plain 'The Ness.' Then more resonant Scotch (or Scots) 'Ness of Ness.' Then 'The MacNess of MacNess.' Then, with 'Eureka' ringing like music in the air, 'The MacNess of that ilk' – which not only would not be derogatory, but might help to drive into the heads of the British Public the fact that 'ilk' does not mean 'sort' or kind.

Of course, if the monster turns out to be a female, with or without a brood of little Monstquharsons, a good deal of my argument will fall to the ground.

Yours obediently,

J. C. SQUIRE

[The MacNess is still being sought]

BBC Pronunciation

[The BBC Advisory Committee on Spoken English was formed in 1926 with Robert Bridges as its chairman. In 1934 its members included Lady Cynthia Asquith, Rose Macaulay, Sir Johnston Forbes-Robertson, Lord David Cecil, Kenneth Clark, Edward Marsh, Logan Pearsall Smith and Professor I. A. Richards]

From Mr Bernard Shaw   *2 January 1934*

Sir,

As chairman of the committee which in the discharge of its frightful responsibility for advising the BBC on the subject of spoken English has incurred your censure as it has incurred everyone else's, may I mention a few circumstances which will help towards the formation of a reasonable judgment of our proceedings?

1. All the members of the committee speak presentably: that is, they are all eligible, as far as their speech is concerned, for the judicial bench, the cathedral pulpit, or the throne.

2. No two of them pronounce the same word in the English language alike.

3. They are quite frequently obliged to decide unanimously in favour of a pronunciation which they would rather die than use themselves in their private lives.

4. As they work with all the leading dictionaries before them they are free from the illusion that these works are either unanimous or up-to-date in a world of rapidly changing usage.

5. They are sufficiently familiar with the works of Chaucer to feel sincerely sorry that the lovely quadrisyllable Christe-masse, the trisyllable neighebore, and the disyllable freendes should have decayed into krussmus, naybr, and frens. We should like to vary the hackneyed set of rhymes to forever by the Shakespearian persever; and we would all, if we dared, slay any actress who, as Cleopatra, would dare degrade a noble line by calling her country's high pyramides pirramids. But if we recommended these pronunciations to the announcers they would, in the unusual event of their paying attention to our notions, gravely mislead the millions of listeners who take them as models of current speech usage.

6. We are not a cockney committee. We are quite aware that Conduit Street is known in the West End as Cundit Street. Elsewhere such a pronunciation is as unintelligible as it is incorrect. We have to dictate a pronunciation that cannot be mistaken, and abide the resultant cockney raillery as best we can.

7. Wireless and the telephone have created a necessity for a fully and clearly articulated spoken English quite different from the lazy vernacular that is called modd'ninglish. We have to get rid not only of imperfect pronunciations but of ambiguous ones. Ambiguity is largely caused by our English habit of attacking the first syllable and sacrificing the second, with the result that many words beginning with prefixes such as ex or dis sound too much alike. This usage claims to be correct; but common sense and euphony are often against it; and it is questionable whether in such cases it is general enough to be accepted as authentic usage. Superior persons stress the first syllable in dissputable, labratory, ecksmplary, desspicable, &c.; and we, being superior persons, talk like that; but as many ordinary and quite respectable people say disputable, labor-ratory, exemmplary, and despickable, we are by no means bound to come down on the side of the pretentious pronunciation if the popular alternative is less likely to be confused with other words by the new human species called listeners-in.

We have to consider sonority also. The short i is much less effective than the long one; and the disturbance I created in the

United States last April by broadcasting privvacy instead of pryvacy was justified. Issolate is a highly superior pronunciation; and wind (rhyming to tinned) is considered more elegant in some quarters than wynd; so that we get the common blunders of trist (rhyming to fist) for tryst and Rozzalind for Rosalynde; but we recommend the long i to the announcers for the sake of sonority.

Some common pronunciations have to be rejected as unbearably ugly. An announcer who pronounced decadent and sonorous as dekkadent and sonnerus would provoke Providence to strike him dumb.

The worst obstacle to our popularity as a committe is the general English conviction that to correct a man's pronunciation is to imply that he is no gentleman. Let me explain therefore that we do not correct anyone's pronunciation unless it is positively criminal. When we recommend an announcer to pronounce disputable with the stress on the second syllable we are neither inciting him to an ungentlemanly action nor insinuating that those who put the stress on the first ought to be ashamed of themselves. We are simply expressing our decision that for the purpose and under the circumstances of the new art of broadcasting the second syllable stress is the more effective.

Yours truly,
G. BERNARD SHAW

[Ten years previously 'issolate' had been the subject of a lively correspondence between Shaw and A. B. Walkley, drama critic of *The Times*, who objected when an actress used this pronunciation in a production of *Back to Methusalah*]

The Provocative Ankle

From Miss Marie Tempest   5 January 1935

[who created the part of Judith Bliss in Noël Coward's *Hay Fever*; DBE 1938]

Sir,

I see that the Bishop of London is protesting against the scantiness of the costumes worn on the stage.

I have memories of Mrs Chant's crusade, and of the wave of indignation and disgust that was roused in every decent-minded person by that prurient, prying, self-righteous campaign. George Moore says somewhere, speaking of a similar wave of puritanism in Dublin:

But let not the stern moralist rejoice unduly, for the good work is still being carried on by a band of enthusiastic amateurs.

Perhaps this is a little beside the point, which is that of costume or the lack of it. Modesty is a very odd, subtle thing. Someone, I forget whom, said it is all a matter of beauty. If we were all perfect we should not mind walking about with no clothes at all. And while I am not quite sure of the entire truth of this, I do remember meeting a very dignified Zulu outside Durban walking at the head of a file of wives, the first of whom, a young girl, wore only a loin cloth, the next a primitive brassiere, and so on, till we came to the eldest, who was completely clad; and I remember thinking how perfectly right and decent the arrangement was.

When I was in a convent in Belgium I had to bathe in a bath which was sheeted over to prevent my guardian angel seeing me. This, and similar precautions, caused a good deal of unhealthy sniggering among us girls. Anatole France has treated the whole subject with Gallic wit and irony in *L'Isle des Penguins*.

I have the greatest respect for the Bishop of London, but I humbly submit that this is not a matter for anyone of mature years. They are apt to argue logically. If an ankle in the nineties thrilled one, as even the most modest can recall, what must a whole leg do in 1934? Well, the answer is that there is no thrill at all and we are going back to the provocative ankle of the period of purity.

The modern young boy and girl are so used to the sight of practically naked bodies that I am confident nudity and indecency have nothing in common to them. Indeed, the only result of this familiarity with the nude has been to induce a tendency to sexlessness. I can see little evidence among the youngsters of today of the obsession of sex which one sensed in Victorian days and of which one has read a great deal in the franker biographies of recent years.

I believe that some girls have objected to the costumes they have to wear, but that later they got used to them. Well, I don't want to appear to be on the side of a certain type of unpleasant manager. I remember that when I first wore tights in *The Red Hussar*, showing about as much leg as a lift girl at

142

Selfridges, I wept for about an hour and then went on in a large cloak to hide my shame. In a few days I realized how silly I was and discarded the cloak. I've no doubt many of our land girls in the War were a little self-conscious at first. What of it? They can laugh at their scruples now without being utterly unsexed.

I am not entirely without feelings of decency; there are things I do object to (I admit to feeling a little old-fashioned at times), but I do protest strongly at any attempt to revive the activities of the Prudes on the Prowl, the spying of the Stigginses, and the chortling of the Chadbands.

Yours faithfully,
MARIE TEMPEST

[Mrs Laura Ormiston Chant also has her place in history. In 1894 she campaigned to erect partitions and so separate the bars of the Empire Theatre from the adjoining promenade where ladies (who would now probably be described as 'singers') flaunted their charms. This provoked the first letter in a national newspaper, the *Westminster Gazette*, of a 19-year-old Sandhurst cadet: 'I submit that the only method of reforming human nature and of obtaining a higher standard of morality is by educating the mind of the individual and improving the social conditions under which he lives.' On 3 November the partitions were pulled down by a mob headed by this same cadet who had signed his letter 'WLSC']

The Ideal Menu

From Sir Nicholas Grattan-Doyle   4 *November 1935*

[Unionist MP for Newcastle-on-Tyne (North) 1918–40]

Sir,

In these days of wars and rumours of wars, much that would otherwise be of moment passes unnoticed. But food is always of interest, so I crave courtesy to propound this question to those among your readers who are still, in spite of vitamin fiends and slimming devotees, among that rapidly diminishing band once known as gourmets – what is the ideal meal?

Sir Frederick Keeble has just told us that no one has enjoyed a perfect meal since our first parents were expelled from the vegetarian bliss of Eden. On the other hand, two notable banquets – 'dinners delectable' I have seen them called – have just been held in Bath, the first in memory of the author of 'Notes on a Cellar Book,' George Saintsbury, the second the annual dinner of the Wine and Food Society, which would indicate that fine feeding, which the two societies exist to encourage, is not yet a lost art. I append the menus for the information of the gastronomically inclined.

Is either the ideal meal? Is there an ideal meal? In what meal, if any, can the succulent steak and the Roast Beef of Old England claim to be included? And when, if ever, may we expect to see the menu of even the 'posh' dinner – the idiom of the younger generation inevitably creeps in – written in English?

I am, Sir, your obedient servant,
NICHOLAS GRATTAN-DOYLE

SAINTSBURY CLUB DINNER

La Tortue Royale
Harvey's Sherry

Les Filets de Sole Nantua
Berncasteler 1921

Le Ris-de-Veau en Cocotte
Château Cheval Blanc, 1923

Le Perdreau roti sur canape
La Salade Parisienne
Clos de Vougeot, 1911

La Bombe Nesselrode
Château d'Yquem, 1921

Les Délices Edenmore
Cockburn, 1912

Dessert
Sercial Madeira, 1850

WINE AND FOOD SOCIETY DINNER

La Veloute de Tomates
Le Consomme Madrilene
Manzanilla Sherry

Les Blanchailles Diablées
Le Suprème de Turbotin
Florentine
Liebfraumilch Imperial
Silver Jubilee, 1929

La Selle d'Agneau, persillée
Les Haricots Verts
Château Clos Fourtet, 1917

Le Faisan Roti à la
Périgourdine
Aloxe Corton, 1919

La Bombe Arlequin
Les Friandises
Martinez, 1908

[Asked to cost the Saintsbury Club menu in mid-1974 terms, a London hotel suggested between £15 and £16 per head. 'The original wines would be very expensive indeed, so if you could let us have your list . . .' The knowledge that *The Times* frowns on extravagance prompted a modest list: Harvey's Sherry, Piesporter

144

Michelsberg 1961, Château Cheval-Blanc 1953, Clos de
Vougeot 1955, Château d'Yquem 1949, Cockburn 1950
... As the menu and wines now totalled £75–£100, no
mention was made of the Malmsley 1885.

Re-costing the Saintsbury Club Dinner in mid-1981
terms, the same London hotel suggested £32 per head for
the menu. After three of the wines recommended had
totalled £150 per head, *The First Cuckoo* swallowed hard
and flew away to the House of Commons dining-room,
where the shade of Sir Nicholas Grattan-Doyle was con-
templating a menu printed in English converting '*Délice
du berger*' into 'Shepherd's Pie'.

A Bath hotelier suggests that the original dinner cost
£3 15s.]

Musical Dogs

From Sir John Squire   *11 January 1936*

Sir,

All dog-lovers must be interested in Lieutenant-Commander
Elwell-Sutton's account of his white whippet which insists on
singing to the accompaniment of his (or, may I hope, his
young son's?) accordion – presumably one of those gigantic
new instruments, invented, I think, in Italy, which make
noises as loud as those made by cinema organs and rather like
them. This dog's taste is low; but a musical ear is a musical
ear.

Some of your readers may think the gallant officer's story a
tall one; so do not I. Of course I have known dogs who simply
could not stand music, dogs who have bayed the moon when
one's nearest and dearest were singing, dogs who have crept
miserably under the chintz valances of sofas and armchairs
when the wireless was turned on. But I have known at least
one dog which had a passion for music no less ardent than that
of the accordion-fan whippet (as some of your contemporaries
would put it), although he was too modest to essay his voice in
public – whether he practised, like so many of us, in private I
do not know.

A good many years ago I was staying with the late Mr
Thomas Hardy at Max Gate. He possessed then, and for long,
a delightful fox terrier who nonchalantly supported the name
of Wessex. His owner said of him that he bit bad poets and

nuzzled good ones; I was let off, so naturally was flattered. During dinner Mr Hardy, a man of free mind who was willing to admit any fact if it was demonstrably a fact, remarked casually that the dog had a passion for the wireless. 'He won't,' he said, 'let us leave this room (the wireless, as Dr Watson might deduce, was in the dining room) until he's had a few minutes of it. He insists on it, even when we don't want it ourselves.' I listened, not incredulous, for Mr Hardy had one of the most accurate minds that ever I encountered. The ladies left the room, and I and that gentlest and most modest of great old poets were left alone with our (or, at that date, it may have been my) port. We talked a little about Chesil Bank, Dead Man's Bay, geology, and the Cerne Abbas giant (the dog meanwhile couched comfortably beneath the silent loudspeaker), and then, as manners bade, but forgetfully, we rose to go and I was graciously ushered towards the door.

Not a bit of it! Wessex's ears were pricked. He would no more go without his Sir (or was it then Mr? – historians must be exact about these things) John Reith than he would go without his breakfast. As Mr Hardy was about to pass out of the room the dog sprang at him, and gave him a fierce nip in the trouser-leg. Mr Hardy turned with that smile that wrinkled all his country face, and said: 'Well, well, Wessex, we forgot you, didn't we?' He closed the door and switched on what was then, I suppose, Daventry; and we resumed our seats. Melodiously forth came – well, I won't say a Bach Fugue, for I do not remember asking Mr Hardy whether his dog's Bach was worse than his bite. We watched the dog with affectionate and solicitous eyes, while the dog, squatting on his haunches with his jaws wide and his tongue hanging out, intently watched the 'set.' After five minutes he had had his ration, and he made no complaint when he was asked to join the general company in another room.

Sir, I am not saying or suggesting that all dogs' tastes in music are the same. One dog's Bartok is another dog's poison. Even among humans there are the tone-deaf: we remember the classic Victorian instance of the man who confessed that he could not tell 'Pop goes the Queen' from 'God save the Weasel.' But is there not a scientific field for investigation here? What percentage of dogs like music? Do particular breeds like particular kinds of music? What variations are there within the breeds themselves? Which kinds of dogs sing best? A hundred such problems await the attentions of research – and we must have many thousands of proved in-

146

stances before we can draw the most provisional of deductions.

Mr Wodehouse's Ukridge, in the course of his many optimistic efforts to turn some kind of a penny, started a farm in Kent where dogs, which their owners thought had developable intelligences, could have their intelligences developed – probably on Montessori lines. Could not some scientist, or body of scientists, more competent and better endowed than Mr Ukridge attack a more limited sphere in a more practical manner, collect a large number of dogs of various kinds, experiment on them with music of various kinds, and assist dogowners who wish to have the sort of dogs who like the sort of music that they like themselves?

I forgot to add that when Mr Hardy was describing his terrier's passion to me he added (with a poet's exactitude): 'Mind you, he doesn't like the talks.'

I replied: 'I can't tell you how I agree with him!' I had just delivered some myself.

Yours faithfully,

J. C. SQUIRE

The Abyssinians' Fate

From Dr Arnold Toynbee   *22 April 1936*

[Companion of Honour 1956; the first three volumes of *A Study of History*, one of the century's masterworks, had appeared in 1934]

Sir,

Which would we rather be? The Abyssinians or our European selves?

The Abyssinians today are dying painfully because they have the courage to fight to the death against an aggressor who is overwhelmingly stronger than they are, and who is using a devilish weapon which he has sworn to renounce. We Europeans (as Mr Baldwin told one European audience last Saturday) are perhaps going to die the same painful death tomorrow because some of us have not scrupled to commit a double breach of faith and morality by making an aggressive war and waging it with poison gas, while the rest of us have not dared to carry out more than a fragment of our covenant, for fear of the immediate risks to which we might expose ourselves by keeping faith completely.

The penalty for these interwoven sins of commission and

omission surely stares us in the face. If we Europeans persist in our present course, we are going to turn our arms against one another and then die in droves, like sheep penned in slaughter-houses, from the poison which European airmen will spray over European cities.

If our death is to be a premature and painful one anyway, which matters more? To make sure of dying it tomorrow instead of today? Or to make sure of dying it with honour instead of with dishonour? This question, which forces itself upon all parties concerned in the present international issue, has been answered by the Abyssinians already. They have chosen to die a painful but honourable death today. Have we Europeans quite made up our minds to take the other option?

I venture to enclose some Greek verses in which I have tried to picture the two choices as they may perhaps appear here-after in the longer perspective of history.

I am, &c.,
ARNOLD J. TOYNBEE

ΑΙΘΙΟΠΩΝ ΚΑΙ ΕΥΡΩΠΑΙΩΝ ΕΠΙΤΑΦΙΟΣ

κεῖνοι μέν, γυμνοὶ καὶ βάρβαροι ἄνδρες ἐόντες,
    ὄργανα φρικώδους οὐκ ἐφοβοῦντ' Ἄρεως,
ἀλλ' αὐτοσχεδίῃ, ἔτ' ἐλεύθεροι, οὐ τι τρέοαντες,
    εἰς Ἀΐδην καλῶς μαρνάμενοι κάτεβαν.
ἡμεῖς δ' οἱ μεγάλοι καὶ καρτεροί, οἱ σοφοί; ἡμῖν
    τῶν αὐτῶν ὀδυνῶν γενσαμένοισι θανεῖν
μοῖρ', αλλ' οὐ θάνατον τὸν Ἀρήϊον οὔποτε τοῖον
    τοῖς ἐπιορκοῦσιν δῶρον ἔδωκε θεός.

AN EPITAPH ON ETHIOPIANS AND EUROPEANS

Without our arms or art, these men could dare
War's utmost frightfulness, since men they were,
And, in close fight, to death untrembling passed,
Still freemen, battling nobly to the last.
But we, whose science makes us strong and great,
Are doomed to share the tortures of their fate.
Yet not their soldier's grave; the gods in scorn
Withhold that privilege from men forsworn.

(translation by Geoffrey Gathorne-Hardy)

The Wooster Chin

From Mr. P. G. Wodehouse   *30 November 1937*

[from 1939 Dr Wodehouse; briefly, in 1975, Sir Pelham]

Sir,

Your correspondent Mr John Hayward is to a great extent right in his statement that Bertie Wooster has a receding chin.

A fishlike face has always been hereditary in the Wooster family. Froissart, speaking of the Sieur de Wooster who did so well in the Crusades – his record of 11 Paynim with 12 whacks of the battleaxe still stands, I believe – mentions that, if he had not had the forethought to conceal himself behind a beard like a burst horsehair sofa, more than one of King Richard's men – who, like all of us, were fond of a good laugh – would have offered him an ant's egg.

On the other hand, everything is relative. Compared with Sir Roderick Glossop, Tuppy Glossop, old Pop Stoker, Mr Blumenfeld, and even Jeeves, Bertie is undoubtedly opisthognathous. But go to the Drones and observe him in the company of Freddie Widgeon, Catsmeat Potter-Pirbright, and – particularly – of Augustus Fink-Nottle, and his chin will seem to stick out like the ram of a battleship.

Your obedient servant,
P. G. WODEHOUSE

The Plural of Rhinoceros

From Dr Julian Huxley   *17 August 1938*

[Secretary, the Zoological Society of London, 1935–42, Sir Julian Huxley was Director-General of Unesco, 1946–8]

Sir,

In your issue of 30 July you employed *rhinoceri* as the plural of rhinoceros. This is surely a barbarism, although on referring to the New Oxford Dictionary I find to my surprise and regret that it is one of the usages cited.

This plural has given writers of English considerable trouble. Besides rhinoceros, rhinoceroses, and the above-mentioned rhinoceri, the N.E.D. quotes rhinocerons, rhinoceroes, rhinocerotes, and rhinocerontes.

Rhinoceroses would appear to be the least objectionable, but even this still has a pedantic sound. Has not the time come when we can discard our etymological prejudices, accept the usage of the ordinary man, and frankly use 'rhinos'? Confusion will not arise, since the slang use of rhino for money is moribund, if not dead.

Zoo for Zoological Gardens has now become accepted usage: I hope we may adopt the same common-sense principle for some of its inmates with embarrassingly long names. In addition to rhino, I would plead for hippo and, with a certain diffidence, for chimp.

Yours faithfully,
JULIAN S. HUXLEY

Henry Irving and Coquelin

From Lady Oxford   *8 February 1938*

Sir,

I knew Henry Irving and his lovely leading lady well. I had a passionate admiration for both of them, and after my marriage my husband and I often joined them at supper.

Irving had the sort of face which I most admire, nor can I recall any face at all like it. He did not seem to be looking at you but through you when he was talking to you. He would have enforced attention even if he had not been famous. There were many criticisms which could be made about his acting – a halting gait, a curious intonation; nevertheless, in some of the parts he played he was unrivalled and was thrilling to all theatregoers. He was the greatest impresario who has ever been connected with the English stage. In spite of his fame and his genius, and even some natural affectation, he was a lovable and authentic person and fundamentally humble.

When I first met him I was a friend of Coquelin, who visited London every season with his company from the Comédie Française. During these short visits he gave me lessons for love in the art of acting. He had made a great hit in a Paris play called *Le Juif Colonais*, which Irving bought and produced at the Lyceum under the title of *The Bells*. After seeing Coquelin perform the tortured part of Mathias – the innkeeper who had thrown one of his lodgers from his sleigh to be devoured by wolves – I went to see Irving. Two more different interpretations of the same part cannot be imagined. Coquelin enjoyed an even greater fame than Irving, and was the most accomplished actor of his day. But he had the sort of face which you could never associate with melodrama. It was as round as a Swiss roll, and had the agricultural smile of a peasant; the cleverest make-up could never have made him look sinister. Well aware of this, he played the part in a rollicking manner. However much his conscience pricked him, he appeared to be always at his ease when surrounded by his boon companions at the bar of his famous inn. He laughed louder and drank deeper when he fancied he heard sleigh-bells in the snow, which, whether they were there or not, were haunting his guilty imagination.

Irving took a different line. He never attempted to calm his conscience. When sitting in the inn with the same boon companions, however much he discoursed and declaimed he shuddered at the sound of sleigh-bells and raised his glass in both hands to distract his listeners from observing the anguish of his face.

When I praised this performance to Coquelin I could see that he was a little jealous and thought that I was exaggerating. (With all his charm and genius he had a certain vanity.) He asked me to take him to see *The Bells* and return afterwards to have supper with him. Sitting alone together, I asked him what he thought of the play, to which he replied that he had been thrilled by Irving's acting and doubtless he was a man of genius.

But, he added, the difference between our two interpretations is that the stupidest detective would have clapped Mathias (Irving) into prison, whereas I would never have been caught.

The last time I talked to Irving was when he came to see me at the end of a London season (I do not remember the date). I said that I was sorry to say goodbye to him, but I might by luck see him at the Palace garden party. He said that no actor was ever invited to a royal party unless he had a title. I told him that there would be no difficulty about this, as all our Royal Family were patronizers of the stage. I am proud to think that it was through my husband's influence that Irving was knighted.

Yours, &c.,
MARGOT OXFORD

[Margot Tennant married H. H. Asquith (later Earl of Oxford and Asquith) in 1894 when he was Home Secretary. Irving was knighted the following year]

Future of the Two Rhodesias

From Miss Margery Perham   *29 July 1939*

[Reader in Colonial Administration at Oxford 1939–48, and Director of the Oxford University Institute of Colonial Studies 1945–8. Dame Margery Perham was BBC Reith Lecturer in 1961]

Sir,

There is danger lest the crisis may distract attention from the deep significance for Africa of the issues which Mr Huggins is now discussing with our Government. These relate to the future of Southern and Northern Rhodesia and Nyasaland.

British Africa today contains two divergent systems. In areas where the European minority is considerable and has political control, the political, economic, and social measures crystallize its present superiority and lead to a stratified or caste type of society based on colour-distinction. In the other system, which obtains where European residents are few or absent, British officials assist Africans to develop in all aspects of life towards a position in which they may ultimately stand by themselves. Discussion of this contrast would be simplified if it could be detached from questions of vice and virtue. The only virtue of the Colonial Service is that it is composed of temporary, expert officials responsible to an impartial, strong and experienced Government. Admittedly the system has defects and is liable, especially in small territories such as the two now in question, to periods of inertia. For these the inadequate interest of the British people and Parliament is largely responsible, and suggestions to remedy this are being considered.

On the other hand, there is no vice in the British community of Southern Rhodesia, least of all in its attractive leader: it is composed of much the same sort of people as ourselves and our Colonial officials. But its position prevents impartiality: it is impelled to its courses by the strongest immediate motives of economic interest and by fears, often subconscious, for its own ultimate preservation. Its most high-minded individuals seek to mitigate the policy of the majority and alleviate it with social services. But those who know what Africans can achieve where they are encouraged to reach to their full stature as persons must contrast this with a system where they figure mainly as cheap, unorganized labour and – the decisive test – where the least qualified white is given the

152

full citizenship and economic opportunity denied to the most highly qualified African.

For Southern Rhodesia, with about 60,000 whites and 1,250,000 Africans, the issue is settled. It has almost complete 'self-government.' The question is as to whether the first steps should be taken to extend the Southern African system to Northern Rhodesia, with 10,600 whites and 1,366,425 Africans and Nyasaland, with 1,800 whites (largely officials and missionaries) and 1,619,530 Africans. A Royal Commission has recently reported in somewhat inconclusive form, and with important reservations by half its members, that these steps should be taken, and that the white minorities of the two northern territories should be given even fuller representation than the considerable measure they possess. Two members of the Commission hope that this, together with closer association with Southern Rhodesia, will lead to the amalgamation of a 'solid *bloc* . . . under one democratically elected Government imbued with British ideals.' This is not in harmony with the report of the highly authoritative Joint Select Committee upon the basically similar problem of East Africa. The great differences in racial numbers and culture in both areas require the continuance of an arbitral impartial Government which can hold the balance between conflicting interests, encourage actively the advance of the Africans, and progressively adjust institutions to that advance.

The representatives of the 3,000,000 northern Africans, who know Southern Africa well from their labour-migrations, have protested strongly and unanimously against the steps proposed. In this dilemma we cannot evade the main issue by compromising upon one modest step when the next ones will be automatic. We cannot salve our conscience with safeguards in native interests, since experience has taught that such safeguards upon otherwise 'responsible' Governments do not work.

Our leading Ministers have recently made before the world very large claims for our Empire as one where subject-peoples advance towards self-government. The steps proposed are not compatible with this claim. They would remove what many of us regard as our only moral justification for retaining so large a Colonial Empire. We may be sure the European claims will be fully and ably voiced. The future interests of the unrepresented Africans are wholly dependent upon the willingness of people in England to study and to urge them.

Yours faithfully,
MARGERY PERHAM

The Dachshund

From Mr D. L. Murray   *29 August 1939*

Sir,

May I, through your columns, appeal to caricaturists and humorous writers to suspend during the present crisis the practice of making the dachshund a symbol of Nazidom or of the German nation? Absurd as it may seem, the prevalence of this idea in the popular imagination has produced a real risk of thoughtless acts of cruelty being committed against harmless little animals which are English by birth and often by generations of breeding.

I am, Sir, yours faithfully,
D. L. MURRAY

[In 1914 owners of dachshunds had given away their dogs for fear of being thought German spies]

The Make-Up of Hitler

[Britain was at war with Germany from 3 September 1939]

From Dr William Brown   *19 October 1939*

[Director, Institute of Experimental Psychology, University of Oxford, 1936–45]

Sir,

A reading of Sir Nevile Henderson's 'Final Report' fully confirms the conclusions to be drawn from a psychological study of Herr Hitler's character. The following tendencies seem to me to be definite ingredients in his mental make-up:

1. An hysterical tendency, shown in his emotional appeal to crowds, in which his mind seems to undergo temporary dissociation through the very intensity of his concentration upon the matter in hand. With his mind so narrowed down on one point, he may be temporarily oblivious of other considerations, and thus may appear perfidious. There is also a probable

hysterical identification, in subconscious phantasy, with Frederick the Great, and a tendency towards a mechanical imitation of the less admirable political manoeuvres of him and of Napoleon, which makes him appear, judged by modern standards, as an atavistic monster.

2. A paranoid tendency, almost amounting to persecutory mania. He is a very aggressive person, and 'projects' this aggressiveness upon the world around him, being acutely on guard against aggression from others, with suspicion and possibly delusions that such hostile aggressiveness is active against himself and his nation. This tendency was favoured in its development by the harsh conditions of his early manhood as a lonely outcast in Vienna, although it must have a strong hereditary basis. One important effect of its presence is the fear of encirclement or of being 'ringed round with enemies,' and where encirclement is already a fact – often the result of the paranoid person's own aggressiveness – there is a great intensification of this fear, with a corresponding intensification of aggressiveness.

3. A growing megalomania, with messianic feelings. This is a further development of his paranoid tendency, making his followers paranoid, and producing a collective paranoia.

4. A compulsive tendency (in his case, a power impulse) towards more and more 'bloodless' victories, in which his latest claim to territory or power is called his last – cf., the alcoholic, who claims his latest drink his last.

In the light of above psychological analysis (which I made many months ago) it is possible to explain, at least in part, the strange reversal of policy shown in the Soviet-German Pact. After the events of last March, and the British and French reactions thereto, Herr Hitler's paranoid fear of encirclement became so intense, and his accompanying aggressiveness so magnified, that the unbearable mental tension could only be relieved by a 'retreat to Moscow.' But by this step he has jettisoned his whole *Weltanschauung*, and made nonsense of 'Mein Kampf.' He has suffered the most overwhelming defeat in the East that has ever occurred without overt fighting. Only by blind stupidity among his followers is even a temporary continuance of his régime possible. His disappearance from the scene, either by abdication, or in some other way, would clear the ground for the negotiated 'peace with justice' which all sane men desire.

Yours faithfully,
WILLIAM BROWN

The 3,000th Crossword

From the Reverend E. A. C. Buckmaster   *10 October 1939*

Sir,

Recently we were greeted for our enjoyment with *The Times* Crossword Puzzle No. 3,000. The puzzle was not – as some of us hoped – of a nature specially appropriate to this remarkable anniversary, but I do not think the occasion should be allowed to pass without suitable comment. There must be thousands of readers of *The Times* – especially cricketers and lovers of Shakespeare – who owe an undying debt of gratitude to the author of our daily 'food.'

At this point, it is interesting to look back and consider which we regard as his cleverest clue. Personally, I still cling to one of his early ones:

Clue. – 'It is topping to kiss a monkey.'

Answer. – Apex.

Bravo! Sir. Kindly carry on through the difficult days that lie ahead.

Yours sincerely,
E. A. C. BUCKMASTER

Grass for the Table

From Mr J. R. B. Branson   *2 May 1940*

Sir,

In view of the publicity you have accorded to Mrs Barrow's letter, I hope that you will spare me space to say, as an advocate for the consumption of grass-mowings, that I have eaten them regularly for over three years, and off many lawns. The sample I am eating at present comes off a golf green on Mitcham Common. I have never suffered from urticaria or any of the symptoms Mrs Barrow mentions. Nor did any of the many of my horses to which I have fed grass-mowings, freshly cut and cleaned from stones, &c. For my own consumption I also wash them well.

Yours faithfully,
J. R. B. BRANSON

[A typical meal *chez* Branson: lawn mowings mixed with lettuce leaves, sultanas, currants, rolled oats, sugar, and chopped rose-petals, with uncut rose-petals sprinkled over the whole]

General de Gaulle

From Mr Robert Cary, MP   *1 July 1940*

[Conservative Member for Eccles, later for the Withington Division of Manchester, Sir Robert Cary contested every general election between 1924 and 1970]

Sir,

May I be allowed to comment on the excellent letter of your Military Correspondent, Captain Cyril Falls?

I too have heard a little of the cautious talk about General de Gaulle. His age is a refreshing innovation in Allied leadership: the quality of his rank can easily be determined by the British Government – particularly if it were coupled to a gracious offer to be designated an honorary aide-de-camp to the supreme head of the British armed forces. General de Gaulle made a bold and superb gesture which was based upon a high strategic comprehension. The widening of the circle of the war away from the land-locked misery of the defensive to a wider perimeter where sea power could play its decisive part would give to France the energy and resource of successful counter-attack. An answer to the Panzer divisions could not be mounted on the soil of France, but their limitations – rooted in one dimension – defined their possibilities. In changing the nature of the war and given the naval and military weaknesses of Italy to bite upon, General de Gaulle discerned the seed of ultimate victory.

I cannot understand that anybody could be dilatory in recognizing General de Gaulle, unless dilatoriness is merely another symptom of those two diseases of the British method – caution and understatement. His recognition should have been automatic. Problems of rank, pay, allowances, and conditions of service for him and his followers were not insurmountable obstacles of negotiation between the British Government and the separated interests of the French Empire.

It would be difficult to find in military history characters more attractive than Hoche or Marceau, than Desaix or Richepanse. Any one of them, had he risen to supreme power, would have served France better than Napoleon. Perhaps it may be reserved to General de Gaulle to occupy the premier place in the military history of the French Republic.

Yours, &c.,

ROBERT CARY

The Countryman in War

From Mr R. D. Blumenfeld   27 December 1940

[for twenty-eight years editor of the *Daily Express*]

Sir,

I am writing this letter from my home in the country. My predecessors, who lived here for hundreds of years, experienced war in its various phases, and met it calmly and bravely during the generations that came and went.

Up to a few years ago portions of age-blackened skin which once covered the body of a raiding Dane were nailed to the door of a church in a neighbouring village. The gruesome trophy was removed shortly before the last War by an American collector of 'curios.' Here in our village there is a tumulus containing the 700-year-old bones of a goodly number of the deceased Dane's countrymen, who in the course of various raids on Essex were so hospitably received by the natives and accorded what may be termed as 'decent burial.' I believe these raiders were not subjected to the rather drastic process of skinning. But there they lie, giving ocular proof of what happens usually to unwanted invaders.

As I write this evening the air is filled with the ominous sounds of hostile aircraft passing over on their way to and from their objectives in London and other points. The sky is agitated with the flashes of exploding AA shells and made weirdly picturesque with the graceful movements of the night-piercing searchlights from various ground points. Our local ARP warden on his bicycle can be heard puffing up the hill, while at intervals he blows his tin whistle to warn us of the alert which we heard from the neighbouring town 20 minutes ago. In the meantime the invaders are over us. The warden, an old friend of mine on the land, stops at times for a little chat. He has a long way to go from farm to farm and cottage to cottage, and by the time he reaches home there will probably be another alarm to whistle for again.

Meanwhile at my gates, while the sky is at war and searchlights search and guns go off in the near distance, while we see the fireworks over London 50 miles away, a little group of six boys are singing Christmas carols. Imagine the scene! They are singing the old carols unperturbed, and not always in tune, as their fathers and forefathers have sung them where they stand, generation after generation. 'Hark! the Herald Angels' to the accompaniment of sirens and AA guns!

158

These little carol singers, the future men of England, walking mile after mile in the darkened country lanes, singing their age-old carols, unmindful of the portents above, are proof that, like the rest of the nation, they are of the Spirit that knows not defeat.

Yours &c.,
R. D. BLUMENFELD

[At Great Easton in Essex, where Blumenfeld and his wife lived for half a century, the bus stop seat has a plaque in their memory]

After the Fires

From Mr Clough Williams-Ellis   *3 January 1941*

[the creator of Portmeirion]

Sir,
  A major architectural disaster has befallen us in the mutilation or destruction of many of Wren's City churches, little masterpieces of English Baroque that we all saluted with affectionate respect even if we failed to know them intimately or learn to love them for their innate intelligence and charm.
  One of our aims in this war, a basic and uncontroversial one, is so to contrive things that apparent calamities may, wherever possible, be turned to our ultimate advantage. Not long since, the ecclesiastical authorities themselves proposed to make away with a number of these churches as 'redundant' and profitably to exploit their sites for secular uses. Now that rebuilding is anyhow thrust upon us – (the supine acceptance of a 'total loss' in this matter is surely unthinkable) – and now that some rationalization of the City's plan will presumably be called for, is there not something to be said for resurrecting these lovely buildings where they will be certain of a welcome, secure of an honoured future, and where their lustre may best illumine our pervading architectural gloom?
  Briefly, where a City clearance really does seem justified, let the old church site be profitably secularized, on the one condition that an adequate sum be set aside for, or towards, the rebuilding of the church itself in some provincial city or town that has honourable scars to be healed, and where a worthy and permanently secured island site can be made ready for it. There could be few towns where the authentic Phoenix-Wren

church would not be the most gracious, notable, and revered building in the place, so giving a more general pleasure and exercising a wider civilizing influence than ever it did as an obscured member of a congested galaxy. Decentralization, diffusion, democratization . . . If the enemy's bombs serve to disperse this cultural heritage more widely and more effectively over our country at large, there will at least be a credit side to the account. The antiquary may object that our reconstructions will not be 'authentic.' I doubt the validity of their obvious arguments.

Apart from original Wren drafts, I believe that pretty well every one of his buildings has been accurately surveyed, measured, and recorded in complete detail, so that, with photographs, far more exhaustive working drawings could probably be handed to the reconstructor than were given to the original builders. All the architect's designs (as always) had to be interpreted, well or ill, through the medium of a multitude of contractors and craftsmen, often with little or no effective supervision from the chief himself. Where parts of the original Wren fabric survive in usable condition, obviously one would piously incorporate them in the new Phoenix, but it seems to me that a stone now hewn faithfully to the master's design is not 'unauthentic' merely because it takes shape posthumously. If that pedantic test be applied to other cooperative arts, then there has been no true Beethoven symphony for over a century, no ginuine play of Shakespeare's for over three.

> I am, Sir, your obedient servant,
> CLOUGH WILLIAMS-ELLIS

[Sir Clough Williams-Ellis recalled (29 July 1974) that his letter provoked considerable reaction, 'some averring that the redundant churches shanghaied into alien surroundings would look ridiculous – many having been most ingeniously designed by the Master to fit into and exploit exceedingly cramped and awkward sites. True, but my retort was that in such cases the new surroundings should of course be modified and adapted to pay due respect to the so distinguished new-comer. Jack Squire – founder of The Architecture Club and then editor of *The London Mercury* was on my side and I recall a poem of his in which he administered a stinging rebuke to the then Bishop of London for his indifference to the fate of Wren's churches. I wish I could remember it – or better – recover it – but I seem to recall the lines:

"An eloquent witness in every street
  That the worship of money was not complete."
Or something like it.']

Official Advice

From the Bishop of Fulham   *3 June 1941*

[the Rt Rev. Staunton Batty]

Sir,
   A few weeks ago I was given official advice as to what action
to take in a gas attack. I was recommended to put both my
hand in my pockets and if I carried an umbrella to put it up.
   This morning the President of the Board of Trade told me
on the wireless that if I found myself without any clothes
owing to a 'blitz' I should appear before the Local Assistance
Board and demand coupons. It is puzzling, but, as Mr A. P.
Herbert has laid down, 'Let us be gay.'

                                    Yours faithfully,
                                    STAUNTON FULHAM

The House of Commons, a Perfect Chamber

[The House of Commons chamber was destroyed by
enemy action on 10 May 1941; the Commons then moved
to the House of Lords, and the Lords to Church House,
Westminster]

From Mr J. Howard Whitehouse   *21 May 1941*

[Liberal MP for Mid-Lanark 1910–18; headmaster of
Bembridge School 1919–54]

Sir,
   Will you allow me to state a few things about the House of
Commons which probably made it the most perfect debating
chamber in the world?
   The most important is the arrangement of its seating. As is
well known, on each side of the Speaker's chair are rows of
benches rising in tiers. The result is that members in any of the
rows are looking at the faces of members opposite to them,
with the community of interest which this means. This arrangement gave an almost unique character to the debates of the
House and enabled the play of emotion and of humour to find
adequate expression. Every member addressing the House

spoke from the place where he was sitting, and his audience could not only see him but could hear him perfectly. If the seats had been arranged, as in so many meeting halls and churches, in long rows, one behind the other, and on the same level, life in the chamber would have been intolerable. To sit for a great part of a normal session of at least eight hours in seats which enable you to look at, but not over, the backs of the heads of those in front of you, would have been intolerable, and the arrangement would have destroyed the character of the House as a debating chamber, though suitable for a meeting of the Reichstag. The seating arrangements are also perfect for the Government and their chief opponents. Only the width of the clerks' table separates them. Both are in positions giving perfect equality and speak with the encouragement of the cheers of their supporters around them.

I have heard many of the greatest speeches made by the present Prime Minister in the House. I do not remember an instance even of comparative failure, but I have always felt that his success as an orator is greater in the House than on the platform. The arrangements of the House are the perfect setting for his superb powers, and he enjoys the opportunity of meeting opposition. There is no greater master of the art of repartee. I think, too, they greatly helped the success of orators like Augustine Birrell, Lord Hugh Cecil, Simon, Bonar Law, Balfour, and Dillon.

If I do not include Mr Lloyd George in this list it is not because I have not heard him make many great speeches in the House of Commons, but because he is the only great orator I have known who was more successful on the public platform than in the House. For his special genius he always seemed to require a large popular audience, and one which in the main was friendly. The chamber is a small one, and this is another vital factor in its success. It is the perfect size, never loses the atmosphere of a free debating assembly, or becomes a public meeting. Freedom, toleration, and equality are its controlling features. To make it larger would weaken some of these things. But it is large enough. Ordinarily there are sufficient seats. On special occasions the side galleries are used, chairs are brought in (though this has happened only once in 10 years), the steps of the gangway are used, and there is not a little standing room. I am quite sure that on these special occasions the interest and the inspiration greatly exceed that which would occur in a larger hall. No member has ever been shut out.

I discussed this matter on one occasion with John Dillon. He generally spoke from the corner seat of the fourth row below the gangway. He had attacked the Government on the Irish question (it was during the last War), and I congratulated him upon the brilliance of his speech. 'I am always helped,' he said, 'by the seating of the House. I am looking at the faces of those I am addressing, and it makes all the difference. Moreover, if I am attacking the Government I am happier in speaking from a seat above them. I am looking down upon them, hurling my defiance.'

There is this further point to be remembered about the size of the House. If it were bigger it would affect vitally the character of the speaking. There is a distinctive feature about the present method of debating, any change in which would be a great loss. Let me explain this. However great the occasion or the eminence of the speaker, our parliamentary tradition permits interruption. I am not now referring to cheers or cries of dissent, but to the fact that any member may rise and ask the member addressing the House to allow him to correct some point or put a question. The member in possession of the House invariably gives way for a moment. I think the canons of courtesy practised in this connexion greatly raise the prestige of the House and the respect – and something greater – which the members feel for it. Such a custom could not be continued in a larger hall or with a different arrangement of seating.

Complaint is made that there are no writing facilities in the chamber. Why should there be? It is a debating chamber, and it would be wholly foolish to attempt to make it at the same time a writing-room and a library. You would require a building twice the size to provide a writing desk for each member. Moreover, it is entirely unnecessary to do so. A member has only to walk through any of the doors leading into the division lobbies to find luxurious and ample writing facilities.

You, Sir, are the editor of a paper which has a great parliamentary tradition. For long decades it has reported fully the debates of the House and, if I may say so, has impartially interpreted the spirit of Parliament. May I beg you to use your influence to see that what I have described as the perfect chamber is rebuilt without substantial alteration?

Yours very truly,
J. HOWARD WHITEHOUSE

[The new Commons chamber, from the designs of Sir Giles Gilbert Scott, was used for the first time on 26 October 1950]

'Esquire'

From Mr L. Pendred   *14 November 1941*

Sir,

Among the minor reforms that are coming would not the suppression of 'Esquire' in general and business correspondence be welcomed? It is a relic of mid-Victorian snobbery, and has little or nothing to commend it. I believe the United Kingdom is the only part of the Empire that uses it.

Yours truly,
LOUGHLAN PENDRED

From Sir Max Beerbohm   *17 November 1941*

Sir,

How right Mr Loughlan Pendred is in denouncing the use of this word as 'a relic of mid-Victorian snobbery' and in demanding its 'suppression'! But why does he not go further? Is not our all too infrequent utterance or inscription of the word 'Mr' an equally gross survival from an era which men of good will can hardly mention without embarrassment and shame? I do hope Pendred *will* go further.

Your obedient servant,
MAX BEERBOHM

From Mr Osbert Sitwell   *21 November 1941*

Sir,

Beerbohm's suggestion that the prefix 'Mr' should be abolished does not go far enough. We are stil left with our surnames, and this is undemocratic. I demand that we should all be called by the same name, as plain a one as possible. If this should render difficult the filling up of forms, a number could be attached to each – or rather the same – name.

Yours faithfully,
OSBERT SITWELL

The Future of Education

From Mr A. L. Rowse   27 February 1942

Sir,

There is a point of view as to the future of our educational system which is of the utmost importance in the present discussions, and yet is hardly represented in them or sufficiently taken account of: that of people who pass through elementary and secondary schools, the vast majority of the nation. It is they who should have the largest say as to the future of education in this country, and we look to *The Times* to give expression to a point of view which was not given consideration in the discussion in the House of Lords.

We do not agree with the Archbishop of Canterbury or Lord Hankey that it will help the nation's education to enable the public schools to play a larger part in it than before. We hold that it is neither practicable nor desirable for any portion of the pupils attending elementary or secondary schools to be taken away to public schools. It is impracticable on financial, still more on social, grounds. Working-class parents will not be prepared to have their children taken away to be educated into a different social stratum, breaking up the unity of their families, when there is a perfectly good day-school system at their doors, which in many cases offers a better education than that at inferior public schools. The proper solution for the difficulties of the public schools, with the decline in the birth-rate and in the incomes of the middle-classes, is not to drain away the pupils from the national schools but for the public schools to concentrate their resources upon the best of their number. The recent amalgamation of Haileybury and the Imperial Service College points the way to the right solution for them.

We want the elementary and secondary schools to develop their own ethos and make their own contribution to the national life. We think that day-school education has its own advantages, and that the education provided at a day-school like Manchester Grammar School, for example, is inferior to none in the country. It is vital that there should not be mere imitations of the public schools. The latter made their great contribution to national life in the nineteenth century; and there are all too evident signs around us that their standards are not wholly adapted to the conditions of the contemporary world. For example, the disproportionate importance they attach to character rather than intelligence: a wrong emphasis for which we are now paying the price in every field of national life, in the conduct of the war, in politics, in administration, in the services, in the Empire. It was not so in the great, creative days of our nation in the age of Elizabeth, of the reign of Anne, of the Pitts, when the Empire was won.

Nor do we agree with the Archbishop that more religious instruction in the schools is going to be our salvation. What we want is more intelligence, putting ability, clear thinking, foresight, aggressive energy first – those standards which your Correspondent in his terrible indictment, found so wanting at Singapore.

Yours sincerely,
A. L. ROWSE

[Dr Rowse was educated at elementary and grammar schools in St Austell and at Christ Church, Oxford]

From Lord David Cecil   *10 March 1942*

[Companion of Honour 1949]

Sir,

Mr Rowse is wrong about religious education. Apart from other considerations, he fails to realize how much the study of Christian truth clears the mind and enriches the imagination.

But he is right about character and intelligence. No doubt character is of the first importance to a nation. But it is not in character that we have shown ourselves inferior to our ancestors. Our leaders during the last 20 years have been men of most respectable character. Morally they compare favourably with Cromwell and Queen Elizabeth. But, alas, they have not shown the same penetration in diagnosing a situation, or the same resource in meeting it. It was lack of intelligence, not lack of character, that made the leaders of the Left advocate, in the same breath, resistance to Fascism and reduction of armaments. It was lack of intelligence, not lack of character, that made the leaders of the Right persist, in spite of repeated failures, in believing it was possible to appease Hitler. It was lack of intelligence, not lack of character, that made the majority of the Conservative Party deaf to the warnings of the present Prime Minister.

Nor can the public schools be acquitted of all responsibility for this intellectual decline. It is mortifying to compare the schoolboys of today with those of a hundred years back. As schoolboys Pitt, Fox, Peel, and Canning, none of them prigs or freaks, were mentally as advanced as boys of 20 today. Already they were talking intelligently about politics and literature and social life; already their interests, transcending the limits of school life, made them citizens of the great world. The human animal does not change so quickly in a hundred years; the change must be due to education. And, indeed, there must be something wrong with an education which spends the larger part of its time teaching boys Latin and sends away 5 per cent at most able to read a Latin book for pleasure. The fact is that public school masters, concentrating on the school rather than the boys, have neglected to encourage curiosity, imagination, mental independence, and enterprise in order to produce 'safe' men, steady, loyal, unquestioning supporters of whatever institution fate has seen fit to place them in. It is such 'safe' men who land others in danger.

Yours truly,
DAVID CECIL

[Lord David Cecil was educated at Eton and Christ Church, Oxford]

Astrology and War

From Mr Tom Harrisson, Director of Mass-Observation
11 June 1942

[who returned to England from Central Borneo and the Western Pacific in 1938 determined – instead of studying primitive people – 'to study the cannibals of Britain'. Hence Mass-Observation]

Sir,

The correspondence on astrology in your columns has drawn attention to a development in British life, the importance of which has hitherto been under-estimated by the serious-minded.

It is not generally recognized that a very large section of the community are involved. In a detailed mass-observation study it was found that more people followed their daily fate in the stars than followed the advice of archbishops, preachers, and parish magazines. In addition to the vast readership of newspaper astrology there are numerous specialized periodicals, privately circulated 'astrological news-letters,' booklet predictions, and envelope predictions available on almost any book-stall and selling in hundreds of thousands, and astrological 'almanacs' (one version of which alone sells 3,000,000 copies annually). Something like four persons in 10 have some degree of interest or belief in astrology, and this is highest among women and working-class people. Both interest and belief have steadily increased in recent years, and especially since the war.

The numerous errors in astrological prediction do not diminish the confidence of the faithful. The basis of mass astrology is favourable prediction for the future – constantly optimistic emphasis, the primrose way. Even when the prediction fails to come true, it has had its sedative, soothing effect. This may have some value in keeping certain people calm and steady, but in the long run it must be dangerous to the war effort that people should continually be lulled by complacency unrelated to reality. The astrologers played a big part before the war in assuring people that there was not going to be one, and their role nowadays is fundamentally the same. The astrologer, though generally sincere, is not tied by any of the traditional, ethical responsibilities of the editor, parson, or politician. He may influence, even if only in small ways, millions of people, without having to take responsibility for the result, and up till now without much fear of contradiction or criticism. The revival of such ancient beliefs, and their growth into mass interests among the British public, is symptomatic of the wide decline in spirituality over the past decades. Surely the symptoms need to be diagnosed and dealt with? They cannot much longer be ignored.

Yours sincerely,
TOM HARRISSON

Conduct of the War

[Shortly before Auchinleck won the first battle of Alamein, Churchill faced a vote of no confidence in the House of Commons. Debated on 1 and 2 July 1942 the motion was defeated by 476 to twenty-five with forty abstentions]

From Captain B. H. Liddell Hart   *9 July 1942*

Sir,

An important point of history, which has a no less important bearing on current affairs, arises out of a passage in the Prime Minister's speech, where he said:

'I must ask the House to allow me to place the salient points of the tank story before them. The idea of the tank was a British conception. The use of armoured forces as they are now being used was largely French, as General de Gaulle's book shows. It was left to the Germans to convert these ideas to their own use.'

Here the Prime Minister, unwittingly, I am sure, did an injustice to our own pioneers of mechanized warfare. For their conception of the use of swift-moving armoured forces, in the way the Germans used them in 1939 and since, was expounded from the early twenties onward – by Colonel Fuller and others. It received widespread attention and translation abroad, especially in Germany and Russia. Indeed, the French was the only great army which remained almost untouched by these new ideas. General de Gaulle's now celebrated little book, 'Vers l'Armée de Métier,' was not published until 1934 – and it remained unfortunately, almost unheeded in French official circles. It was an excellent argument on the need for armoured forces, aimed to convert French public opinion, but did not go at all deeply into the technique of mechanized tactics – for which there was no basis of experimental experience in France.

Our own exponents of the new conception had proved, comparatively at least, more effective. By 1927 they had succeeded in persuading the War Office to create an Experimental Mechanized Force (next year re-christened the Armoured Force) – the first that the world had seen. Its component elements, and its proportions, were similar to those adopted in the eventual German panzer division. It was practised in the same roles. And, in its earliest exercises, the concentrated tank thrusts were covered by synchronized dive-attacks from air squadrons working with them.

In 1929 the first official manual on mechanized warfare was issued by the War Office, embodying the new conception. By the time General de Gaulle's book was published, in the endeavour to arouse the French public to its significance, we had seven years' experience of practical tests behind us. Indeed, that same year the new technique had attained a high-water mark in the exercises of our first permanent armoured formation under Brigadier Hobart. There is ample evidence that the Germans were already far more advanced than the French in developing the new conception. (Field-Marshal von Reichenau, of whom Hitler said, on his death early this year, that he 'would go down in history as the first commander of an armoured army,' had been the translator of my own books more than 10 years before.)

Mr Churchill's mistake about 'the salient points of the tank story' is presumably due to a lapse of memory. For in September, 1927, he was the first member of the Cabinet to visit the trials of our original mechanized force. I gather, not directly, that he subsequently proposed the conversion of the cavalry into a modern mechanized force – only to find the forces of tradition too strong. Two regiments only were mechanized, one at home and one in Egypt, during 1928–9, and in the latter year Mr Churchill went out of office, not to return until war had come. Subsequent steps were deplorably slow, and the full conversion was not carried out until 1937–8, Mr Hore-Belisha's first year of office as War Minister, when our first two armoured divisions were formed, one at home and one in Egypt.

The mechanized technique with which the Germans won their victories did not go beyond our own earlier practice in any important respect. On the other hand, our conception went beyond their subsequent practice in a number of ways. So there is still room to leap ahead of the enemy's technique – if we draw upon our own fund of ideas – instead of merely trying to tackle him in 1943 with an imitation of his 1940 methods. To the historian of the future the most astonishing feature of the first three years of this war – three of the most critical years in our history – may appear to be our own neglect to make adequate use of the tank-minded soldiers who had developed the technique which our enemy so strikingly exploited and vindicated.

Yours, &c.,
B. H. LIDDELL HART

['To my mind [Sir Basil Liddell Hart] is the military historian *non pareil*.' – Field-Marshal Viscount Montgomery of Alamein, *A History of Warfare*, 1968]

The Beveridge Report

[The *Report on Social Insurance and Allied Services* was published on 2 December 1942. Its aim was 'freedom from want']

Sir,

   In my opinion the way of the Beveridge Report is the road
to the moral ruin of the nation, it is the way tending to weaken
still further the spirit of initiative and adventure, the stimulus
of competition, courage, and self-reliance. It substitutes emphasis on rights for emphasis on obligations, and collective impersonal charity for private personal charity. It is a blow at the
heart of the nation with the weapon of a seductive opiate. It
is the way of sleep, not a symptom of the vitality of our
civilization but of its approaching end.

Yours, &c.,
OSWALD T. FALK

From Sir Walter Benton Jones   *9 March 1943*

Sir,

   What is it in the Beveridge Report which has gripped the
whole nation? It is the expounding of a moral principle. If
those who live in Great Britain deserve the place in civilization
which they claim to have reached, they should accept the
principle that no living soul among them should be compelled
to starve so long as any other of them has more than enough
to avoid starvation, and starvation means the want of what is
necessary to prevent body, mind, and spirit from sinking below
a vital standard.

   But while we are talking about questions of cost, may we
not be jeopardizing the great reaction to the Beveridge exposi-
tion, the common bond it made clear to us, the hopes it raised
for some, the willingness to sacrifice it engendered in others?
The cost will be the amount required to augment the incomes
which do not come up to the fixed line. The real question
therefore is, how can we arrange that every one may produce
goods or perform services which, taken over his whole lifetime,
will be not less in value than what is required to keep him
above the line? If we can find the answer to this question the
cost will be nil. If we cannot find a complete answer the cost
will be measured by the extent to which we fail, and it will be
borne by those who are able to live above the line. The answer
does not depend on governments, political parties, or even
Parliament, it depends upon the people. Beveridge has lighted
a beacon of faith, faith in our country, in ourselves, and in

the triumph of what is good over evil. Are we going to let it die out, or are we going to fan it into flame? Are we a little people or are we a big people? We must all put our shoulders to the wheel, and with new inspiration and renewed faith in our genius and in our tradition we cannot fail to find the answer.

The debates in Parliament suggest a prevailing fear of return to mass unemployment instead of a determination to prevent it. Few are sufficiently well informed to express an opinion about all the recommendations contained in the report, but the setting up of the suggested Ministry of Social Security, not only to deal with the report but also to examine means of making employment reasonably secure, would restore hope to many to whom the debates were a disappointment.

Yours faithfully,
WALTER BENTON JONES

Bones and the Dog

From Mrs N. O. Pegg   5 December 1942

Sir,

Mr Morrison, chairman of the Waste Food Board, in his letter in *The Times* of 2 December, says that thousands of tons of bones are being lost annually through being buried by dogs, and that they should go to salvage instead. But why not both? Our Scottie invariably has her bone – spends a glorious time gnawing it, then entreats us to let her out – spends an even happier time burying it, and comes in content. After a time, which may be days, or even a week or two, she digs up the bone, and another long gnaw leaves it all clean and 'nice' again. It is then left, usually lying about the lawn, all interest in it from her point of view having gone. But after it has been washed and dried salvage comes into its own.

Yours truly,
N. O. PEGG

Art and the Film

From Mr Nicolas Bentley   9 March 1943

Sir,

Your critic, commenting on *The Magnificent Ambersons*,

172

is hopeful that 'one day the film may become an important art.' I do not know what is his definition of art, and I admit my own confusion on this elusive topic. But there need surely be no dispute between us in acknowledging the truth of Ruskin's broad assertion that it is the language of the imagination; a language in which the best film directors, actors, and technicians of Britain, America, France, and Russia are often exquisitely fluent. (Fifteen years ago the inclusion of Germany would also have been possible.) The apparent disdain with which your critic dismisses their inspiration and ability, and his condescension towards all that the cinema, in its short history, has achieved aesthetically needs no comment.

His oblique denial of the cinema's importance as an art seems as difficult to follow as to justify. The ubiquity of the film, whether good or bad, assures its affecting the ideas and emotions of a far greater number of people than is at present influenced by any other form of art. To dismiss it, therefore, as unimportant admits a degree of oblivion or partiality which is painful to observe in one who speaks with the authority of a critic.

I remain, Sir, yours truly,
NICOLAS BENTLEY

[*The Magnificent Ambersons* was the second film made by Orson Welles but, unlike *Citizen Kane*, it divided critical opinion. Both are now generally regarded as masterpieces]

A Labour MP on Public Schools

From Mr George Muff, MP   8 July 1943

Sir,

We look forward to seeing what the President of the Board of Education has to say to us in his proposals. By the courtesy of various headmasters of our public schools, 11 Labour members of Parliament, mostly new members, have been visiting Christ's Hospital, Eton, Harrow, Charterhouse, and Winchester. I also privately visited Stonyhurst.

We were miners or textile workers– all with ripe experience of public administration in Liverpool, the LCC, Hindley, Manchester, the West Riding, Lanark, Durham, Hull, Bradford, and South Wales. We were of the opinion that the 'two nations,' vividly portrayed by Disraeli, were nurtured on prejudice and foolish class distinctions. Some of us believed that class separation of the people commenced in our middle school years. There was a gulf between the public school and the elementary school – a caste system; when all the while we knew the child of the worker was neither 'untouchable' nor belonged to a depressed class. The free places in our great grammar schools have proved, by the output to our universities, that given an equal chance, the son of a bricklayer can take his place as a mental equal with the son of a barrister.

We went to the public schools. We stipulated that we wanted to mix with the boys and not the masters. In certain instances we stayed overnight to enjoy the free and easy of a 'round table conference.' We went and joined in the boys' evening prayers. What did we find? We found an utter absence of snobbery. After all, the average normal boy is the same all England over. Whether rich or poor, the young lad has to be made, under duress, to wash his neck as well as his face. We found wholesome, vivid youth flourishing under the best conditions. We found no pampering. Indeed, there was a fine simplicity of living: most of the boys made their own beds, and took their turn in the service of meals. We heard in various schools the loud cry of 'Boy.' I, at any rate, realized that being of service does not mean servitude. Those who cried for a boy had themselves been fags. These public schools breed character. The motto of Winchester is common to all: 'Manners makyth Man.'

In the mass these boys have independence and poise. They think for themselves most vigorously in the higher forms. We were treated with deference, more so than we get at times from our constituents. We also realized – again in the mass – that there was a spiritual background to the education plan. Who can forget Charterhouse Chapel and morning prayers? The unassuming part the boys took themselves in the inspiring worship at Winchester College? The friendliness of Harrow? Its war memorial, which is a gathering ground – a commonroom – for old and new boys? The invitation of all men of good will over the portal of the refectory of the memorial, 'Pass Friend'? We passed: and found that two sorrowing but proud parents had sacrificed some of their priceless belongings to furnish a room of welcome to all who cared to enter. There was the portrait of their boy of 19 who died in the last war. The whole conception is an inspiration to the boys of today and tomorrow. Who can forget the glorious equality of 'Duckers' and 'Gunners' – that is if you could swim?'

We want more boys to share in the heritage of our public schools. We want the boy from an industrial home to be as proud of the school tie as his dad is of his trade union badge. Can it be done? Christ's Hospital has partially solved the problem. A goodly number of the boys are 'presented' from the London education authority. These boys qualify by examination and are then interviewed. The parents are asked if they will agree to the boys living away in a boarding school. Christ's Hospital, like Stonyhurst, has the great advantage of having its own preparatory school. Boys can be admitted at nine or ten. I assume the admittance age for a public school is 13 or thereabouts. I am not pleading for boys to be taken away from a secondary or grammar school. I ask the door to be at least ajar for the boy who has passed the entrance examination to the local grammar school, whose parents are ready for their boy to go to a boarding school, and who is temperamentally suitable.

Eton has its scholars and its greater proportion of 'outsiders' – the 'Oppidans.' Winchester has its proportion – a big one– of 'Commoners' and its 70 scholars. What chance has a lad from a post-primary school to be a scholar when Latin is one of the subjects? So the expensive preparatory schools have almost the monopoly of winning the scholarships at our public schools. What is the difference between a preparatory school and a 'cramming' school? Apply the means test! Let the son of wealthy parents have the honour of being a scholar and pass on the scholarship to his poorer friend. (The Board of Education should inquire into the usefulness of some preparatory schools.) Moreover we should make it possible for a maintenance scholarship to be available outside the boundaries of the rating authority. The Board should extend the principle of direct grants which are now made to 51 combined boarding and day grammar schools. I ask – nay, challenge – all headmasters and governors to see how far part of their endowments can be used to educate boys from working-class homes.

In conclusion, I wish to emphasize that we MPs went on a serious pilgrimage. We went not to orate to the boys, or be on exhibition as prize rabbits or vegetables. The nearest approach to talking was when we all were heckled hours on end in the various 'houses.' I did take one period of the senior science form at Winchester in history and economics. I was so emboldened when I saw the text-book was by that great man, George M. Trevelyan. I also noticed other text-books used. They were the volumes of cartoons published in *Punch* for the past 60 years. This was most revealing and human.

Boys – normal average boys – do not suffer from inferiority or other complexes. Neither do they deal out 'dope' to members of Parliament. We thank the many hundreds we have met for their hospitality. We hope to meet them again.

I am yours truly,
GEORGE MUFF

[In 1945 Muff became the first Baron Calverley. His son and heir was educated at Bradford Grammar School]

Foreign Policy

From Professor R. W. Seton-Watson   *2 December 1943*

[Masaryk Professor of Central European History in the University of London 1922–45]

Sir,

There is one important aspect of the war which was not mentioned in your three remarkable articles on foreign policy. This war is not only a war between Germany and the English-speaking world, but also that war of Teuton and Slav which Bethmann Hollweg foretold in 1913. In 1918 Germany overran Tsarist territories equal in area to those overrun by Hitler in 1941–42 – the main booty in each case being the black earth of the Ukraine, to be converted into a vast colonial *Lebensraum*. Hitler, more ambitious than William, hopes to hold what he calls 'the fortress of Europe' against all comers, and finally to dismember three of the four lesser Slav States – Czechoslovakia, Poland, and Yugoslavia, perhaps even the fourth, her Bulgarian vassal. He would then be free to evict their present population, especially in Bohemia and in Poland, west of the Vistula, and to settle German colonists in their place. The success of this policy, as crudely stated in 'Mein Kampf', means the creation, by the end of this century, of a Germany of 250,000,000 people, and the relegation of Russia to the steppes of Asia.

The Moscow agreement now recognizes the absolutely vital function of Russia in the European balance of power. From this standpoint our interest in the restoration of the Slav States is scarcely second to that of Russia herself: and it is incumbent on us to help her in achieving a settlement such as will make another German invasion of Russia impossible. It is thus that the great problem of security presents itself to Russian eyes.

176

The zone of small or medium States which lie between Russia and Germany, between the Baltic and the Aegean, and which number not less than 100,000,000 people, must also be vitally interested in Russia being strong enough to prevent, in conjunction with her allies, any resumption of German aggression. The alternative – that they should ally themselves with Berlin – is no alternative at all.

It would be folly to suppose that these nations all see eye to eye with Moscow; but it is clear that the twin problems of their liberty and of Russian security have to be solved by parallel action within the framework of the Atlantic Charter. This is the delicate task which faces the statesmen of the Grand Alliance, in the most Slav of all wars.

Yours, &c.,
R. W. SETON-WATSON

Beatrix Potter

[whose death was mourned on 24 December 1943]

From Mrs E. Atthill   *28 December 1943*

Sir,

On reading your charming leading article on Beatrix Potter yesterday, I was surprised to find reference to the 'only' self-portrait of Miss Potter as that in 'The Roly-Poly Pudding.' I was able to confirm my suspicion when I looked into the volume of 'Pigling Bland' which my son found in his stocking this morning.

There, on page 22 – 'I pinned the papers for safety inside their waistcoat pockets' – the same long-skirted figure is saying 'Good-bye' to Pigling. Unfortunately there is no illustration of 'I whipped them myself and led them out by the ears. Crosspatch tried to bite me.'

Yours, &c.,
ELIZABETH ATTHILL

Equal Pay

From Mr R. F. Harrod   *31 March 1944*

[at this time serving in the Prime Minister's office in an advisory capacity. Sir Roy Harrod wrote numerous books, including *The Life of John Maynard Keynes*]

Sir,

If the favour shown by the House of Commons to equal pay on 28 March reflects national opinion, no doubt that principle will sooner or later be adopted not only by the Government but also in due course in all sections of industry, trade and finance, where the two sexes do similar work. In drawing attention to an important corollary, I do not wish to add to the distractions of the authorities in the hour of supreme endeavour, but rather to give food for thought to the friends of equal pay.

The majority of active women are engaged on the tasks of motherhood. Even under the old system these have had an unfair deal, and we have recently been thinking of family allowances as a method of redressing the balance in their favour. But the most generous proposals so far suggested would barely cover out-of-pocket expenses incurred on behalf of the children. If the remuneration for women's work outside the home is to be improved, we shall have to go farther and think in terms of the endowment of motherhood as such. The work of bringing up children is probably harder and certainly more valuable to the community and more skilled than any work done in factory or schoolroom. No woman should be allowed to suffer financially for choosing the better path.

So long as woman are paid considerably less than men in their occupations, it is arguable that a woman may not lose very much by giving up her work on marriage, since a married couple can live on less than twice what is required for a single person. Where equal pay operates women will inevitably lose on renouncing their outside work.

To ask whether we could afford to endow motherhood is to misconceive the issue. It is not a question of supplying something extra, but of redistributing what we already have. That is also true of equal pay. For some time – namely until our industrial efficiency had increased in proportion to the increase in total pay-roll involved – equal pay would mean reducing (through higher prices and taxes) the spending power available for men, married or single, for married women employed on their domestic duties and for children, and it would mean reducing the relative amounts going to these classes permanently. Thus by itself it would be a retrograde measure. But if it were accompanied by a proportionate endowment of motherhood, the burden would be shifted off the families on to bachelors, unoccupied spinsters, and married people without dependent children where the wife was unoccupied. Thus equal pay and the endowment of motherhood should be indissolubly linked

178

in projects of reform.

But the matter is not simple. For example, the injustice to mothers would not be removed by offering the same endowment for an ex-school mistress as for an ex-waitress. And how would those who marry before taking up any settled occupation be graded? It is easier to legislate for equal pay than for an adequate endowment of motherhood: before returning to the charge it is incumbent on those who urge the former to offer proposals for giving simultaneous effect to the latter.

I am, &c.,

R. F. HARROD

A Trinity Jump

From the Master of Trinity College, Cambridge
16 March 1944

Sir,

On a recent visit to Cambridge, General Montgomery, on entering the Great Court at this college, pointed to the hall steps and said to me, 'Those were the steps my father jumped up at one bound.' The general's father, Henry Hutchinson Montgomery, afterwards Bishop, was an undergraduate at Trinity from 1866 to 1870. He came here from Dr Butler's Harrow with a great reputation as a runner and jumper.

The feat of leaping up the eight steps at a single bound has often been attempted by athletes, hurdlers, and jumpers without success. The only person to succeed of whom I know was the gigantic Whewell, when he was Master of the college; he clapped his mortar-board firmly on his head, picked up his gown with one hand, and leapt. The late Sir George Young, Bt., saw him do this, and many years later told his son Geoffrey Winthrop Young, who allows me to make this statement. I have heard that the feat was accomplished once or twice in this century; once, I was told, an American succeeded, but I have not the facts or names. It has certainly been done very seldom.

Now we have a fully authenticated case of which I had not heard. Bishop Montgomery himself told his son the general, and the story was often told in the family. The general has asked me to send the facts to you in the hope that publication may elicit further facts.

Yours, &c.,

G. M. TREVELYAN

179

[Whewell accomplished his feat at about the same age as Lord Butler of Saffron Walden on his election to the Master's Lodge]

Gefreiter

[Commander-in-Chief of the German Army, Adolf Hitler committed suicide on 30 April 1945]

From Dr S. E. Michael   *7 May 1945*

Sir,

I read with interest your article on Hitler's career, and I came across a slight inaccuracy in your description which might seem quite insignificant, but which you may perhaps allow me to point out in a few words. You say that Hitler obtained the rank of corporal in the German Army in the last war. This is not correct. In fact, he was only lance-corporal (*Gefreiter*, a rank which is not that of an n.c.o. in the German Army). I was told by the German officer in whose company Hitler served throughout the war that on more than one occasion when necessary promotions to n.c.o.s were discussed in his battalion Hitler was turned down as altogether too empty headed and irresponsible to be trusted with the job of an n.c.o.

I am, Sir, your obedient servant,
S. E. MICHAEL

Re-educating Germany

From the Headmaster of Charterhouse   *8 May 1945*

[Educational Adviser to the Military Governor, Control Commission of Germany 1947–9, Sir Robert Birley was later headmaster of Eton]

Sir,

It is becoming clear that the 're-education' of Germany by the allies will not be a pious aspiration, but an unavoidable duty. To administer an entirely shattered nation involves educating it, whether one likes it or not. If so, it is surely necessary to think out carefully what is meant by the term.

There are certain lines of policy about Germany on which all are agreed, *e.g.* that the criminals should be punished and the nation completely disarmed. Would it not be well to consider this problem of re-education, on which there seems to be little agreement, except on the fact that it will take a long time, and especially to decide what kind of country we expect a 're-educated' Germany to be? It is in the hope of raising this issue that I make these three suggestions, which do not pretend to cover more than a part of the field.

First, although the German people certainly did know about the horrors of the concentration camps, their real crime was not that they failed to stop them when all power was in the hands of the Nazis, for this would have been practically impossible, but that they ever allowed the Nazis, whom they knew to be villains, to rise to power at all. They allowed this because they were politically irresponsible. For a century they have been fatally ready to accept any government which would save them from having to make decisions for themselves. The first task is to teach the Germans to face responsibility. In planning their education this is even more important than the provision of the right text-books or broadcast information. It will mean that the proof that Germany is being successfully re-educated will not be that she is submissive to the allies, but that she is found capable of producing a stable democratic government.

Secondly, it is no use hoping to build anything except on some foundation of national tradition. Germany will not be a *tabula rasa.* Every means should be taken to persuade the Germans that they themselves have such a tradition, however completely forgotten now, on which a decent society can be based. There was once a Germany of Goethe, a country which the young Meredith visited because it was a land of liberal thinkers, one with universities which inspired Americans like George Bancroft. 'It was in part the influence of American scholars who had caught the flame in Germany that made Harvard, as early as the 1830's, a steadfast defender of the scholar's freedom from political and religious pressure.' (Morrison and Commager: 'The Growth of the American Republic' – I, 412.) Germany will not be truly re-educated until she is once more proud of that tradition.

Thirdly, the Germans must learn to respect the Slavs. In Western Europe it is not generally recognized that one of the main traditions in German history, and the most sinister, is that of the conquest and colonization of Slav lands. As a result the ordinary German has come to regard the Slav as an inferior being and he has never begun to adapt himself to the Slav renaissance of the last 100 years. The victory of Russia is probably the most valuable, as it is the hardest, lesson the Germans have learnt in this war. Perhaps the acid test of German re-education will be their readiness to accept the Czechs and the Poles as people with cultures and traditions of their own.

Yours faithfully,
R. BIRLEY

British Air Power

From Lord Brabazon of Tara   *12 May 1945*

[as a pioneer airman, J. T. S. Moore-Brabazon held Number One Certificate granted by the Royal Aero Club for Pilots]

Sir,

We ended the last war supreme in the air. Through lack of vision we threw away the advantage that might well have prevented this one. The scars borne by so many of our great cities have been a costly lesson, but inspired this country into turning the tables, and in doing so made aircraft manufacture its greatest industry. Terrible as was the attack upon this country it was puny compared with the raids by our own Air Force upon the enemy, made possible by the willing hands of the men and women of this country.

A curious corollary of superiority is that as danger disappears so the evidence of air power recedes. Neither London nor indeed any of our great cities has ever seen what to the enemy must have been a terrifying sight – namely, the approach of thousands of heavy bombers with their escort. Before it is too late and our vast concourse of machines moves to other spheres could we be given – to remind us of what we have escaped – a mass parade over London? I want to see the RAF, so skilled in timing concerted bombing, show itself in all its grandeur. I want to see squadron after squadron, wing after wing, converge on London from every quarter, all to cross at a predetermined time over Buckingham Palace, at their scheduled heights. I do not believe such a spectacle would ever be forgotten or the implication that we are no longer an island more graphically realized. I need hardly say that other great cities should be similarly treated. With the modern range of machines, one consecutive flight on the one day could well be arranged to cover most of our great cities. It would indeed add to the glory of this demonstration if our American friends would join in with their great white machines and escorts inter-mingled with our sinister and dark weight-carrying bombers.

We Cockneys and dwellers in great cities will never see the Fleet assembled, we could never see the Army, but here is a possibility for all of us to see, at least once, the might of Britain and her allies in the air. Defeated generals may with truth tell the story of why they were beaten, but as a humble man in the street, I want myself a demonstration of how it was that mira-cles occurred and what the force looked like that made all our dreams come true. Lest we again forget.

Your obedient servant,
BRABAZON OF TARA

Thanksgiving

From Mr Frank Dugdale   *12 May 1945*

Sir,

Truly we are an odd race. Having read that churches would be open on VE Day for thanksgiving, I went to St Paul's Cathedral at 2 p.m. on Tuesday and found the entrance steps thronged with people listening to a Guards band seated below who at that moment were giving a spritely rendering of 'Roll Out the Barrel.' Excusable, perhaps, but hardly the place even on VE Day.

Yours,
FRANK DUGDALE

[Doubtless the barrel had first been emptied]

Arrival of the Scaup

From Mr C. J. Purnell   *19 December 1945*

Sir,

In your issue of 5 December 1944, you recorded the arrival of the scaup on its annual visit to St James's Park late. This year he has come nearly a fortnight later.

Yours faithfully,
C. J. PURNELL

Into the Welfare State
1946-1953

THE first full year of peace began with an attack on Picasso whose work seemed as indecent to some as the threatened Nationalization. Reform of the House of Lords was touched on, prayers were urged for a mission to India. The inability of Arab and Jew to work together in Palestine was regretted. Non-talking carriages seemed a good way to make rail travel bearable. German prisoners working on the land were not allowed sufficient baths, a bricklayer dealt satisfactorily with 5,000 bricks in five days. The BBC radio hero Dick Barton interfered with children's homework. An increase in juvenile crime greeted 1947, so did a fuel crisis which compelled the shut-down of the Third Programme. Rail fares went up, houses did not. Towards the end of the Walker Cup golf match the British wilted, the blame being placed on lack of food. The Dean of Canterbury, Dr Hewlett Johnson, spoke often, so giving common ground to Christians and atheists. 1948 saw a petrol shortage; coincidentally it was observed that thatching seemed to be a dying craft. On 31 January an increase in the weekly fat ration of one ounce (so making eight ounces) reminded some that Germans were starving. MPs for the University seats heard they would soon be without parliamentary employment, BOAC was criticized for showing a deficit. The groundnuts scheme evoked indignation and merriment, the value of the pound grave concern. The controversy over comprehensive schools began. It was also revealed that 60 per cent of rejects for the higher civil service had been scholars of their universities and colleges.

Who was to rule Africa? The answer of 1949 was 'anyone but intellectuals'. Anglo-Irish relations were examined, so was dismantling in Germany. Devaluation caused an uproar, clearly MPs were overpaid. The case against recognizing the Communist government in China was argued. 1950 was viewed as the fulcrum of the twentieth century. Graduates seemed to be entering business instead of teaching, higher civil servants suffered from financial injustices. To make things worse, the BBC showed brutalized plays on television. London lamp-posts grew more ugly, something was manifestly wrong when the Coronation stone could be stolen. There was only one thing left for correspondents in 1951: unanimously they called for a national effort. But apathy was shown over recruiting for civil defence, and far too many men attended Covent Garden (where Fonteyn reigned supreme) clad in loud check sports coats. Their women wore trousers. Talk of taking the stymie out of golf showed how debased our standards had become. Train windows were dirtier than ever, the pound lacked stability. For the record: was the editor of *The Times* aware that although Victorians spoke much as he did, they orated differently?

Ingenuity triumphed in 1952: why should not the same man read both gas and electricity meters? The £25 travel allowance irked, so did another sterling crisis. The Government met with caustic response when it announced that in spite of power cuts, things were getting better; translated, power cuts were fewer than they had been the previous year. Some male correspondents registered misgivings when they heard the cry of 'equal pay for equal work', others remarked on the aggressiveness of the blue tit. Flying saucers and anxiety over Suez afflicted 1953. Cricket was no longer worth watching, a building near St Paul's horrified, NATO needed strengthening; the farthing (worth about one-fifth of the modern $\frac{1}{2}$p) was eulogized. As 2 June, the day of Queen Elizabeth II's Coronation, approached, the nation gave itself over to various manifestations of hysteria. The following morning, before the streets had been swept, *The Times* remembered its Victorian self and thundered in a famous leading article – 'And After?'

Spectacles on Nose

From the Reverend R. J. E. Boggis   *1 February 1946*

Sir,

After your description of spectacled faces on the tomb of Henry VII in Westminster Abbey, it is interesting to note the mention of a pair about two centuries before.

Walter de Stapeldon, a good man and an eminent bishop, fell a victim to mob law in 1326, sharing the unpopularity of his master, Edward II. A full inventory of his effects has been preserved, and in his *camera* in Exeter Palace there was found a pair of spectacles (*unum spectaculum cum duplici oculo*) valued at 2s. – a considerable sum (a mirror was reckoned as worth one penny). Spectacles are said to have been invented shortly before the end of the thirteenth century, probably by Roger Bacon, so Stapeldon's must have been an early specimen. (Stapeldon's *Register*, p. 565.)

Furthermore, the benefit derived from wearing spectacles is not limited to humans, as is shown by this amusing description in the *Banner* of 13 January 1888: 'A correspondent of the *Manchester Sporting Chronicle*, thinking that his horse was shortsighted, had his eyes examined by an oculist, who certified that the horse had a No. 7 eye, and required concave glasses. These were obtained and fitted on to the horse's head. At first the horse was a little surprised, but rapidly shewed signs of the keenest pleasure, and he now stands all the morning, looking over the half-door of his stable with his spectacles on, gazing around him with an air of sedate enjoyment; when driven his manner is altogether changed from his former timidity, but if pastured without his spectacles on he hangs about the gate whinnying in a plaintive minor key. If the spectacles are replaced he kicks up his heels and scampers up and down the pastures with delight.'

Yours, &c.,
R. J. E. BOGGIS

The Future of Germany

From Mr Robert Boothby, MP   *16 May 1946*

[represented East Aberdeenshire as a Unionist 1924–58,
now Baron Boothby of Buchan and Rattray Head]

Sir,

There is an alternative policy for Germany to that put forward in your leading article of 9 May, and by Mr Stokes. It is to bring the British, French, and American zones into a Western European Federation. And it has the merit of being based upon the realities of the present situation, and not merely upon wishful thinking.

What is done cannot be undone. At Teheran, at Yalta, and at Potsdam we accepted solutions of the frontier problems of eastern Europe which had no geographical or ethnical justification, and took no account of economic facts. Further, we acquiesced in the policy of forcible mass deportations as the only method of implementing the arrangements that were then made. Today the eastern zone of Germany has been, for all practical purposes, incorporated in the Soviet Union. Russia has already imposed upon the German territories under her control her own political system, and brought them within her closed economy. Indeed, we may well be told, when the Peace Conference comes eventually to be held – and with considerable justification – that the population of eastern Germany is now predominantly Slav; and we shall not seek to probe too deeply into the events which have brought about this remarkable transformation.

In such a situation, phrases in Mr Stokes's letter such as 'Germans must be allowed to form their own political parties independent of zones,' and 'Elections should be held as soon as possible,' are perfectly meaningless. If Mr Stokes seriously believes that Russia will now hand back Eastern Germany to social democracy and free capitalist multilateral trade, he is the victim of an illusion. On the other hand, he is quite right in emphasizing the incredible folly of limiting German industrial production in the west.

The truth of the matter is that, flanked by the tremendous aggregations of political and economic strength represented by a federated Soviet Union and a federated United States, the countries of Western Europe cannot hope to survive as separate and isolated units in the modern world. Unless they get together in pursuit of common policies, based on social justice, individual freedom, and a deliberately planned economic expansion, social democracy on the continent of Europe is doomed. And the inclusion of Western and Southern Germany is absolutely vital to the security and economic strength of any Western regional *bloc*.

The first essential is an agreement between Great Britain and France. We are separated by only 20 miles of water. But for the last two years we might have been inhabiting different planets. The French demand that the industries of the Ruhr should not be returned to German control is justified. They should be administered by an international authority; and co-ordinated with the heavy industries not only of Belgium, Luxemburg, the Saar, and Lorraine, but also of this country. This was Rathenau's vision 25 years ago. Its realization now is a necessary condition of the renaissance of Western Europe. As Mr Walter Lippmann recently observed: 'The security and the power of the Empire based on the British Isles cannot be divorced from the countries across the English Channel. Nor can the reconstruction of British industry be planned intelligently without a clear understanding of how far it will collaborate with, how far it must compete with, Western European industry.'

We must face the fact that any practical policy designed to create a western *bloc* in Europe will meet with some initial opposition both from the Americans and the Russians – from the former because they are making a final attempt to revive the *laissez-faire* economic system of the nineteenth century, based on promiscuous unplanned international trade, within the framework of fixed exchanges; and from the latter because it would set a limit to their westward expansion. The United States would, however, very soon find that a stable and unified Western European economy could provide far better markets for her export surplus than a number of small, weak, poverty-stricken, and conflicting national units. And the Kremlin well knows that the main purposes of such a federation would be economic rather than strategic. It could in no sense be a coalition directed against the Soviet Union. Moreover, they have done precisely the same thing themselves in Eastern Europe; and imitation is the sincerest form of flattery.

What is the alternative? For the continental democracies of Europe, a gradual absorption by the Communist *bloc*. For us, a gradual absorption by the American *bloc*. We should cease to be a world Power, and become a bastion – a kind of Aden – of the American strategic and economic system. The emergence of two *blocs*, based on diametrically opposed political and economic systems, and culminating in a struggle for world power, is a terrifying prospect. The case for a third *bloc*, subject to the over-riding authority of the Security Council, which would steer a middle course between the extremes of collectivism and individualism, is, in my submission, overwhelming.

Your obedient servant,
ROBERT BOOTHBY

Horse and Hen

From Mr T. L. Ward   *1 June 1946*

Sir,

The Parliamentary Secretary to the Ministry of Agriculture stated in Parliament recently that the amount of oats issued to racehorses in April was 556 tons, which was considered a comparatively small quantity of grain to divert from human consumption. He did not say, however, that it would have been an adequate grain ration for 300,000 hens which, in April, would have laid at least 6,000,000 eggs. .

Yours faithfully,
T. L. WARD

Two Sentences

From Mrs Norah Lofts   *25 January 1947*

Sir,

This is England today. A woman beats her five-year-old child until her head is swollen, her forehead protruding, and her nose injured. The mother is fined £10. Another woman is found in possession of more ration books than her family of three children entitles her to. She is sent to gaol for six months.

Comment is superfluous, but a public expression of disgust is imperative.

Yours faithfully,
NORAH LOFTS

Grey Squirrels

From Sir Stephen Tallents   *25 January 1947*

[an eminent civil servant whose interests included the collection of thistledown for pillows and the science and art of scything]

Sir,

May I, as an executor of the grey squirrel whose fatal crossing of my lawn and successful emergence in a casserole you recorded on 2 December, thank you for the posthumous fame which your obituary notice has brought to the deceased?

Its canonization began with telephone inquiries from several of your London contemporaries and a local paper's request for a biography of our cook. Then, with some appeals for advice, recipes began to arrive. Some of their kindly senders drew from American cookery books: others recorded personal experiments, and the Ministry of Agriculture and the Wine and Food Society both contributed. One correspondent registered on an anonymous post-card contempt for the 'clodhopper' who would take a gun to a squirrel. Another reported more than 150 Chiltern squirrels stalked and shot within a few months by a man with a ·22 rifle. Yet another experienced hunter advised the sinking of a baited barrel in the ground. From Surrey I heard of Canadian troops astonished at our neglect of squirrel meat. Was I wrong in detecting an echo of the saga when Lord Marshmallow's heir, at the high point of his Christmas shooting party, located two squirrels in the home covert (ruthlessly exposed by Mr Gillie Potter as 'the holly bush behind the wood shed')?

A resident of the Channel Islands told how during the occupation he tricked a *Gestapo* man, in return for hints about the stalking of inferior prey, into giving him the grey squirrels he shot. A British officer, writing from Seremban, in Malaya, described how a growing queue of villagers, begging him in four different tongues to kill for their supper the pest that was damaging their coconut trees, embarrassed his shooting. A handsome private Christmas card was sent me, which had chanced to include a quotation from Brillat-Savarin commending these squirrels as 'highly prized' in Connecticut, and describing how six or seven of them, which his party shot, were stewed in Madeira and served at a 'distinguished reception.' A correspondent in Lyons sent me independently the precise reference of this quotation. Several writers recalled nostalgically feasts of fried or roasted squirrel in the hill-billy country of the Southern States. An admirably vivid letter from the editor of the *Talladega Daily Home* reported that the creature was still regarded in the woods of Alabama as 'one of our major game animals' and 'something of a delicacy.' The country folk there cherished their 'squirrel dogs,' the best of them often mongrels, trained to ignore all other breeds of game.

I am today the richer by much new knowledge and several good dinners. I needed no such proof that, to students of an obscure subject, a letter published in *The Times* was as good as a travelling scholarship. It had not occurred to me, till a puzzled railwayman delivered at our door a timely bunch of grey corpses from a Sussex shoot, that it could also be an insurance against meat ration deficiencies during a lorry-drivers' strike.

Yours, &c.,
STEPHEN TALLENTS

[The heir to the Hogsnorton estate was, of course, Twister Marshmallow]

Politicians in 1947

[The heaviest five weeks of snow since 1880–1, no power for industry in the south-east or north-west of England, the Government was apparently helpless]

From Sir Waldron Smithers, MP   *1 March 1947*

[Conservative Member for Chislehurst 1924–45, for Orpington 1945–54]

Sir,
Britain is faced with the biggest catastrophe in her long and glorious history. This is due to the application of wrong principles of Government. May I ask all bishops, priests, and deacons to re-read Article XXXVIII of their Articles of Religion, and to proclaim the principle therein from every pulpit?
Your obedient servant,
WALDRON SMITHERS

['The Riches and Goods of Christians are not common, as touching the right, title, and possession of the same, as

192

certain Anabaptists do falsely boast. Notwithstanding, every man ought, of such things as he possesseth, liberally to give alms to the poor, according to his ability.' (Article XXXVIII)]

[A few months later the Attorney-General, Sir Hartley Shawcross, rebuked certain women who deplored the collapse in our standard of life. They were either 'politically ignorant or politically dishonest']

From Mrs I. D. Shawcross   *17 June 1947*

Sir,

May I, as a middle-class 'impertinent housewife' add two or three more instances of the lowering of our standard of living to the excellent list supplied by your correspondent Mrs Williams?

(1) We still have to fetch our bits of meat, fish, &c., ourselves, and wrap them up in newspaper. (2) Few of us have more than one bath a week now, owing to shortage of fuel. Surely a sad lowering of the former universal standard of cleanliness as practised by Englishmen? (3) The shabby condition not only of our clothing but of our houses, owing to shortage of materials and coupons. We are willing to cooperate and help with all this, but resent being told our standard of living is as good as in 1938.

However, if my illustrious namesake considers it a 'good thing' for us to accept the lowest standard of living without grumbling, there is nothing more to be said.

Yours faithfully
IRIS D. SHAWCROSS

[By now the weather was glorious]

The Interrupted Symphony

From Mr Clifford Curzon   *11 September 1947*

[Knighted 1977]

Sir,

Last evening the Home Service broadcast a concert from the Edinburgh International Festival given by the Vienna Philharmonic Orchestra, reunited for the first time since the war with its former conductor Bruno Walter. The fact that the programme was announced in three languages indicated that the BBC considered this a special event, intended also for listeners abroad. As the orchestra reached the last page but one of Beethoven's Pastoral Symphony (one of the most superb performances England has heard for some time), it was suddenly 'faded out' and we were told in silken tones that we would now 'leave the Edinburgh Festival,' but that the entertainment would continue with . . . 'Twenty Questions: a New Kind of Parlour Game'!

We go to the trouble of promoting an International Festival which arouses world-wide interest and then behave with a Philistinism that must surely dissipate any prestige the venture has brought us. Apart from this, can nothing be done to stop an institution which officially represents the nation from insulting distinguished guests in this way by cutting off the sublime to make way for the ridiculous? Are even English manners to succumb to the general decline, and must we become as fit a subject for caricature in the cultural world as we are fast becoming in several others?

Yours faithfully,
CLIFFORD CURZON

Christian Names in 1947

From Mr J. W. Leaver   *9 January 1948*

Sir,

It may be of interest to you to know that to children born in 1947 whose birth and Christian names were announced in the appropriate column of your paper the following were the most popular names given:

BOYS			GIRLS		
John ...	...	... 250	Ann (107) or Anne (96) 203		
Michael	...	... 142	Elizabeth	...	... 158
Richard	...	... 133	Mary ...	...	... 148
David ...	...	... 117	Jane ...	...	... 139
Anthony	...	... 113	Susan ...	...	... 98
Peter ...	...	... 101	Margaret	...	... 97
Charles	...	... 99	Jennifer	...	... 60
James ...	...	... 97	Caroline	...	... 48
Christopher	...	... 95	Diana ...	...	... 45

Yours faithfully,

J. W. LEAVER

[See letter for 10 January 1974]

A Change at Rugby

[In 1948 Sir Arthur fforde, a solicitor, was appointed headmaster of Rugby School]

From Commander C. B. Fry   *20 January 1948*

[who took a First in Classical Moderations, captained England at cricket, held the world long jump record, wrote Latin verses for *The Times*, ran the TS *Mercury* for over forty years – and talked]

Sir,

The controversy about the headmastership of Rugby was sure to drift into side-issues – may I assist?

I hold, on some experience, that the most important matter in school life is efficient and happy domestic economy. That good, all is good.

I hold that any educated and cultivated man can teach a sixth form some one subject: preferably the English language and effective expression of thought. An eminent lawyer could be as good at that as any academic.

The art of teaching *qua* teaching can only be acquired by doing it. Some men are born teachers. What matters most in a schoolmaster, head or assistant, is the sort of man he is as a man. A really successful head master could have run a departmental store, a battleship, or a brigade with success. And vice versa.

The difficulty about schools is that schoolmastering since the

Greek and Roman paedagogos has been a despised profession – except in Scotland and India. When James Pigg in 'Jorrocks' wished to be particularly insulting he called his adversary a 'schulemaster.'

Yours, &c.,
C. B. FRY

Turkish Delight

From Imam S. M. Abdullah   *31 March 1948*

Sir,

Sometimes very interesting and amusing letters addressed to the doctors appear in the columns of your paper. This has tempted me to send you a copy of a letter received by me as Imam, that is, leader of the Mosque at Woking. It shows that it is not the doctors alone who have to look after all the various needs of their patients but we, the religious heads who administer spiritual food to human beings, are also required to attend to the various desires of our followers. The letter runs:

'Dear Imam, – I shall be most grateful to you if you will kindly let me know if you supply Turkish Delight, or any kind of sweet similar to it. If you do not keep any sweets, would you be so kind as to let me have the address of any other Mosque where I may obtain it? If you do keep it, will you please let me know the price, &c.?'

Yours truly,
S. M. ABDULLAH, Imam

The Name of Britain

From Professor D. W. Brogan   *3 January 1949*

[more generally concerned with French or American affairs, Sir Denis Brogan was Professor of Political Science at Cambridge 1939–67]

Sir,

In a world in danger of death because of pathological nationalistic nonsense, it is perhaps being unduly severe to comment on the letter addressed to you by the representatives of the St Andrew's and St George's Societies. Yet their protest against the use of 'Britain' for 'Great Britain' is surely a symptom of the disease, if in a very mild form. It is also, I think, mistaken, even from a nationalist point of view. Britain has been the name of our island since the beginning of recorded history. Great Britain is a new term, useful in law but not in any other department of life. I was told more than once by that deeply patriotic Scot, the late Sir Robert Rait (Historiographer Royal for Scotland) that the term was invented by one of his predecessors as head of Glasgow University, John Major (or Mair), as a punning title for his history of Britain (*Historia Majoris Britanniae*).

When James the Sixth was graciously pleased to become James the First of England, he invented the term Great Britain, ostensibly to distinguish it from Brittany. It was as if his colleague, Henri IV of France and Navarre, had called his kingdoms Transalpine Gaul. To insist now that, in ordinary speech or writing, we should use 'Great Britain' is like telling the inhabitants of York that they must write 'Old York.' In France, it is true that in writing it is necessary to use 'la Grande Bretagne' to avoid confusion with 'la Bretagne.' In speech, of course, in spite of 'the auld alliance,' the French always say 'l'Angleterre,' unless they specifically mean Scotland. Let our island keep the name it has had.

'Since Britain first at heaven's command, Arose from out the azure main.'

Yours faithfully,
D. W. BROGAN

The Lady and Her Hat

From Miss Silvia Risolo   *29 June 1949*

Sir,
Please forgive my English. I am not English and have been in England for two months only. Two days ago I was in the London Bridge underground station. I went out of the train and began to go upstairs. Suddenly a gush of wind blew away my hat, and I ran downstairs to the platform, but the hat went down between the rails. Then I too went down between the rails and, since the hat had stopped finally, I took it and climbed on the platform again. Nobody told me anything. Today a friend of mine told me that the rails are electrified

and that I could die very easily. But why, if so, is there no advertisement near the rails? I did not know that the rails were electrified. I simply took my hat. Since I am in a rather difficult situation at present, some people might have thought that I had committed suicide – instead I was following my hat only. This story is comical and strange, but it is a little dreadful also.

Yours sincerely,
SILVIA RISOLO

British Manners Abroad

From Mr Terence Prittie   *6 August 1949*

[at this time chief correspondent in Germany of the *Manchester Guardian*]

Sir,

I have just returned from five weeks in France, Italy, and Switzerland. Along with a universal concern in these countries over Britain's parlous financial position and the febrile handling of the recent dock strike by his Majesty's Government, there is a growing distress with the manners of British tourists on the Continent. At an exclusive country club outside Rome I watched British guests taking part in a bear-garden tumble which consisted of throwing each other into the swimming-pool, cannonading into Italian hosts trying to swim, and sousing Roman matrons and débutantes whose tables flanked the pool. At Lugano I watched British visitors appropriate all the boats belonging to a large hotel for all the afternoon, indulging in a regatta which involved ramming each other just off-shore. When tired of this sport, they handed their boats to other British visitors. The 80 per cent of the hotel guests who were Swiss had the alternative of watching this unedifying water-gala or of risking a bat over the head with a paddle if they ventured into the water. At two other places in Switzerland I heard complaints of British tourists who jostled, elbowed, and stomach-charged their way through hotels and restaurants.

These are no isolated incidents. Obviously the bulk of British visitors to the Continent travel in order to enjoy themselves and do so with the tact and good manners which have formerly made them the most welcome of all foreign guests. But an increasing number of Britons are giving grounds for criticism and complaint, particularly from their habit of moving about in gangs which, if by no means so lethal as those of Chicago and the Bowery, are superficially far more offensive. This is a serious matter. I am convinced that Englishmen are becoming less welcome abroad than ever before – not because austerity has reduced the size of their purses, but because they are failing to behave with their habitual restraint, good breeding, and understanding.

I am your, &c.,
TERENCE PRITTIE

Death of a Mouse

From Sir Charles Jeffries   *31 October 1949*

[Joint Deputy Under-Secretary of State, Colonial Office, 1947–56]

Sir,

Several years ago I bought a very ingenious mousetrap which actually caught one mouse. The cheese was placed in a cage approached through a small doorway. When the mouse had entered, the door automatically closed behind him. When, bored with trying to get at the cheese, he sought to depart, the only way open was up a sloping tunnel. At the top he came out on to a platform, which tipped over under his weight and deposited him in a tank of water. As the platform returned to level, it released a catch which opened the front door for the next victim. It is only fair to the mice to say that the one caught by this apparatus was too young to know any better.

Yours faithfully,
C. J. JEFFRIES

Skiing Today

From Field-Marshal Viscount Montgomery of Alamein
13 February 1950

Sir,

I paid my first visit to Switzerland 47 years ago. I first began to ski in 1925, and in my opinion the general standard of skiing was far higher in those days than it is today. By 'skiing' I mean, of course, real skiing, and not rattling down prepared pistes.

In 1925 a man was regarded as a good skier if he could find his way about the mountains and if he could run fast and steadily on all kinds of snow – soft snow, breakable crust, and unbreakable crust. Today, the one standard of excellence appears to be speed down a prepared course from which every vestige of natural snow has been removed: the result is that modern skiers are for the most part incompetent in soft snow and, therefore, inferior to their predecessors. What are the main reasons for this decline? In my opinion they are commercial. A ski teacher would waste his time hunting for soft snow: he can teach more people and earn more money by sticking to the practice slopes. The kind of worthless badge given for speed down pistes, 'Cresta skiing', is easy to obtain; and as hotel keepers like their clients to be happy, badges which increase the sum total of happy clients are encouraged by Kurvereins.

Against this decadence the Ski Club of Great Britain and the Kandahar are fighting a desperate rearguard action. The Ski Club of Great Britain still includes soft snow in its tests and still demands a list of expeditions from candidates for the higher tests. The Kandahar Ski Club, which originated the modern downhill racing movement (the slalom is a British invention worked out at Mürren), still insists that its candidates shall pass a test in soft snow. It is no credit to the leaders of the various Alpine schools (and I am assured that there is no difference in this respect between any of them) that they should acquiesce in the degeneration of skiing into a kind of glorified tobogganing on wood. I know that many teachers still teach soft snow skiing, but no determined and organized effort is made by those in control of the Alpine schools to stress the infinite superiority of mountain skiing.

Recently I saw the Inferno Race in Mürren: I also saw it in 1949. This race, like all modern innovations in ski racing, originated with the Kandahar. The Inferno is a test of real skiing. Most other races, including world championships, are only a test of piste skiing, a debased and impoverished variant of the real thing. The Inferno Race starts from the summit of the Schilthorn and finishes at Lauterbrunnen, 7,000ft. below: the course from start to finish is on natural snow as shaped by sun, wind, and frost. As a soldier, this type of race appeals to me immensely; it calls for quick decisions; these have to be taken almost instinctively, and this can be done only against a background of knowledge which is acquired only by hard work and study of snow conditions. We want more races like the Inferno and more badges like those of the Ski Club of Great Britain and Kandahar, which still stand for real skiing as opposed to 'Cresta skiing.' I appeal to the leaders of the Alpine schools to do something to arrest the decadence of a noble sport.

Yours faithfully,
MONTGOMERY OF ALAMEIN, FM

A Link with Wellington

From Major P. J. M. Rous   *10 March 1950*

Sir,

I should like to place on record that at my son's baptism today there was present one lady whose father, born in 1794, had fought under Wellington in the Peninsular War.

If this boy or others of my children live the allotted 70 years they will be able to claim to be among the very few people who in 2020 will say: 'I had a friend once who told me how cross her father had been at the postal delays when he was in Spain with Wellington 200 years ago.'

I am, Sir, your obedient servant,
P. J. M. ROUS

The Electoral System

From Mr Christopher Hollis, MP   *10 March 1950*

[Conservative Member for Devizes 1945–55]

Sir,

People are asking whether our traditional electoral system can survive. Many do not seem to understand how largely that system has already perished. According to the traditional system – the system, for instance, of the nineteenth century – their constituents elected some 600-odd gentlemen to serve in Parliament, to legislate, and perform the business of the House of Commons.

It is true that most of those members were, more or less vaguely, attached to one or other of the political parties and that those parties had made more or less vague statements of their political philosophies. But there were no detailed political programmes, no talk of there being a mandate for this and not

201

being a mandate for that. It would have been impossible to appeal back against the verdict of the House to the votes of the electorate – first, because so many of the members were returned unopposed; secondly, because candidates made their own promises and programmes and did not merely repeat the syndicated programmes of their central offices.

The modern custom of checking the majority of seats in Parliament against the majority of votes in the country is an innovation. It may be good or bad. One great difficulty about it is that the electorate almost always casts more votes against anything than for it. The National Government of 1931 is, I think, the only Government of recent years that received the support of the majority of the electorate. If all Independent candidates are to be almost automatically rejected, if no member is ever to vote against his party, if no party is ever to do anything for which it has not got the support of the majority of the electorate, and if the majority of the electorate are never going to support anything, it is a little difficult to see how the King's Government is going to be carried on. It is still more difficult to see what is the importance of a member of Parliament. Lecky, perhaps the wisest of our historians who ever sat in the House of Commons, said that most of the duties of its members could be better performed by 'a fairly intelligent poodle-dog.'

Yours faithfully,
CHRISTOPHER HOLLIS

['I have never understood how a man [Hollis] with so withering a contempt for ambition and so keen a zest for entertainment could have endured ten years in the House of Commons.' – Robert Speaight, *The Property Basket*, 1970]

The Television Habit

From Mr T. S. Eliot, OM   *20 December 1950*

Sir,

In your issue of 17 December you announce that the BBC proposes to spend over £4m during the next three years on the development of television. I have just returned from a visit to the United States, where television (though not, I believe, more highly developed technically) has become an habitual form of entertainment in many more households than here. Among persons of my own acquaintance I found only anxiety and apprehension about the social effects of this pastime, and especially about its effect (mentally, morally, and physically) upon small children.

Before we endeavour to popularize it still further in this country, might it not be as well if we investigated its consequences for American society and took counsel with informed American opinion about possible safeguards and limitations? The fears expressed by my American friends were not such as could be allayed by the provision of only superior and harmless programmes: they were concerned with the television habit, whatever the programme might be.

Your obedient servant,

T. S. ELIOT

Rebuked by Man . . .

From Mr Peter Allison   *24 February 1951*

Sir,

I must protest! That a journal so rich in tradition, with so many distinguished readers, and which expresses itself so well upon every branch of world affairs should fall down on this one vital issue which affects every household in the country is unforgivable. I have tried three times already, but before cancelling my order I will make one more attempt. However, I can assure you, Sir, that if my fire refuses to light this time I shall without compunction transfer my custom to a newspaper which shows more readily combustible qualities.

I am, Sir, &c.,

PETER ALLISON

[A single sheet of *The Times* for 3 November, 1938 has just disproved the heretical views expressed above. Indeed the flames danced most spitefully around 'HOUSE facing Park, convenient Richmond; 3 reception, 5 bedrooms; perfect condition, £895']

. . . But Praised by Cat

From Mr A. H. Walker   *2 March 1951*

Sir,

Combustibility is all very well, but our cat detects more important, more abiding virtues in your paper. There was a choice before her on the couch of morning and evening papers, various oddly assorted weeklies, and a couple of glossy magazines, but she moved confidently towards yesterday's issue of *The Times*, made a nest out of the personal column, covered herself with the leading articles, and overnight produced five kittens.

I am, Sir, your obedient servant,
A. H. WALKER

[The first leading article dealt with Defence]

Fainting on Parade

From Dr E. P. Sharpey-Schafer   *4 July 1951*

[who held the chair of medicine at St Thomas's Hospital, London, from 1948 until his death in 1963]

Sir,

From time to time a great State occasion coincides with a break in the normal cool English summer weather. Under these conditions young soldiers on parade may faint in large numbers. Serious or even fatal accidents have resulted: the head may strike the parade ground or, as happened on a recent occasion, a bayonet may pierce the body. A number of beliefs on the cause of fainting seem to be held. There is a general feeling that only weaklings faint. Indulgence in alcohol the night before and lack of breakfast on the day itself have been blamed, while pressure of the bearskin on the brain was thought by one member of Parliament to be the deciding factor. Something, however, is now known of the physiology of this phenomenon. Perhaps the most important relevant fact is that all normal men and women will faint, even in the supine position, if a suffcient quantity of blood is lost. The faint is due to a sudden fall in blood pressure which diminishes the blood supply to the brain.

The erect posture in man is maintained only precariously.

204

Standing quite still for long periods causes blood to accumulate in the lower part of the body and is equivalent to a large haemorrhage: this effect is accentuated if the leg blood vessels are dilated by heat. Indeed, there appears to be a direct relationship between the environmental temperature and the number of persons who faint. 'Standing to attention' introduces an additional factor, since it causes obstruction to the great vein below the heart and further accumulation of blood in the lower half of the body. In the course of his biological history man seems to have developed no defence against this posture: it is all the more remarkable that it should have been chosen for military ceremonial. It is, perhaps, too much to hope that we are sufficiently civilized to abandon an established tradition. At least the authorities might think twice before punishing the victims for what is no more than normal physiological behaviour.

I am, Sir, &c.,
E. P. SHARPEY-SCHAFER

Left-Handed Kippers

From Mr John Christie   *12 June 1951*

[Companion of Honour 1954]

Sir,
If at breakfast a kipper is spread out on your plate with its tail on the right, the backbone is found sometimes on one side, sometimes on the other. Does this mean that – for want of a better term – some kippers are left-handed?

Yours, &c.,
JOHN CHRISTIE

[In 1947 Glyndebourne had performed *Albert Herring*]

Football Pool Statistics

From Mr Hubert Phillips   *16 May 1952*

Sir,
As one who has devoted a good deal of time to the statistical investigation of the football pools, I should like, if I may, to comment on recent correspondence.

The evidence which I gave to the Royal Commission on Betting, Lotteries, and Gaming (16 June 1950) was not, to my surprise, reported in *The Times;* but the Royal Commission devoted Appendix III of its report to a detailed examination of my conclusions, and went nearly all the way towards accepting them. And even such criticisms as are offered in this appendix can, in fact, be answered; and were answered by me in the course of the discussion at a recent meeting of the Royal Statistical Society.

I made the following points in my evidence: (1) The winning of dividends in the football pools follows exactly the pattern of random selection. For (2) if even a scintilla of skill were brought to bear, the dividends would inevitably be smaller and more numerous. Yet, in 1949–50, prizes in a four selections pool averaged 49s., as against a theoretical average of 40s. 6d., and prizes in a six selections pool averaged 350s. as against a theoretical average of 364s. 6d. Again, on the basis of 'random selection' (*i.e.,* regarding the pools as pure lotteries) the number of winners in one penny points pool, throughout the season 1949–50, should have been 326,985: in fact, it was 302,764. And the average first dividend was £5,440, against a theoretical average (in a lottery) of £4,800. Finally (3) pool tipsters' forecasts, which I analysed exhaustively, produce exactly the same results as Sir Alan Herbert's pin. One much publicised 'tipster' averaged 4.60 correct results, over the season, in one of the penny points pools; my average, with a pin, was 5.00; the theoretical average is 4.67. The whole business of forecasting, study of form, permutations, and all the rest of it is, in fact, pure nonsense, and involves the community in an indefensible waste of paper, time, and energy.

In short, football pools are indistinguishable from lotteries, and it is from that point of view that I criticize them. I am not fanatically opposed to lotteries as such. But I think it deplorable that the State, while condemning sweepstakes and so forth as illegal, should tolerate the continuance of these gigantic lotteries – incidentally collecting some £16m. in taxes – on the ground that participation in them may involve an element of skill. Hence arises the grotesque illusion, shared by most of those who participate, that enormous prizes can be won by 'hard work' and the application of judgment. They do not understand the laws of chance or how fantastic are the odds against success.

The reason why skill cannot enter into the business is that

winning prizes in all the significant pools involves the forecasting of draws. Now no one can forecast a single draw, let alone eight draws, as is necessary in the so-called treble chance. The *a priori* odds against any eight matches being drawn are about 60,000 to one; and if, in fact, only eight matches are drawn in the course of a single Saturday, the odds against forecasting them correctly are over 750,000,000 to one. This last season the money available for one first dividend amounted, I believe, to about £130,000. This meant that, to make so huge a prize possible, some 24 million sixpences must have gone into the kitty.

The average 'investor' (note the subtlety of that term, as of the corresponding word 'dividend') does not in the least realize that there are these astronomical odds against him. He does not grasp that he can hope to win a £75,000 prize once every 200,000 years or so. Nor does he realize that, of all the money subscribed, only 50 per cent is returned to subscribers; that perhaps two-thirds of those who play the pools win nothing from one year's end to another; that not more than one in 40 can hope to show a profit at the end of the year; and that in pool betting, which at present is entirely unregulated, 'there are' (to quote the Royal Commission) 'special opportunities for fraud on the part of the promoter.'

I am, Sir, yours faithfully,
HUBERT PHILLIPS

[In February 1974 a correspondent asked why 'windfall' profits made by banks, and 'unearned' fortunes reaped by property speculators, were considered 'obscene', while the £680,967 just won by someone on the pools was 'all right']

Gynes

From Sir Henry Tizard   30 January 1952

[chairman of the Advisory Council on Scientific Policy 1947–52]

Sir,
What a pity that that remarkable man Gynes, messenger at Magdalen in my undergraduate days and afterwards promoted to higher ranks, is not alive today. He would have been the obvious choice for the Chair of Ghost-writing at Washington University. Scratch golfer, literary and art critic, he would

whip off an essay on any subject at short notice in a style admirably adapted to the capacity of his client. 'I say, Gynes,' an old Etonian would say, rushing into the Lodge, 'I haven't started my essay yet and I have to show it up tonight. Can you do it?' 'Yes, Sir,' Gynes would reply, 'Let's see, gamma minus, isn't it?' But he could do 'top level' alpha pluses just as well. Dear Gynes – what a loss to Congress and the White House, as well as to Oxford.

Yours truly,
H. T. TIZARD

Supersonic Flight

From Mr A. H. Yates   *14 May 1953*

Sir,

The Minister of Supply told the House of Commons on 11 May that 'there was no solution in sight to the problem of the supersonic bang, and in fact we were probably in for some rather noisy times.' The steady noise of traffic, even of underground railway trains and of aircraft flying low overhead is much less objectionable to most people than the sudden, unexpected bang of a rifle shot or of a car back-firing. The prospect of unexpected and startingly loud bangs from a hitherto silent sky is not a welcome one, and the Minister of Supply was right to warn us that no solution was in sight.

The phenomenon is now well understood, and it is known that whenever an aircraft flies at a speed greater than that of sound in air (some 660 to 760 miles an hour, depending on its height) it creates shock waves in the air which move away from it as do the bow waves from a ship travelling fast through water. The waves travel on, losing strength only slowly, until they strike the ear on the ground beneath (or break upon the beach). At present aircraft can fly supersonically only in dives at high altitudes and usually slow down to the subsonic speeds at which no shock waves are formed before getting within three miles of our ears. For this reason the bangs we hear do not cause aural discomfort; the pressure jump has been calculated and measured and found to be of the order of only one pound a square foot.

Within a few years, however, aircraft will be capable of exceeding the speed of sound in level flight, and spectators at the Farnborough air displays of recent years will realize that the sudden noise from a fast, low-flying aircraft would then have grave consequences. The aircraft at Farnborough have so far been traced by their own noise, so that our ears have been able to give us some warning of their approach, and we were prepared for the rapid pressure rise which hurt our ears a few moments later. An aircraft flying low at supersonic speeds, perhaps only 100 miles an hour faster than at present, would create havoc not only with our eardrums but by material damage to our homes.

Calculations of the pressure rise caused by the shock wave from aircraft flying supersonically 1,000ft. above the ground show a sudden change of about 10 pounds a square foot when the shock wave passes. Besides being damaging to the ear this is sufficient to break most windows. Since the shock wave is being created constantly (and not merely during the acceleration through the 'sound barrier') a level-flying aircraft could devastate a large area during a low, fast flight.

It is clear that supersonic flying can be permitted only over the sea or at great heights, and disciplinary action against low flying will have to be much stricter than it is today. The danger of an enemy, or a thoughtless friend, raising the roof merely by flying past is a very real one.

Your faithfully,
A. H. YATES

[In 1910 a correspondent had asked the editor of *The Times* if an aeroplane could be sued for trespass when passing over one's garden]

Sussex Surnames

From Mr Aytoun Ellis   *17 January 1953*

Sir,

Can any county claim more curious surnames than Sussex? Pitchfork, Slybody, Devil, Lies, Hogsflesh, Sweetname, Juglery, Hollowbone, Stillborne, Fidge, Padge, Beatup, Wildgoose, and Whiskey are a few in the county archives that would certainly have interested Dickens. As for the names adopted during the Puritan revolution, there can surely be none so odd as those to be found in the Sussex registers. In 1632 Master Performe-thy-Vowes Seers, of Maresfield, married Thomasine Edwards; when his death was recorded his name had by then been abbreviated to Vowes Seers. A Heathfield wench was named More-fruits, and there are also on record Stand-fast-on-high Stringer, of Crowhurst; Weep-not Billing, of Lewes; Fight-the-good-fight-of-faith White, of Ewhurst; Kill-sin Pemble, of Withyam; and Fly-fornication Richardson, of Waldron.

I am, Sir, &c.,

AYTOUN ELLIS

Concern for the National Psyche
1953-1965

———————◆———————

THE remainder of 1953 concerned itself with the fight against inflation and the doping of athletes. Bath's newly opened Pleasure Gardens struck some as an insult to culture, the spot where Jane Austen had once taken breakfast being occupied by a model gorilla clad in red trousers. 1954 expressed indignation that pornographic reading matter should be so readily available; it also grew irritated by a dock strike and the sound made by counter-tenors. The following year turned to religion in schools and television sets in hotel lounges, correspondents insisting that the scintillating talk to which they had long been accustomed had dried up in the face of poor programmes. This amounted to a moral crisis. Outside hotel lounges the air was demonstrably not clean. In May 1956, as the cost of living soared, the Government decided there should be incentives for exporters; this dismayed as much as the news from Cyprus and Suez. The railways continued to deteriorate, the Duke of Bedford was denounced for referring to 'dustmen' when he should have said 'refuse collectors' (a passion for euphemism dated from this time). The year closed with *The Times*' readership split over the Anglo-French action at Suez. The Russian invasion of Hungary was regretted.

A cut in the Third Programme annoyed 1957, though few seemed interested in reforming the House of Lords. Many offered advice on how to deal with inflation. Leopold Stokowski revealed a consummate knowledge of concert hall acoustics. The Teddy Boy phenomenon was explained to 1958, age had succeeded class as the social barrier. Race riots took place, diesel fumes choked, the only opera to merit a U certificate was *Die Meistersinger*. A sit-in by passengers on the London underground greeted 1959; Wolfenden considered homosexuality, educationalists the desirability of compulsory Latin. Correspondents were naturally as one on the serving of Burgundy at room temperature until someone asked if this was the temperature of British or American rooms. As de Gaulle turned to the problem of Algeria, he was advised what to do. More vital, however, was the proposed larger golf ball, the dedicated not being disturbed when a weaker mortal said *he* wanted a larger hole. A walk-out of typists did not unduly dismay 1960; however, love letters composed on a typewriter were held to be less indecent than love letters written in shorthand. The habit of saying 'yeah' or 'yep' was seen as subversive. Lady Chatterley's trial was duly divisive on this side of the Atlantic, from the other a courteous letter asked why *The Times* review of the year had ignored the election of the future President Kennedy but not a decision permitting scouts to wear long trousers. Invited by the International Council for Bird Preservation to name a British emblem, correspondents voted 17 per cent for the robin and 11 per cent for the grouse.

Anxiety of different kinds afflicted 1961: the shortage of British-born doctors, the likelihood that Fahrenheit would give way to Centigrade, the way in which religion at the universities was under fire from philosophy dons. The next year questioned Post Office priorities (always deliver football pools trivia before parcels), bewailed the rise in rail fares, and regretted violence on television, a strike on the railways, and bad manners at Covent Garden where *la coiffure bouffante* held sway. The Crowther Report, which advocated 16 as the school leaving age, was criticized; not until December, when Dean Acheson said that Britain had lost an empire but had not yet found a new role, was the country reunited. In 1963 Common Market discussion divided, likewise opinions of King Richard III. The Thirty-Nine Articles were attacked, the entrance to Oxford and Cambridge adjudged too exclusive. 1964 debated the right to strike, and reproved the BBC for depicting army officers in plays as idiots. Chaos in the docks ushered in 1965. We were living beyond our means. Eton was surely a comprehensive, workers marched forth with their transistors. As the financial crisis worsened, and goods sent by rail arrived tardily (if at all), a cry went up: 'What we need is the spirit of Dunkirk.'

'To See Oursels'

From Mrs James P. Dean   *19 September 1953*

[writing from New York]

Sir,

At last, you English are achieving the impossible – you are making us lose our national sense of humour. For years, insults and sneers have been wafted across the ocean at us and we even imported lecturers who told us in clipped, forceful speech that we were braggarts, uneducated, money-mad, homicidal, crude. Then a lot of us began to travel in England. We searched almost in vain for the Oxford and Cambridge accent we had admired in the movies – it appeared once in a while, but the rest of the time it was smothered under the broad Lancashire and Yorkshire speech and the amazing, almost foreign, accent of the Cockney. We met people who told us we 'didn't sound American' – that being a wondrous compliment.

We met a man who kept £10,000 in his safe and counted it for us, not once but three times. We read about whole families being poisoned and attended the trial of a murderer who made Jack the Ripper sound mild. A woman expectorated out of the window of a crowded bus, and we thought longingly of the $50 fine that she would have received in America. We had tepid baths in cracked bathtubs, almost swallowed pits [stones] that loitered in plum puddings, choked over watery brussels sprouts, and watched butchers chasing flies from meat left exposed to the elements. We attended vaudeville shows which for sheer vulgarity could not be matched in any country – and the chief comedian invariably did an American characterization which was unfunny and untrue. We spent one unforgettable day at Blackpool and decided that our counterpart, Coney Island, is a model town of chivalry and refinement.

We rowed on the Thames with an ex-colonel who blamed us for both wars, and played darts with a mole-catcher who told us the citizens of Chicago were mowed down by machine-guns every day. We were asked by a delightful, bedridden lady if we knew some people named Smith in New York, and if there were any hospitals in Philadelphia.

We visited a large estate and the hostess asked us, while the maid was serving tea, if we had as much difficulty in America with our servants as she did with hers . . . and we immediately thought of our Swedish gem who called us by our first names and received $35 a week for telling us what to do and when to do it. We watched a four-year-old boy pick up a discarded cigarette and smoke it. We questioned children of 14 or 15 who had left school and were working and thought of the law that keeps our children in school until they are 18 years of age. And we searched in vain for one woman or one man who was serving on a charitable committee and thought of the long hours and days and years we had spent collecting money and clothes for unfortunate people of other countries.

We came home and forgot all this. The remembrance of the smiling policemen, the fascinating Tower, the succulent beef (we forgot the flies) – the statute of our George Washington – the people who were genuinely interested in America – the beautiful children – was stronger than the disagreeable experiences. But now – the cartoons and the speeches and the newspaper articles from England that are flooding this country – are bringing them all back. And we are forgetting that a strong Britain and a strong Europe are necessary for our survival. We are beginning to wonder if the large slice deducted from our salaries is worth the survival of a lot of alphabetical absurdities.

We might suggest a remedy – just ignore us. Forget the 'Bundles for Britain' and the 'Flood Relief' and the help that has helped you to regain some sort of economic steadiness – we have forgotten your marvellous bravery during the last war and the delight we shared with you when your Queen was crowned. If you ignore us, we may be able to regain the friendship which is so necessary – when you are tempted to tell us our shortcomings, remember you have a few of your own. Above all, ignore us – and we can regain our sense of humour – we know people who turn the dial on TV when an English movie comes on!

Sincerely yours,
STELLA DEAN

The Quick Brown Fox

From Mr N. H. New   *21 September 1953*

Sir,
I am embarking on a project to teach a young African French, and to allow him to practise typing at the same time. But is there a French equivalent for 'the quick brown fox jumps over the lazy dog'?

Yours faithfully,
NEVILL H. NEW

From Mr E. A. Paterson   23 September 1953

Sir,

On the margin of the instruction card of a portable type-writer I bought in Calcutta in May 1949, was typed: 'Zoë ma grande fille veut que je boive ce whisky dont je ne veux pas.'

Your obedient servant,

E. A. PATERSON

Personal Baths

From Mr Jonathan Routh   30 March 1954

Sir,

With regard to your leading article on 2 April on 'Personal Baths,' it was not in my knowledge any Cambridge don but Dr Martin Routh, President of Magdalen, Oxford, from 1791 to 1854, who could see no reason for the installation of baths in the college since the young men were up for only eight weeks at a stretch. Dr Routh also refused to believe in the existence of railways, dismissing undergraduates who told him that they had travelled from London to Oxford in two hours as 'conspirators bent on making him take leave of his senses.'

Yours faithfully,

JONATHAN ROUTH

[The Didcot to Oxford branch line was opened in 1844 when Dr Routh was in his 89th year]

Formative Years

From Mr W. O. Lake   9 April 1954

Sir,

Not everyone in *Who's Who* tells us to what school he went, but from those who do, a list of schools represented and the number of alumni might be of interest. Eton has 1,421. Then follows Winchester 472, Harrow 437, Rugby 435, Marlborough 373, Charterhouse 302, Wellington 260, St Paul's 250, Clifton 249, Cheltenham 242, Westminster 213, Haileybury 207, Dulwich 200, Uppingham 159, Bedford 146, Shrewsbury 138, Tonbridge 137, Malvern and Merchant Taylor's 135 each, Repton 129, and so on.

The first four are possibly national institutions (their old boys will give affirmation to this bold statement, no doubt), and Wellington and Cheltenham may be above the average in major-generals, brigadiers, and colonels. The Midland group of Shrewsbury, Repton, Uppingham, Bedford, and Malvern make five corners of a pentagon in the heart of England and the figures are astonishingly similar. If numbers passing through the schools are any guide, Repton and Uppingham are neck and neck (their rivalry is intense in anything where the ball is the same shape). Is Clifton's success due to the addition of Polack's House, which is inhabited by a race who have contributed so much to the arts, science, and business? She may have poached on Bristol Grammar School, which might explain why the latter school is not quite so well represented as other great day schools like Manchester Grammar School, King Edward's, Birmingham, the City of London School, and George Watson's College.

Averages can be dangerous, but it is not unreasonable to assume that if one had been to a public school for five years between 1890 and 1950 one would have had at least a 30 to one chance of joining the ranks of the eminent. One could speculate indefinitely upon why these institutions are so successful. But would *Who's Who* be so bulky a tome without them?

I am, Sir, your obedient servant,

W. O. LAKE

[If the schools mentioned were of the same size, then of every 1,000 old boys in *Who's Who*, Eton would claim 139, Winchester 103, Harrow 74, Rugby 73 and Cheltenham 67]

In Praise of Hookahs

From Sir Hugh Rankin   *13 May 1954*

Sir,

So much has been said recently about the ill-effects of smoking. But if the British could only take to smoking the various forms of Indian hookah, then there would be no danger of ill-health. For, in the hookah, all tobacco smoke passes through a vessel which is filled with water *en route* to the smoker's

216

mouth. All nicotine is left in that water and none reaches the mouth.

Yours faithfully,
HUGH RHYS RANKIN

[BR (Southern Region) state that rush-hour commuters will be expected to rest hookahs on their laps]

A Vanishing Craft

From Mr J. G. Strachan   *9 April 1954*

Sir,

It has been brought to my notice that the once flourishing craft of swaging is rapidly becoming forgotten. In my grandfather's lifetime the swager was a familiar figure in the West Country, mentioned several times in his diaries. Workshops like the one he describes at Chetnole must have continued to fascinate, while such individual crafts were still scarcely affected by nineteenth-century industrialism. Today a swaging iron is something of a curiosity, and the old swagers, still working with scud and fossick, are few and far between. Cannot something be done to preserve this craft from extinction?

Yours faithfully,
J. G. STRACHAN

† 'Swaging' is the shaping or working of cold metal, wrought iron, &c., by hammering it on a suitably grooved or perforated block.

Population and Resources

From Sir Charles Darwin, FRS   *15 January 1955*

[theoretical physicist; Master of Christ's College, Cambridge 1936–8, Director of the National Physical Laboratory 1938–49; grandson of the author of *Origin of Species*]

Sir,

In the letters of Mr Stern on 10 January and Mr Bunker yesterday on the subject raised by Lord Simon of Wythenshawe on 7 January a line of uninformed optimism is taken against which a strong protest must be made. The cheerful doctrine that 'Something always turns up' is admissible only in a condition of profound ignorance, and we are now far past that condition – perhaps unhappily for ourselves.

As Lord Simon says, the earth's resources are being rapidly used up, and it is not a question merely concerning the far distant future, but rather the question is how much many of the younger people now living will have their standards of life materially lowered by these shortages.

It is, of course, true that not every acre of the earth's surface has been explored, but in a looser sense we do know what it contains, and that looser sense is enough. First, take an example near home. There are rich coal fields under us in parts of England, and it is not impossible that there are some more not yet discovered, but nobody would be likely to maintain that there is any chance whatever that there is 10 times as much undiscovered but mineable coal under us as that already known. In this loose sense we do know the amount of English coal.

Now apply the same idea to Lord Simon's case of copper. There are at present a number of great ore fields being worked. They have been well explored, and it is unlikely but still it is possible that they might have large but unknown reserves of ore. They might perhaps have as much again as the known amounts or even double that, but it is practically certain that there is not 10 times as much. So, too, there may turn out to be great ore fields in the unexplored parts of the earth; it is possible but unlikely that there might be three or four such, and certainly there cannot be 10 of them. It is in this general sense that we know how much copper there is in the earth. Our present estimates may prove too low, but it is practically certain that they are not 10 times too low. This knowledge suffices to show the difficulties we are soon going to be in. The world has simply got to get on without demanding so much copper.

The usual suggestion to meet the difficulty is to propose substitutes. Now the electrical industry is the most important user of copper, and it is undoubtedly true that an electric generator will work with wires made of other metals, but only at a distinctly lowered efficiency; that is why copper is always used. The physicist can say with absolute confidence that there is no good substitute for copper for this purpose; the only possible one is silver, which would be even better, but it is, of course, much too expensive. In nearly everything the substitute will be inferior, and it is this inferiority that will make one of the main difficulties for the future. It is impossible to go here into this question of substitutes, but one of the most formidable short-

218

ages of all must be mentioned; this is energy, which it is hoped to relieve by the use of atomic energy. It can be said that, though this looks promising, it will certainly take time to develop it, and there may well be a close race between this development and the exhaustion of our stocks of oil and coal.

Of course, the most formidable part of the whole problem is the increase of world population. Short of the sort of catastrophe that would hardly be invoked by any optimist as a solution, it is practically certain that the world will have a population of nearly 4,000 million by the end of the twentieth century, as compared with the present 2,400 million. It is going to be a problem even to feed them, and in the present connexion it signifies that the shortages will produce their effects even more rapidly than would be deduced from considering the demands of the present population.

The serious student of these matters is forced to the conclusion that the principle that 'Something will turn up' is a wild gamble not to be taken by any wise man. There is surely a better prospect for us and our successors of at least mitigating some of our coming troubles, if we recognize the dangers, and do not follow the lead of the optimists by merely turning a blind eye to them.

Yours faithfully,
CHARLES DARWIN

After Henley

From Mr E. R. Thompson   9 July 1955

Sir,

We have had another thrilling Henley; and those who value what is left of sport in the old sense can surely feel nothing but gratitude to the authorities, who have steadily refused to compromise the traditional character of that great regatta. The entrants, British and foreign, are expected to take Henley as they find it. To judge by the regularity with which they return, and the zest with which they race when they get there, they find it very good indeed.

But to acknowledge this is not necessarily to allay a certain anxiety about the way things are going from our own national point of view. It would hardly be too much to claim that eight-oared rowing, in its modern form, was invented in this country, in the nineteenth century, by an *élite*, who made up in physical prowess and voluntary discipline what they lacked in numbers. Viewed historically, their achievement has been quite astonishing. The heirs to their inheritance, at Oxford and Cambridge and on the Thames tideway, have maintained over the past 100 years a standard of performance which, when considered in relation to their resources, may well rank as outstanding by any comparison.

In particular, it would surely be necessary to dig deep in the annals to find anything like the record of one or two Cambridge college boat clubs, which have contrived, decade after decade, with nothing more than a handful of undergraduates and an incomparable tradition, to put forth crews of Grand Challenge Cup class, or near it. These, with the great clubs on the tideway, are now the custodians of British rowing prestige, in the face of the mighty forces, massed, graded, professionally coached, subsidized, and geared to international competition, of the United States and Russia.

They are splendid. And yet – let us face it – in such company they can no longer hope to win. Their numbers are against it; their finances are against it; and their rowing calendar is against it. And the vista now opens up of a future in which we provide the traditional trappings of an annual rowing festival, and the aura of past greatness, while the real battles are fought out by others and elsewhere. One need not be obsessed by the importance of Olympic gold medals to feel some reluctance to resign one's self to this. No doubt we have not the resources of America or Russia.

But are we making the best use of the resources we have? No one would wish to interfere with, or to dilute, what might be described as the Leander tradition. But those of us who look at these things from the detachment of the towpath may surely be allowed to wonder whether that tradition might now be augmented and diversified? There must be tens of thousands of young men, at universities other than Oxford and Cambridge, and at no university, from whom potential crews might be drawn.

The demands of rowing are such that it must always remain a minority sport. But we surely have the men at least to prevent the Thames Cup from remaining permanently in America; and perhaps to double the British entry for the Grand. If so, what are the obstacles that prevent them coming together? Are they social, physical, economic? And ought they not now to be investigated, with a view to overcoming them, if at all possible?

I am, Sir, yours, &c.,

E. R. THOMPSON

220

Voles Prefer Cox's

From Mr David Garnett   *13 December 1955*

Sir,

If, as you report in your leading article of 10 December
water voles eat the bark of Cox's Orange Pippins in Denmark
and show no such preference in England, it is perhaps because
the Danish nurseryman grafts his apple tree as close to the root-
stock as possible, whereas the English nurseryman works the
standard tree from the top. Thus the vole can only find the
bark of crab, Paradise, or E. Malling, unless he climbs to the
branches. But though voles can be outwitted, nothing can prevent the sybaritic bullfinch from taking the buds of greengage
and Doyenne du Comice in preference to those of damson and
cooking plums and stewing pears. The standard of living rises
among the animal as fast as among the human population.

Yours, &c.,
DAVID GARNETT

Space Travel

From Mr G. V. E. Thompson   *6 January 1956*
Sir,

I am surprised that, according to your report of 3 January,
our new Astronomer Royal has stated that the prospect of
interplanetary travel is 'utter bilge,' although he apparently
admits both that it is technically possible and that he has no
idea how much it would cost.

Surely it is unwise for him to prophesy that nobody will ever
put up enough money to do such a thing, when he himself can
exert little or no influence on the persons who seem most likely
to have to decide whether or not to finance the first expedition
– namely, the next two or three Presidents of the United States,
or the corresponding wielders of power in the Kremlin? While
it is obvious that the next war could not be won by the first
man – or even the first regiment – getting to the moon, the cold
war might well be decisively influenced. The propaganda value
is obvious: a landing on the moon would unquestionably be
man's greatest material achievement, and would no doubt be
claimed to demonstrate its technical superiority by the nation
concerned. It is hardly necessary for the expedition to be a

financial success, any more than it is for the present Trans-Antarctic Expedition.

There are many fields of human endeavour which are more worthy of support – cancer research is an example which springs immediately to one's mind. Nevertheless we cannot confine our activities to one or two narrow branches of knowledge. We now seem to be approaching the stage at which we both need to colonize the other planets (where suitable), and have the means to do so. Interest in and research into space travel are not confined to this country but are world-wide. When the moment of history arrives no doubt some organisations will be prepared to play the part of Queen Isabella. Perhaps the real question facing us in this country so far as space travel is concerned is for us to decide whether we are content that it should come about under the spur of national rivalry or whether to press for its being undertaken under the aegis of the United Nations.

I am, Sir, &c.,
G. V. E. Thompson

['That's one small step for man but one giant leap for mankind.' – Neil Armstrong on the moon, 3.56 a.m. (BST), 21 July 1969]

Secretarial Staff

From Mrs M. Trevett   *21 January 1956*

Sir,

By all means let salaries for secretarial staff be stabilized at an economic level; but in this process let us not lose sight of economic justice.

A financial distinction should surely be made between the great majority of unskilled and semi-skilled typewriter punchers of little or no education, and the women of genuine education and background who bring a professional skill, sense of responsibility and capacity for initiative to bear on their work.

For women of this calibre a minimum salary in the region of £600 would not be excessive, and in any case that salary is below what a man of comparable attainments would expect, or receive. Your issue, of today, for example, carries an advertisement for a young male private secretary 'at a four-figure commencing salary, together with bonus and non-contributory pension scheme.' I entirely agree with Mr Nesbitt, whose letter you print this morning, that £9 and over, plus 'perks,' is excessively generous remuneration for the 'half-baked flibbertigibbets.'

An adequate type of skilled secretarial assistant could be ensured by certain responsible bodies – the Institute of Management and the Federation of British Industries, for example – holding examinations for executive secretaries/personal assistants (as opposed to company secretaries), such examination to be taken after the usual training and some years of general office experience, the passing of which would rank as a professional qualification.

Such a qualification would ensure that the secretary: (1) was capable of relieving her employer of the burden of correspondence, other than that relating to technical or policy matters; (2) was able to collate material for and draft reports; (3) was experienced in committee/board work, the taking of minutes, &c.; (4) could, in her employer's absence, conduct responsible interviews on his behalf, as opposed to receptionist duties; and (5) was capable of administering her office efficiently. If the present somewhat nebulous term and status of 'secretary' were defined by such an examination, a different type of young woman would surely come forward, thus ensuring an adequate supply of candidates for what would then rank as a profession.

My feelings on this subject are strong, for I am of the secretary as opposed to the 'sekketary' class, as many young women now call themselves. My own experience is that employers are aghast at the idea of paying women like myself a salary genuinely commensurate with our abilities: they often employ two flibbertigibbets when one woman of proven capacity would, in spite of a higher individual salary, ultimately prove the more advantageous proposition.

I am, Sir, yours faithfully,
MARIE TREVETT

[By 1980 this sort of advertisement was appearing in *The Times*:

NO SHORTHAND!
A job awaits for an attractive girl of 21, Salary £5,500, with great fringe benefits, working to Hi-fi Vivaldi. Hankypanky: nil!]

Glimpse of Philately

From Miss V. Sackville-West, CH   *31 January 1956*

Sir,

I am no philatelist, but if pre-natal influence counts for anything I ought to be. My mother amused herself during the months before my birth by papering a small room at Knole with stamps arranged in strips and patterns. As the date was, I regret to say, 1892, many of those stamps must now be of some interest and value. I remember that there were many Russian stamps of the Tsarist régime, and there were some early Victorian stamps also.

Yours, &c.,
V. SACKVILLE-WEST

Spirit of the Olympics

From Mr John Crammond   *6 January 1956*

Sir,

In 1948, in my forty-second year, I won a bronze medal in the Winter Olympic Games. The discipline in which I had the honour to participate was a two-day event, on the first day I was placed first but, on the first and second days' results, my final position was third.

I was entirely delighted but not for long. On my return to this country three people referred to the matter. The first was a very young lady and a close relation, who, throwing her arms around my neck and bursting into tears, said: 'Only third!' The second, an eminent accountant, said: 'It is not clear to me whether we are to commiserate or congratulate you.' The third, the editor of a Sunday newspaper, asked, 'Why didn't you win?' Therefore, until this moment, I have been careful never to refer in public to 'this dark page in my career,' although I find that privately I am still entirely delighted.

I do now mention these matters because I think that the attitude revealed by your correspondents on this subject can only be damaging to our athletes' morale and obstructive to the spirit of the Games. I suggest that the importance of coming first is an obsession of professionals and the very young. Baron de Coubertin's dictum is the correct one.

There must be tens of thousands of athletes who enter and

re-enter their fields of play well content in the knowledge that among the other hundreds and thousands playing they, the chosen 10,000 are likely to come in leggy last. Nor are they thereby put off – on the contrary, they welcome the challenge to renew their style and bearing.

I submit, and this submission is based on the observation over a period of 30 years of many hundreds of international events on the Cresta Run, that national prestige is advanced by good style and bearing far more than by a total of points scored. If some competitors are playing hookey with the amateur status clause and ours are not, then two things can happen – our athletes can (1) enjoy the fun of beating the sponsored or (2) reinforce our national reputation of being good losers.

If your correspondents are correct we have to choose between (*a*) sponsoring our athletes or (*b*) denying the truth of (2) above. I beg to disagree. There is a third course. We can send our athletes off to the Games telling them to have fun and leave the rest to them.

I am, Sir, your obedient servant,
JOHN G. CRAMMOND

Operatic Standards

[Karl Rankl was Musical Director of the Royal Opera House 1946–51, Rafael Kubelik was appointed in 1955]

From Sir Thomas Beecham, CH   *27 June 1956*

Sir,

If it is Mr Rafael Kubelik's contention, as expressed in his letter on 23 June, that there is a host of latter day English singers capable either of competing with their foreign rivals or of filling the large auditorium of Covent Garden I should like to know who and where they are. Nearly 50 years have passed since I first started looking for them, and I am still occupied with the same pursuit. I have always freely admitted the excellence of many native vocalists, but have consistently pointed out that nearly all of them have light voices more suited to a smaller building than the so-called Royal Opera House. In my English seasons of the past I avoided Covent Garden as much as possible, and gave them preferentially at such theatres as Drury Lane, His Majesty's and the Aldwych. And those were the days when we had a few voices, but only a few, able to vocalize in what the late Mr Richard Capell used to call the 'Royal Manner.'

During the past 25 years only one English soprano has appeared in Covent Garden who fulfils this condition – namely, Miss Eva Turner, who was trained in Italy and sang only in Italian opera. During this same period, where have been and where are now the voices of an English Brünnhilde, Isolda,* Salome, Electra, Aida or indeed any of the weightier roles? And thinking of men where are those of Siegfried, Tristan, Tannhäuser, Lohengrin, Wotan, Hans Sachs, or in another direction those of Othello, Radames, Manrico, Don Carlos, Don José and Des Grieux? They are certainly not heard at Covent Garden, so perhaps they are elsewhere. But I scan in vain the lists of singers at such opera houses as the Metropolitan of New York, the Colon of Buenos Aires, La Scala of Milan, Vienna, Paris or 50 lesser establishments for the sign of any of our native vocalists filling any important roles in the international repertoire.

I submit, therefore, that to support Mr Kubelik's contention along this line is futile; indeed, it would be dangerously misleading and contrary to our true interests. This gentleman appears to think that all would be well with our singers if they were encouraged to overcome their native inhibitions and to project their voices more scientifically. I join with Mr Martin Cooper, whose letter you print today, in expressing wonder that no one at Covent Garden has ever thought of this before. In my humble experience, I have always found that these two disabilities can be largely overcome by a due appreciation of the strong as well as the weak points of our language. This should be the prime consideration of anyone taking charge of the English side of opera, be it at Covent Garden or anywhere else. But how did the management of our national institution set about this task? In defiance of all common sense they engaged as Musical Director a foreigner, and let him loose upon the unhappy creatures who had been led to expect beneficial results from this monumental stroke of stupidity.

After the departure of this gentleman from the London scene there followed a period of interregnum during which the misguided Directors had plenty of time and opportunity to select some Englishman of musical attainment and general culture to meet this supreme need. Now we have another foreigner in charge. But does he possess any of the qualifications essential for the creation of a truly national organization? It is not a question only of conducting; the modern world positively teems with conductors of every nationality and nearly all of them are highly praised by the Press.

What we have all got to realize is that Covent Garden has neither accomplished the purpose for which it was established, nor is it ever likely to do so while it remains in the hands of those who are now in charge of it. The time has come for a full and enlightened inquiry into every branch of its activities, and this should be undertaken by an independent body, not one of whom has any association with it, or who has an axe to grind of a material kind.

The dignity of our nation is today at stake and we are presenting a sorry spectacle to the outside world. I have indicated elsewhere what are the necessary and fitting alternatives to this present overgrown, over-staffed, and over-confident musical machine, and I am prepared to re-state them in much greater detail before a competent body of assessment. Incidentally, they are the results of 54 years' association with the lyric theatre and 46 of them as impresario, manager, and musical director.

I am, Sir, yours obediently,
THOMAS BEECHAM

[*The spelling suggests Sir Thomas, doubtless clad in a dressing-gown and enjoying a cigar, dictated this letter. Having dominated the English opera scene for thirty years prior to 1939, he afterwards conducted only a handful of performances at Covent Garden. Toscanini, of course. never conducted there at all.]

A Taxing Question

From Mr Terry-Thomas   *16 February 1957*

Sir,
Inspectors of taxes have acquired a reputation for wanting not only the greater part of one's income, but also the very clothes off one's back. I thought until today that this reputation was quite undeserved and indeed that it was probably the invention of some low, music-hall comedian. I am now told by my accountant, who is professionally impeccable, that my own

tax inspector now wishes to know whether I sell my old suits. Unbelievable, isn't it! I wonder if they ask deep-sea divers the same question.

Yours faithfully,
TERRY-THOMAS

A Disordered Society

From Mr Graham Hutton   *11 January 1957*

Sir,

There is a deep and wide *malaise*, akin to despair, among us. All who regularly move among all social groupings are struck by it. It is in the news: a sixfold increase in applications to emigrate, the increasing loss of expensively trained young scientists and other skilled men, exasperation of the middle class shown by abstention from voting in by-elections, a state of affairs among the doctors unimaginable up to 1948, senseless unofficial 'strikes against redundancy' (the worst moment for them), and disbelief (in all political quarters) in short-term and 'short-time' palliatives like 'sharing the work.' These items tell much more on a natively shrewd people than synthetic pep-talking. Everyone knows things are badly wrong here, and will take a lot of imagination, courage, and work to put right.

In these columns you, Sir, have allowed many authorities in the past decade to say, time and again, that uninterrupted inflation would produce such a disordered society. But – in spite of the Government's exercises over the past two years – total public expenditure goes on rising, along with borrowing from the banking system (and colonies); so taxes cannot be reduced (in real terms, *i.e.*, more than the rise in the cost of living); so that, in turn, no material incentives can be given to persons paying the full rate of income tax and/or surtax.

The trade unionist has more than kept pace with the cost of living since the war (on Socialist economists' showing, he is the only element in the population to have raised his and his family's real consumption, by an average of 20 per cent, since 1939). But the professional men, Judges, senior Civil servants, technologists, managers, and others on whom our national future depends for productive and constructive leadership, have steadily lost ground. Resignation and exasperation are rife among them. Many of our younger trained, talented folk take a look at their lot – at the apex of our pyramid of earned

228

rewards – and emigrate. Many of those who stay do not blench at the vision of a static, managed society – a 'social engineer's paradise.'

Sir, I was a student in Germany in the 1920s when the inflation knocked out an upright, austere, hardworking, public-spirited (if dull) middle class. I saw lack of belief in any worthwhile future lead to despair; and despair to the destruction of moral fibre in what was the backbone of Germany. Europe has not recovered from that. Yet we persist in policies which wrecked central European societies. I may be thought tasteless to breathe this in a British context. But however peculiar our nature, we British are human. Driven far, fast, and unfairly enough, any society – or group of it – will rebel, even if the prospect be as grim as in Hungary. And ways of revolt today allow minorities more power to paralyze the State. Much more despair, sense of inequity, and feeling of penalization among the necessary minority of responsible, skilled, and trained leaders in Britain, will, I think, quickly produce a bigger loss to us (and gain to foreigners) of talents, a not necessarily deliberate going-slow in management and administration, and a decline in the whole nation's standards of living.

But I also think that our present hopelessness, disbelief, and *malaise* could instantly be turned to creative account, if only Tories and Socialists – to start with, the thinkers among them – revised their ends, ways, and means. (Physicians and psychiatrists know that responses are often energetic when stimuli are applied to patients in a 'low' state.) Any Government has to run the State for all of us – not for the majority that have made no material sacrifices since the war, nor for the better-off minority who have. Why should the latter, the most productive and constructive group of earners, make all material sacrifices only for their own extinction through inflation? That is poor social building, and poor cement.

I am, Sir, your obedient servant,

GRAHAM HUTTON

[Variations on this theme have since been a regular feature of letters to *The Times*]

Value of the Third Programme

[The BBC had launched its Third Programme on 29 September 1946 with 'How to Listen' by Stephen Potter and Joyce Grenfell, Bach's Goldberg Variations, talks by Field-

Marshal Smuts and Sir William Haley (the Corporation's Director-General), orchestral music, and a recording of Sir Max Beerbohm's 1935 'London Revisited.' Inevitably there was an Epilogue – from St Mark's, North Audley Street]

From Mr T. G. Miller   *16 February 1957*

Sir,

We must be indebted to the distinguished American critic, Mr R. P. Blackmur, for pointing, a few years ago, to the rise, side by side with the spread of general education, of a sinister, blind, and powerful force in the world – the 'new illiteracy.'

Mr Blackmur saw a steadily increasing proportion of the world's steadily increasing population learning to read, without knowing, and of course without wanting or needing to know, what to read. In fact, not knowing that there might *be* anything to read, with profit, beyond the advertisement, the pay-check, and the 'comic.'

More ominous still, Mr Blackmur demonstrated the invasion of the world of learning itself by the 'new illiteracy,' as that world falls more and more under the domination of the scientists and the technologists and the humanist occupiers of the more narrowly gated ivory towers. An unwillingness – an inability – to become in any intelligently human way committed to humanity spreads and multiplies its devastating tentacles. In this process the possibility of the disappearance of the BBC's Third Programme is the latest appalling symptom.

One does not need to be a slavish and uncritical admirer of the Third Programme to fear the prospect of its foundering. Its simple existence is a strong-point in the struggle to maintain our standards against the spread of the 'new illiteracy.' Whatever one's private views on coteries and cliques and charmed circles there has come now the time to close the ranks and to declare that all who value our ancient heritage and who are able to fight for it must straightly do so. Moreover, it is not just the poets, the musicians, and the political economists who must fight this action, but all who feel themselves involved and concerned to keep the values and standards and aims of a cultivated society, whether physicists, engineers, historians, dramatists, biologists, linguists, chemists, or whatever.

If we allow the Third Programme to be sapped away in an atmosphere of self-centred apathy then we in our turn deserve to be submerged by the flood of the dull, the rootless, the vulgar, the second- or third- or tenth-rate – ultimately and completely the valueless. The full and strong expression of opinion in this situation cannot be anything but academically respectable.

I am, Sir, your obedient servant,
T. G. MILLER

Diplomacy in a Changing World

From Mr K. C. Johnson-Davies   *11 May 1957*

Sir,

A comparison of some 'Public Appointment' vacancies notified in your columns on 6 May indicates an unbelievable lack of realism in the Foreign Office.

The Foreign Office seeks the services of a Principal Instructor in Arabic – a senior appointment – to teach a vital but one of the most difficult foreign languages to our Middle Eastern diplomats and industrialists. For this they offer a starting salary of the wholly unrealistic sum of £605 a year, subject to United Kingdom income tax, for service in a British Government college operated in the non-British territory of Lebanon, a country not merely non-British but not even in the sterling area, and one where the cost of living is notoriously high. The appointment is non-pensionable and carries no gratuity. The living accommodation is sub-standard and the leave does not begin to compare with other Middle Eastern appointments. Small wonder that Britain's influence in the Middle East is in eclipse.

In contradistinction, the State of Qatar seeks an engineer. For this it offers £3,780 a year, no income tax, a five-year contract with a gratuity on conclusion, good leave and free accommodation, fuel, light, and water. Even Cyprus offers £2,277 a year for a trade union official.

Yours faithfully,
K. C. JOHNSON-DAVIES

The St James's Theatre

[whose glory had been enhanced by the actor-managers George Alexander, Laurence Olivier and John Clements]

231

From Mr Alan Dent   *28 June 1957*

Sir,

'Zealacious commerciality!' murmured Wells's Mr Polly when the ironmonger opposite took no notice of his 'Good morning!' – being far too busy arranging his shop. The St James's Theatre is to be pulled down and a block of offices reared in its place. At the confirmation of this threat, I can only repeat – 'Zealacious commerciality!' But the deplorable decision merits far more than a whimsical jest. It is an occasion for dismay and outcry.

As a Londoner by adoption (and in view of my present address), I may be permitted to end this roar of indignation on a personal note and as a practising dramatic critic. For 18 years I lived in Covent Garden, which I liked because I was close to most of the theatres. For the past three years I have lived in St James's which I like because it is close to St James's Theatre. On the day the demolition-man removes the first stone of this theatre, I shall sell the lease of my present flat at whatsoever personal loss. This will not, of course, matter to anyone but myself. But the loss of this old, endeared theatre will matter tremendously to the whole community – or at least to that section of it which persists in thinking that grace and glory and tradition are things worth striving to maintain.

Not until the demolition actually begins shall I really believe that this world has grown so bad, or that this town has grown so mad.

Yours faithfully,
ALAN DENT

[The world grown bad and the town so mad, Mr Dent moved]

What's Wrong with Thomas?

From Dr Thomas Bodkin   *14 January 1958*

Sir,

On reading Mr Leaver's interesting letter about the Christian names of the year, I am prompted, not for the first time, to ask: What's wrong with Thomas? He never gets a look in. Yet Thomas à Becket and Thomas More should both prove to be good patron saints, particularly for Englishmen; and Thomas the Apostle and Thomas Aquinas are surely more worthy of popularity than the Jeremys, Jonathans and the like who have high places in the annual lists.

The name Thomas has usually been borne by some member of my own family since the Bodkins took their place among the Twelve Tribes of Galway in the twelfth century. If I am asked why I have failed to maintain this tradition I can only reply that my wife demurred to having any of our five daughters christened Thomasina, and I hoped until it was too late they might have had a brother. All five are now the mothers of sons, not one of whom is a Thomas. It seems that the name is slighted by the modern mother. 'Poor Tom's a cold.'

I am, Sir, your obedient servant,

THOMAS BODKIN

[The shade of Dr Bodkin has doubtless been placated by the letter for 10 January 1974]

Dr Pauling's Visit

From Lord Russell, OM, FRS 5 September 1958

Sir,

I am writing to report an incident which must bring shame to all who value the fair name of Britain. The incident concerns the dealings of the Home Office with Dr Linus Pauling, a very distinguished native-born American, Honorary Fellow of the Royal Society, recipient of honorary degrees from the Universities of Oxford, Cambridge, and London, Nobel Prizeman, and well known throughout the scientific world as a man of outstanding intellect and integrity. He came to the United Kingdom on 31 August for two main purposes, to deliver an address which he has been invited to give on 15 September at the Kekulé Symposium of the Chemical Society of London and to address a meeting organized for the Campaign for Nuclear Disarmament which is to take place on 22 September.

On arrival at London Airport he was separated from the other passengers by the immigration authorities, and his son, who had come to meet him, was refused information as to whether he had arrived. He was closely questioned as to the purposes of his visit. When he mentioned the Chemical Society, he was asked whether he had any evidence that they had invited him. He replied that the evidence was in his baggage which was in the customs shed, and asked whether they accused him of lying. At the moment, they did not answer, but at a later stage they made this accusation. At first they said that he must leave the United Kingdom on 15 September. He pointed out that this made his address to the Chemical Society impossible, and they reluctantly extended his permit to the next day, 16 September. They stated as the ground of their action: 'We do not admit people to Great Britain who come principally to take part in public meetings, especially when against Government policy.'

This action by the British authorities is shocking. First, for the gross discourtesy of subjecting a man of great intellectual eminence, who has been honoured by many learned bodies in this country, to insult at the hands of ignorant officials. In the United States McCarthyism has lost its vigour, but one is compelled to believe that it is being taken up in this country.

Second, if Government policy is as stated to Dr Pauling, free speech has been abandoned and the only freedom left is that of supporting the Government.

Third, on the particular issue of nuclear weapons the Government have laid themselves open to very damaging criticism. It will be said that they know their policy to be such as no well-informed person could support. Apparently their watchword is: 'Democracy, yes, but only ignorant democracy, for our policy is one which no well-informed democracy would tolerate.'

Yours, etc.,
BERTRAND RUSSELL

[Dr Pauling received two Nobel Prizes, for Chemistry in 1954, and for Peace in 1962]

Clashes in the Streets

From Dr B. R. Wilson   *5 September 1958*

Sir,

The widespread attention given to the sadly misnamed 'race riots' in Nottingham and Notting Hill, and the utterance of MPs and public men, have all apparently misconstrued the really significant issues at stake.

The solitary solution proposed is for some sort of restriction of immigration to this country – as if the coloured people were in some sense responsible for the disturbances. All the evidence suggests that this is not the case. What value can there be to a measure which would undoubtedly discomfort immigrants already here by stigmatizing them and giving the appearance of justification to the riotous white elements; which would make excellent propaganda material for those who would choose to see such a measure as essentially Fascist, and which would provide retrospective vindication for the racial politicians of South Africa, Southern Rhodesia, and the southern states of the United States for their own more pernicious legislation?

The real factors demanding attention in these disturbances (and in some of them coloured people have been involved, if at all, only as defenceless victims of aggression) are the social causes of the mob behaviour of the white population. The usual explanations of racial tensions – employment anxiety or sexual jealousy – are surely appropriate to only a limited extent in these sudden outbursts. The real causes appear to be principally in the boredom and frustrations experienced by our own Teddy boys, who are, today, a very sizable proportion of British youth. Coloured people are simply a convenient, and often defenceless, target for the aggression arising from mass-frustration of this kind.

Clearly the causes of frustration cannot be stated *a priori*, and sound sociological research should be directed to this problem. One might, however, suggest that the following factors play a part:

(a) The development of a high wage economy for unskilled, untrained, socially illiterate youths, too young to have acquired social responsibilities to absorb the money they earn, and whose 'big money' cannot effectively buy the social importance which is craved. An alternative is to gain self-importance and prestige within the peer-group by acts of bravado.

(b) The development of an American-type 'youth culture' in which parental discipline has grown lax, and in any case is undermined by social and economic changes which have steadily destroyed the traditional basis of social respect by giving young people too much independence before they are properly equipped for it.

(c) The glorification of high-powered violence and alien acts of daring by the Press and the mass-entertainment industry, whose products are increasingly available to the new moneyed adolescent class; and which provide the basis of their standards of behaviour.

(d) The absence of creative purpose, and of the need for real effort in the lives of young people to whom society has promised full economic security, and for whom it has, perhaps, succeeded in producing ennui. (This is not necessarily to condemn the welfare state, but rather to suggest that our educational system has not yet effectively come to grips with the release of energy, once used in the struggle for existence, and with the mass-culture which has replaced our traditional way of life.)

What needs to be clearly set on record, for the benefit of the citizens of Bulawayo, Pretoria, and Little Rock – whose comment has already been forthcoming – is that there is no widespread hostility towards coloured people in Britain: that they are not our basic problem, but rather an ill-disciplined, overpaid, frustrated youth, whose life chances have been vastly improved moneywise without commensurate social adjustment either to preserve our traditional values, or to effectively forge for them a new way of life.

Yours, &c.,
B. R. WILSON

Television Breaks

From Mr E. H. Dare   *11 March 1959*

Sir,
When consideration is being given to a third television channel could not a way be found out of the 'advertising break' problem by devoting the new channel entirely to advertising? In that way the present commercial channel could be left free from programme breaks (natural or otherwise), thus satisfying those of us who object to these interruptions while those millions who are alleged to prefer 'the adverts' will also be made more happy in their viewing.

Yours faithfully,
E. H. DARE

Converted Cuckoo

From Dr H. Motz   *29 May 1959*

[Professor of Engineering in the University of Oxford, 1972–7]

Sir,

I know that it is rather late in the season to report on cuckoos; nor is it the usual story we have to tell. We have a cuckoo in the Oxford University Engineering Laboratory, too young to issue its familiar call. It fell out of its nest – we can only think that the other young birds ganged up and threw out the false brother this time. The foster mother, a blackbird, comes dutifully down to feed him. Indeed, who could resist its desperate cries, not yet cuckoo-like but unmistakable in their purpose?

It fell into a basement in front of our high energy accelerator, out in the open, where we usually direct the X-ray beam. We dare not run the machine for fear of hurting the bird. Latinists or not, we are not inhuman, we scientists. But, who knows, maybe the X-rays would induce mutations which might make the wretched bird build its own nest in future?

Yours, &c.,

H. Motz

Definition of Pakistan

[The *Concise Oxford Dictionary* had been banned in Pakistan on account of its definition of that country's name]

From Mr J. M. Wyllie   *15 September 1959*

Sir,

The definition of Pakistan in the *Concise Oxford Dictionary* should read, 'Until 1947, a proposed separate Moslem State in India, Moslem autonomy; after 1947, the independent Moslem Dominion in the Indian sub-continent.' The mistakes in the fourth edition of *COD* are due to the fact that for this edition the definition in the 1944 Addenda to the third edition was touched up instead of being entirely rewritten.

I say 'mistakes' because the etymology is also faulty, and was given more correctly by *The Times* Own Correspondent in Pakistan in a special article in *The Times* of 26 February 1948, on 'The Rise of Pakistan,' in these words: 'Pakistan means "Land of the Pure." It was often incorrectly said that its first three letters were chosen from the initials of Punjab, Assam and Kashmir . . .' I reported this to the Clarendon Press on 21 April 1951, concluding my letter with these words:

'*The Times* Correspondent in Pakistan should have been in a position to ascertain the truth – which as you know is what etymology means.'

A fuller investigation which I made into this interesting word, with the help of my friend Dr C. C. Davies, Lecturer in Indian History in the University of Oxford, showed that it had been coined in 1933 by the late Sir C. Rhamat Ali, and a further letter to the Clarendon Press is relevant not only to this question of etymology, but also to the problem of dealing with the action which the Pakistan Government has now seen fit to take. I give this letter in full. The quotation is from the third edition of *Pakistan* (1947).

'4895/Corm/D.M.D., New Bodleian, Oxford, 27 April, 1951.
'Dear Davin. – Here is the extract from Sir C. Rhamat Ali's book *Pakistan*.

" 'Pakistan' is both a Persian and an Urdu word. It is composed of letters taken from the names of all our homelands – 'Indian' and 'Asian.' That is, *P*anjab, *A*fghania (North-West Frontier Province), *K*ashmir, *I*ran, *S*indh (including Kachch and Kathiawar), *T*ukharistan, *A*fghanistan and Balochista*n*. It means the land of the Paks – the spiritually pure and clean. It symbolizes the religious beliefs and the ethnical stocks of our people; and it stands for all the territorial constituents of our original Fatherland. It has no other origin and no other meaning; and it does not admit of any other interpretation. Those writers who have tried to interpret it in more than one way have done so either through love of casuistry, or through ignorance of its inspiration, origin and composition."

'As Sir Rhamat Ali was responsible both for the idea of Pakistan and the word itself, this statement of his should be regarded not only as the last word on the question but (literally) as the last letter. All subsequent disclaimers emanating from official circles in the Pakistan Government ought to be discounted. Even the gods cannot change the past.

Yours sincerely,
(signed) J. M. WYLLIE
(Editor of the *Oxford Latin Dictionary*.)'

It must be a rare occurrence for a professional lexicographer to be able to say that the etymology of a word given by the coiner of it is erroneous; and it would be more accurate to call this confusion than error in the case of Sir C. Rhamat Ali. But what can definitely be said is that the *Concise Oxford Diction-ary* is wrong and *The Times* Own Correspondent right.

Yours faithfully,
J. M. WYLLIE

Education for Girls

From Mr J. Grimond, MP   *21 January 1960*

[Liberal Member for Orkney and Shetland since 1950; former Scholar of Balliol College, Oxford]

Sir,

No doubt my views on the education of girls are exaggerated – probably also unfair and inaccurate. From such experience as I have had, however, the fault lies not in the girls nor in what they are taught but in how they are taught.

They are stuffed with the belief that academic failure is immoral. They are then subjected to a course of examinations in which the competition is far fiercer than that to which any male has to submit. Girls, if they are not utterly frivolous, are alarmingly conscientious. They are still brought up to believe that their education is a special benefit which it would be un-grateful to waste by one moment's relaxation. As a result they are often reduced to a nervous and unnatural state by the time they take their finals.

To accentuate this torture, in the older universities at least, women are still treated as an adjunct to a man's world, they are relegated to suburban mausoleums which have none of the graces of men's colleges, and they are seldom taught by men. No doubt in time women tutors will be as good as men. At present many of them are not. Too often they lack a sense of proportion. They are seldom gay. Their attempts to help girls driven almost insane by ploughing acres of text-books are often disastrous.

We shall be able to judge better of women's education when there are three or four times the number of places available to them, when women's colleges cease to be so gloomily monastic, and when there is mixed teaching as well as mixed learning.

Yours faithfully,
J. GRIMOND

From Dr Glyn Daniel   *26 January 1960*

[Fellow of St John's College, later Disney Professor of Archaeology in the University of Cambridge]

239

Sir,

Mr Grimond's letter on the education of girls is, as he feared himself, 'exaggerated . . . unfair and inaccurate.' It is nonsense, and rather irresponsible nonsense in a person of Mr Grimond's political stature, to say that 'in the older universities . . . women are still treated as an adjunct to a man's world.' This is certainly not true in Cambridge, where women tutors are quite as good as tutors in men's Colleges – taking infinite care of those to whom they are *in loco parentis*, and where supervision by women is of a very high standard.

Women are frequently taught by men, and in the 15 years since the war when I have been back in Cambridge teaching, no year has passed in which I have not taught, with pleasure and profit, girls from Newnham and Girton. I agree that there should be more places for women in Oxford and Cambridge, that there should be more women's colleges – but I have never seen any reason why admission to the existing Cambridge colleges traditionally called 'men's colleges' should not be opened to women. In most colleges it would involve only a minor change in Statute which would have to be approved by the Queen in Council. It might however involve a major out-break of apoplexy among old male Fellows of Colleges.

But I cannot agree that female students in this or any other University known to me 'lack a sense of proportion' and 'are seldom gay' – or any more so than a comparable sample of male university students. Is Mr Grimond's view of education as out of date as are, perhaps, his politics – and I write as a former Welsh Liberal who knows that Lloyd George is dead, like Queen Anne and Queen Boudicca. Ah, there's a woman for you. What a good head of a House Boudicca would have made, and what a liberal education she would have encouraged in her College and University.

But, seriously, one of the ways forward in Oxford and Cambridge is to open places in all Colleges to men and women. What was wrong with Fontevrault?

Yours faithfully,
GLYN DANIEL

[Although the mixed community of Fontevrault was founded with an abbess at its head, Dr Daniel's college has yet to elect a Mistress]

Let the Eagle Soar

From Mrs James P. Sharrock   6 *April 1960*

[writing from Florida]

Sir,

All of the furor over the golden eagle which is to perch atop the United States Embaassy in London is very amusing. I haven't heard such a to-do over a foreign symbol since Russia's hammer and sickle towered over everything else at the New York World's Fair. Such a tempest in a teapot.

England's attitude towards the States reminds me of an aristocratic family whose son has run away from home. He is referred to in hushed tones as the 'black sheep' or 'that ungrateful whelp' and dire things are predicted for him. Instead, the wayward son strikes it rich and as much as it galls the family, they call on him to pay off the mortgage on the old homestead. Of course, he is not really accepted back into the family. Heavens no – not with the boisterous ways and vulgar accent he has picked up while absent from the parental roof! He doesn't even wear the right school tie and he indulges in trade! For shame! ... The poor boob pays and pays trying to buy his way back into the good graces of the family. He is tolerated at best, laughed at behind his back, criticized to his face. But he takes it – blood is thicker than water – all of that rot!

Can't you accept us for what we are? We're young; we're brash. We run instead of walk and we love our flashy toys. We have all the vigor and all the imperfections of youth but we're growing. We may mellow with age – though I hope not too much.

Won't you please let us have our oversized eagle? Youth must have its toys and that will be a lollapalooza!

Yours, with tongue in cheek,

CORINNE SHARROCK

From Mrs Helen Reid   13 *April 1960*

Sir,

Is it not likely that the London pigeon will dominate the American eagle?

I have the honour to be, Sir, your obedient servant,

HELEN REID

A Lesson for Pavlov

From Dr William Sargant   *18 May 1960*

[honorary consulting psychiatrist to St Thomas's Hospital, London]

Sir,

With the Summit Conference now upon us, and because of the state of disturbed judgment to which Mr Khrushchev's propaganda exploitation of the recent air spy incident reduced at least some sections of both the public and the press in Britain and America alike, it is becoming more and more important that we should all start to get a better understanding of Russian methods of psychological warfare, otherwise the battle for men's minds being waged so intensively at the present time will result in a resounding defeat for the western nations, and this could be far more devastating in its subsequent effects than the outcome of the present race for rocket supremacy.

Obviously, Russian propaganda methods, like others, are based to a large extent on past experience of what works, but, if any expert advice is taken on methods of psychological warfare, it has to come in Russia from scientists versed in Pavlovian theory and practice. This is because in general medicine, and especially in psychological medicine, no other scientific approach is generally considered valid, apart from a Pavlovian one. And it has also, after all, paid some very valuable dividends in recent years in the political field.

Now, Pavlov showed long ago – and this work has been confirmed time and again since – that one of the surest ways of breaking down the nervous stability of the dog and of other animals, and producing in them states of uncontrolled neurotic excitement, which may later lead on to hysterical and submissive behaviour, and finally even to depressive apathy, is to give a trained, cooperative but anxious animal a random series of positive and negative conditioned stimuli or signals. A hungry, tense animal, for instance, who has been used to an orderly laboratory existence, in which certain given signals are followed by food, and others by no food, can quickly become neurotic and confused when he tries to sort out a sequence of positive and negative food signals, followed indiscriminately by food or no food, which do not, and were never intended to, make sense to him from the beginning.

This quite simple physiological technique, taken from Pavlov's laboratory, has been found just as applicable to man and has been repeatedly used on British and American politicians, press, and public alike in recent years. For instance, when the original sputnik was launched amidst world excitement, we were first of all told that it had no military significance and was merely an interesting scientific experiment. Then, soon afterwards, we were reminded that it meant that any part of the United States could be wiped off the face of the earth at will. Again we were quickly reassured of its purely pacific intent, and yet later again of the devastating effects of this development on any future war.

Then a dog was dramatically sent up in another sputnik to keep tension at a high level. We were told that it would live, then that it would die, then it was going to live again, and so on alternately for days on end until its death was finally announced. These positive and negative signals were applied with such precision and skill that some of the British and American press and public alike became, temporarily, just as bewildered, confused and suggestible as did Pavlov's dogs in the presence of a similar barrage of their own special conditioning signals. Numerous other examples could be given of the same technique being used in recent years, and it is unlikely that these have all been just accidental happenings.

Again, before the Summit Conference, we saw the same sort of method being put into action and we have fallen for it yet again. We know perfectly well that every country uses spies of all sorts, and that there is nothing very abnormal about this. Sensibly, Mr Khrushchev again chose a particularly violent and dramatic form of positive rocket signal to fire off his present psychological cannonade, and we were afterwards also quickly informed of the dire consequences to future cooperation between East and West of this particular air spy happening.

Soon, however, we were told that it need not affect in any way the approaching Summit Conference. The following day we were again being warned that nations who harbour such American spy bases would be violently attacked. Then again we were told not to worry, but almost immediately afterwards warned about atom bombs which could rain on America. And we can quite confidently expect, right through the Summit Conference and afterwards, a series of such positive and negative conditioning signals to be put out quite indiscriminately, which are simply not meant to make any sense at all to those who will vainly try to understand them.

There is one way to avoid neurotic breakdown, the inevitable disturbances of judgment, the increase in hysterical suggestibility which can result from the skilled use of these powerful physiological processes on the nervous systems of either man or animals. This is to deliberately *ignore* the signals and stop trying to make any sense of them. Pavlov could not break down dogs who took no notice at all of all the experimental flashing lights specially provided for their undoing; it was only the dog who did his best to cooperate with the experimenter and tried to sort out the signals who was so easily broken down. Unfortunately, the press of both our countries has to relay all these confusing and alternating signals, without also explaining what may really be happening, thus tending unwittingly to play the Russian propaganda game for them.

It is probable that Mr Macmillan was warned about these techniques before he last visited Russia, for he wisely ignored all the deliberately alternating attitudes adopted by Mr Khrushchev, who, during the whole of this visit, was blowing so violently hot and cold in a way that must have seemed absolutely bewildering to the Pavlovian uninitiated. But by just ignoring the whole thing, Mr Macmillan won the day. Let us hope that, with a greater understanding of what is happening, the public, the press and politicians alike will also now try to follow his example.

Yours faithfully,
WILLIAM SARGANT

Cocking a Snook

From Sir Carleton Allen, QC   *5 December 1961*

[Warden of Rhodes House, Oxford, 1931–52]

Sir,

The Lord Chief Justice is shocked, not surprisingly, because a boy who had just been fined five shillings for his third offence submitted to the majesty of the law by cocking a snook at the court. Very rude, very 'deviant', very 'anti-social'; but what, my lord, was the court to do? Give him 'a good dressing-down'? He would have cocked another snook, probably a double one this time.

Contempt? Juvenile Courts, and indeed all courts of summary jurisdiction, have no powers in contempt. Insulting behaviour? That would mean issuing a fresh summons and taking a steam-hammer to crack the nut of going through the whole business again and perhaps fining him as much as *ten* shillings.

Order him a dozen of the best? Illegal! Barbarous! What would Mr Butler's Advisory Committee and the Howard League say? A well-directed cuff by a policeman? An assault, which would probably cause some champion of liberty to press for a Tribunal of Inquiry, costing some thousands of pounds.

No, this poor boy is a subject of pity rather than of indignation. He is obviously 'maladjusted'. Some secret sorrow is gnawing at him, and cocking snooks is his only way of expressing his personality. And if the Ingleby Report becomes law, and if he is under 12, he will not be a *bad* boy at all, but simply in need of 'discipline' or of 'care and protection'. A little care and protection for the public and for courts of justice would not come amiss.

Yours faithfully,
C. K. ALLEN

Thinking in Octals

[The United Kingdom was the last major country in the world to adopt a decimal currency – on 15 February 1971]

From Professor Fred Hoyle, FRS   *28 December 1961*

[Plumian Professor of Astronomy and Experimental Philosophy at Cambridge 1958–73, Sir Fred Hoyle is now Research Professor, Manchester University]

Sir,
If we are being forced by economic reasons into a decimalization of our coinage, and of other units, then plainly we must go ahead. But if, as one suspects, much of the impulse towards decimalization comes from the wish not to appear impossibly archaic in the eyes of the world, then this is the moment to reflect on whether the decimal system is likely to survive into the future as the operative form of practical arithmetic.

It appears safe to say that the electronic digital computer, using binary arithmetic, will become steadily more important to technology. It is likely that 50 years hence the computer will play an indispensable part in human society, much as electricity itself does today. And just as the increasing importance of electricity has modified our educational curricula – nowadays schoolchildren are introduced to ideas that were considered esoteric 50 years ago – so we can expect a modification to meet the needs of a population employing computers as normal

245

articles of everyday life. One emphatic need will be an easy interchange between ordinary numbers and binary numbers.

Conversion from decimal to binary is at best an awkward process, even to most professional mathematicians. Conversion from octal to binary, on the other hand, is simple and quick – for example, an hour's practice is sufficient to enable most non-mathematicians to convert a six digit octal number to binary in a matter of seconds. During the next few decades the octal system is certain, for this reason, to come into widespread use. (Octal is based on eight, so that 100 in octal is 64 in decimal.)

It is often said that scientists are ardent decimalizers. While this may have been the case 20 years ago, it has no force as an argument today. Today, the calculations of greatest scientific complexity are made in binary – with its close relation to octal. It is true that, having carried through our calculations, we still prefer to convert our answers to decimal, but the fault lies in us not in the octal system. We have not yet learnt to think naturally in octal.

Although adults reared on decimal find octal thinking strange, this would not be so for children. A new generation could learn to think naturally in octal. Indeed, octal could be learned more easily since multiplication tables would only be about half the burden they are in decimal. Perhaps as much as a year's mathematical education could be gained by the average pupil, a 10-year-old being the equal in octal of an 11-year-old in decimal.

One notices, with a sense of irony, that our present monetary reckoning from an octal point of view is superior to decimal coinage, since eight half-crowns make up the pound. Sir, there is the very real danger that in attempting to get ourselves up to date we may find ourselves falling behind the times.

F. HOYLE

Surtax in Numbers

From Sir Alan Herbert   *21 March 1961*

Sir,

Some years ago one of your leader-writers regretted that verse was so little used in ordinary life. I hope that the following true tale will please him.

(1) Two years ago I earned enough money to qualify for

surtax in the sum of £84 17s. 6d. A correspondence with the Special Commissioners of Income Tax concerning the nature of surtax, my financial position, and an appropriate date for settlement ended thus:

> but I am to add that if it is not received within that period the papers will be referred to the Solicitors, Inland Revenue, without further warning.

(2) I sent them a cheque, duly stamped and crossed 'Inland Revenue A/c'. The words in capitals were prettily typed in red.

To NATIONAL AND GRINDLAY'S BANK LIMITED
54, Parliament Street, S.W.1.
Dear Bankers, PAY the undermentioned hounds
The shameful sum of FIVE-AND-EIGHTY POUNDS.
£85. 0. 0.
By 'hound', of course, by custom, one refers
To SPECIAL (INCOME TAX) COMMISSIONERS:
And these progenitors of woe and worry
You'll find at LYNWOOD ROAD, THAMES DITTON, SURREY.
This is the *second* lot of tax, you know,
On money that I earned two years ago
(The shark, they say, by no means Nature's knight,
Will rest contented with a single bite;
The barracuda, who's a fish more fell,
Comes back and takes the other leg as well).
Two years ago. But things have changed since then.
I've reached the age of three-score years and ten.
My earnings dwindle; and the kindly State
Gives me a tiny pension – with my mate
You'd think the State would generously roar
'At least he shan't pay SURTAX any more'.
Instead by this unChristian attack
They get two-thirds of my poor pension back.
Oh, very well. No doubt it's for the best;
At all events, pray do as I request:
And let the good old customs be enforced –
Don't cash this cheque, unless it is endorsed.

Alan P. Herbert

(3) The cheque was cashed; and I received not one but two replies in verse from the Office of the Special Commissioners of Income Tax. The official reply was as follows:

S.T.H.31097/40

Dear Sir,
It is with pleasure that I thank

You for your letter, and the order to your bank
To pay the sum of five and eighty pounds
To those here whom you designate as hounds.
Their appetite is satisfied. In fact,
You paid too much and I am forced to act,
Not to repay you, as perchance you dream,
Though such a course is easy, it would seem.
Your liability for later years
Is giving your accountants many tears:
And till such time as they and we can come
To amicable settlement on the sum
That represents your tax bill to the State
I'll leave the overpayment to its fate.
I do not think this step will make you frown;
The sum involved is only half-a-crown.

Yours faithfully,
A. L. Grove

(4) I replied:

Your Ref. S.T.H.31097/40

I thank you, Sir, but am afraid
Of such a rival in my trade:
One never should encourage those –
In future I shall pay in prose.

We must all be delighted by this evidence of humour and humanity in that quarter: but the arguments set out in my cheque, I submit, are sound.

I am, Sir, yours respectfully,
A. P. HERBERT

Sweet Harmony

From Mr Ernest Bradbury   *19 June 1962*

[music critic, *The Yorkshire Post*]

Sir,

I write to you at 3 am, my sleep having been broken beyond the possibility of recovery by a group of what you aptly call transistor louts (actually, in this instance, university students) doing the twist outside my front gate, which is on a main road. An appeal to them to take their music elsewhere met with the response that this is a free country. Your timely leader on 12 June will also be supported, I am sure, by many fellow-musicians who, by instinct as well as training, are unhappily compelled to attend to sounds that are impinged on their hearing, from whatever source.

On three successive Saturday journeys to London transistor louts caused annoyance and unhappiness to railway passengers. On the first occasion an elderly traveller called in the inspector at Wakefield. A brusque 'Turn that thing off: it's illegal on here' surprisingly met with obedience – mutinous, but obedience none the less. On the two later occasions, there being no official at all in attendance, passengers' requests for a similar peace met only with hostility, ridicule and abuse.

The remedy on railway trains and other public vehicles seems simple: warning notices should be carried drawing attention to the by-law and the penalties for infringement, and these should be rigidly enforced. One feels that if, long ago, similar stringent methods had been employed, there would be no need, in 1962, for anti-litter campaigns.

Yoours sincerely,
ERNEST BRADBURY

From Mr Spike Hughes   *15 June 1962*

Sir,

All thrushes (not only those in this neck of the Glyndebourne woods) sooner or later sing the tune of the first subject of Mozart's G minor Symphony (K.550) – and, what's more, phrase it a sight better than most conductors. The tempo is always dead right and there is no suggestion of an unauthorized accent on the ninth note of the phrase.

Yours &c.,
SPIKE HUGHES

From the Warden of New College, Oxford   *7 March 1963*

Sir,

Now that the Admiralty is to disappear, may we also hope for the early physical disappearance of its hideous extension, in mud-coloured concrete, which so disfigures Horse Guards Parade? In no other capital that I know does so ferociously ugly a relic of the war continue to disgrace an important public space.

I am, Sir, your obedient servant,
W. G. HAYTER

Reading in Bed

From Mr H. Malcolm Carter   *10 January 1962*

Sir,

I am surprised that none of your correspondents has proposed the obvious solution – the provision of a series of slits in the bedclothes through which the hands may be projected in the manner of the old-fashioned Turkish bath box. When not in use the slits may be closed by zips or buttons, or even by a handful of straw, barley for preference, as being softer than wheat or oats. It should, however, come from the binder, as the combine generally breaks it up and makes it rather untidy for indoor use.

I am, Sir, faithfully yours,

H. MALCOLM CARTER

The Maturing of Children

From Dr G. A. Wray   *3 October 1963*

Sir,

It is said to be a fact that children nowadays mature physically if not psychologically at a much earlier age.

I wonder what is the evidence for this assertion which is now so freely accepted? Who, in 1863 or subsequently, was making careful statistical studies of the age of onset of puberty in boys and girls in different social groups, because without some basis of comparison there is no foundation for the theory? There may be some way of estimating the development of puberty in girls, there is none in the case of boys. As to psychological maturity there is no method of assessment in either sex.

Stranger still is the explanation, and one apparently accepted without question, revealed in a recent television discussion. It is said to be due to increased standards of nutrition. By this strange token the children of classes formerly underprivileged and under-nourished are now catching up sexually with the boys at Eton and the girls at Roedean. The truth is that there can be no real evidence for this theory and it may well be completely false. Nevertheless, it is of great importance because it underlies the discussions of the learned men at Harrogate and elsewhere who are avowedly setting out to decide on a sensible attitude to sex on the part of the young. There may be, of course, other reasons, such as the rise in the rates of illegitimacy and venereal disease, but I am told that these figures still need much careful study and for a longer period before any valid conclusions can be drawn from them.

I work extensively with delinquent youth and know something of the problems of conformity. I wonder how it is proposed to get the standard accepted when the experts have decided upon it. I mention this because it is sad to see a young psychiatrist making fun of the efforts of Church leaders and others who are trying to do this very thing. Sadder still is it to think that the publicity given to his efforts can only make matters worse.

When you and I were young there were no committees seeking to decide about sexual attitudes and outlets. No doubt there are reasons why they are necessary now but you would be doing a very great service if you brought the investigators back to a careful scrutiny of the factual basis for their discussions.

Yours faithfully,
G. A. WRAY

Googly

[An off-break bowled with a leg-break action, the googly is still known to Australians as the 'bosie', a tribute to its inventor]

From Mr Nigel Dennis   *13 May 1963*

Sir,
Do you want to be torn to pieces by nettled Bosanquets? That family claims two major innovations; (1) the introduction into Oxford of Hegel and 'German idealism', (2) the introduction into cricket of the googly. It is obvious that (2) was merely the sporting consequence of (1): but just as Bradley must be granted to have helped with the philosophical juggle, so must my dear mother (née Louise Bosanquet) be allowed her share in the bowling one.

As a little girl she hero-worshipped her cousin, 'BJT', and paid for it in the 1890s by being made to stand at one end of a lawn for hours, retrieving his experimental googlies. A tennis ball was always used – 'Not a *billiard* ball, a *tennis* ball' were among my mother's last words to me. As she knew nothing about German idealism, I must append the following highly significant dates off my own bat:

1886. Publication of B. Bosanquet's *The Introduction to Hegel's Philosophy of Fine Art*.

1890. The googly ideal conceived by B. J. T. Bosanquet.

1893. Publication of Bradley's *Appearance & Reality*.

1893–1900. Intensive work, helped by my mother, to hide the reality behind the googly's appearance.

1903. The Ashes regained by the googly – German idealism's first and last sporting victory.

Yours faithfully,
NIGEL DENNIS

[Reality insists the Ashes were regained on 3 March 1904]

From Canon Alan Richardson   *18 May 1963*

[Professor of Christian Theology in the University of Nottingham, later Dean of York]

Sir,

Mr Nigel Dennis rightly points out the connexion between Hegelian Idealism and the philosophy of cricket at the turn of the century. It was well understood that the game was a necessary incident in the evolution of the Absolute Idea, in which all differences are reconciled, and that in every cricket match the Absolute was achieving self-realization. You will recall the lines of Andrew Lang, which indicate the ultimate reality behind the invention of the googly:

> 'If the wild bowler thinks he bowls,
>   Or if the batsman think he's bowled,
> They know not, poor misguided souls,
>   They too shall perish unconsoled.
> *I* am the batsman and the bat,
>   *I* am the bowler and the ball,
> The umpire, the pavilion cat,
>   The roller, pitch, and stumps and all.'

Yours faithfully,
ALAN RICHARDSON

From Dr R. W. Cockshut   *10 May 1963*
[chairman, The Cricket Society]

Sir,

The word 'googly' was first used in a newspaper article in New Zealand in 1903 to describe Bosanquet's new ball. The word means uncanny, weird, ghostly, and is supposed to be of Maori origin. There are many words with the ō or oo vowel sound associated especially with k, j or g, which express the same quality of fear and wonder. Bogey, boogey-woogey, spook, etc., and Lewis Carroll must have been aware of this when he coined the word Boojum.

A more apt word to describe a leg break from the off could not be imagined, and we remain indebted to an unknown New Zealand journalist.

Yours faithfully,
R. W. COCKSHUT

'Temporary' Civil Servants

From Mr W. H. T. Porter   *1 May 1964*

Sir,

I am reminded of the temporary Civil Servant who was put on the established staff. Overjoyed, he broke the glad news to his wife, who, womanlike, asked what pay increase was involved. When told that the pay was precisely the same she exclaimed: 'Oh! that is ridiculous. Why, we are living in poverty now.' 'I know,' replied the lucky fellow, 'but thank God, it's permanent!'

Yours faithfully,
W. H. T. PORTER

Called to Mind

From the President of Trinity College, Oxford   *1 October 1964*
[now Sir Arthur Norrington]

Sir,

Mr Sylvester, in his article on Joan Miró on 22 September, suggests that the theme of 'Blue II' is interval and proportion.

'The series of blobs . . . call to mind a medieval musical score . . . painting is *seen* to aspire towards the condition of music.' They also call to mind, in fact they are almost indistinguishable from, the break-up of a thread of liquid issuing

from the tip of a vibrating hypodermic needle, a phenomenon illustrated in an article by Professor B. J. Mason in the September number of *Endeavour* on 'The collision, coalescence and disruption of drops'. I enclose the two illustrations for comparison.

Could anything be more encouraging than this collision and coalescence of two cultures? 'Painting *is seen* to aspire to the condition of physics.'

Yours faithfully,
A. L. P. NORRINGTON

Olivier's Othello

From Professor J. Dover Wilson, CH   *17 October 1964*

Sir,
All the world is flocking in relays to the National Theatre to see our greatest actor performing a part which he had hitherto not attempted, the title role of Shakespeare's greatest tragedy; and having just returned from this exciting spectacle I think that perhaps some of your readers may care for a word from one who has been editing Shakespeare's plays for over 40 years, especially if you number one or two of my contemporaries still alive among them.
Ay there's the rub! For in 1964 I am 50 years out of date;

I am still a believer in the essential dignity of man which is the basic assumption of dramatic tragedy as Bradley taught us, and for him Othello was the greatest of tragic heroes. Such was the reading of his character in all performances of the play that I had yet seen, including that of the noble African Paul Robeson with Peggy Ashcroft as Desdemona.

How proud then must be Dr Lewis when he finds himself the inspirer of this Othello quite new to the theatre! That it was a Leavis Othello was made clear to all spectators when they bought the Book of the Play with the programme as they entered, for there was the quotation from his famous essay in *Scrutiny* as they opened it; and as they watched Sir Laurence's performance it became clearer still.

Unhappily I could not follow the expressions on his face with my imperfect sight except every now and then, but I saw enough to glean a strong impression that the whole conception of the character he was attempting to give us was a Leavis one, which incidentally had also been made in an essay by T. S. Eliot, first published in 1919. Its upshot is that the 'nobility' upon which Bradley insisted (as did Shakespeare) gives place to a 'habit of approving self-dramatization' which is often a 'disguise for the man's obtuse and brutal egotism'; and at the theatre this became especially evident in the second half of the play in which I could discover no dignity in the character at all while the end was to me, not terrible, but horrible beyond words.

Every age rediscovers its own Shakespeare and I suppose that after two great wars and the Nazi eruption from the nether region which seemed to drag our poor human nature through the loathsome filth of the cencentration camps, to say nothing of the disintegrating influence of Freud, it is difficult to think nobly of Man. Yet it was surely not necessary for a Bradley to teach us, what Aristotle had long since taught us, that the essence of Greek tragedy, as of all great tragedy, is to think of the hero as *heroic*, through scene after scene that harrows us with terror and pity until in the end we are purged by the catastrophe which leaves us reconciled, even exalted.

Must be give up Shakespeare's heroes? Must we refuse to admit that the basis of his tragedy was his belief in the integrity of Man? If so, *nunc dimittis* – or I might say so if I were not certain that the whirligig of time would bring in his revenges, that Shakespearian criticism would presently emerge from its 'dark house' and learn again to 'think nobly of the soul'.

Yours, &c.,

J. DOVER WILSON

[*Othello*, 'Shakespeare's greatest tragedy': in *The Essential Shakespeare*, 1932, Dover Wilson awarded the palm to *King Lear*. Had thirty years changed the critic's mind, or was it an unconscious tribute to the power of Olivier's performance?]

For Service, the Beatles

From Mr K. S. Nash   *16 June 1965*

Sir,

What *is* the point of serving a country that awards the MBE to a group of young pop singers?

Yours faithfully,

K. S. NASH

†*The Times* has received a number of other letters to the same effect.

[The average age of Messrs George Harrison, John Lennon, Paul McCartney and Richard Starkey was 23 years and 8 months]

The Duke's Medals

From Mr Michael Levey   *3 June 1965*

[Director of the National Gallery since 1973; knighted 1981]

Sir,

Mr George Savage and Mr Colin Simpson have raised the question of the medals worn by the Duke of Wellington in the portrait by Goya in the National Gallery.

The main facts about these were established some years ago, thanks to the research of staff at the National Portrait Gallery, and I am grateful to Mr David Piper, the present Director, for aiding me in this statement concerning them.

The Duke wears uppermost the Golden Fleece (awarded to him in August 1812). The sashes he wears are those of the Order of the Bath (red) and, underneath, of the Tower and Sword (blue), a Portuguese order which he received in 1811.

He had received the Bath in 1804; the upper star on his coat is of this order. The left hand of the two lower stars is that of the Tower and Sword. That at the right, partly obscured, corresponds well enough with the Duke's regalia to be identifiable with the star of the Order of St Ferdinand of Spain (awarded on 29 April 1812).

The Cross with three bars hanging from a ribbon is the Peninsula Gold Cross. Radiographs confirm that the bars cover a *pentimento* – apparent to the naked eye – of a circular medal. It seems likely that Goya first showed, or planned to show, the Duke wearing the medal and not the Cross; that is how he appears in a drawing at Hamburg and also in the British Museum drawing. This medal is the Peninsula Medal (instituted on 9 September 1810); the Duke's own medal, inscribed *Salamanca*, is at Apsley House.

It had been customary to gain an additional medal for each battle, but in October 1811 Wellington proposed, and it was agreed, that only one medal should be awarded, additional battles to be engraved on it. By a General Order of 7 October 1813, it was further specified that 'upon a claim being admitted to a fourth mark of distinction, a Cross shall be borne by each Officer, with the names of the four battles or sieges respectively inscribed thereon' (see J. Horsley Mayo, *Medals and Decorations of the British Army and Navy*, 1897, page 192). This cross was to be supplemented with clasps where necessary. It is known that a good many questions arose about granting both crosses and medals. That the Cross was under discussion as a decoration by 24 February 1813 is shown by letters exchanged between Wellington and Lord Bathurst (partial text in N. H. Nicolas, *History of the Orders of Knighthood*, 1842, Vol. IV, p. 52). On 16 April that year Bathurst dispatched the actual Crosses for Wellington and his senior commanders.

That Wellington wears three clasps in the Goya portrait indicates that he had received the clasp for Salamanca (battle of 22 July 1812) but not yet that for Vittoria (battle of 21 June 1813). He wears four clasps in the portrait, dated 1814, by Thomas Phillips (reproduced in Lord Gerald Wellesley and John Steegmann, *Iconography of the First Duke of Wellington*, 1935, plate 15).

Thus the National Gallery portrait, though showing the alteration from medal to Cross, records no more than the honours the Duke was already entitled to in August 1812. It seems not possible to say when the alteration was made: whether the Duke returned the picture to Goya for it to be done, or whether the painter had retained the picture and executed what was basically a minor change before handing it over. The above facts reveal that the questions raised regarding the Duke's medals have no relevance to the picture's authorship. Its authenticity has, of course, never been doubted by leading Goya scholars.

Yours faithfully,
MICHAEL LEVEY

What Ought We To Do?

From Baroness Wootton of Abinger　　　　*23 August 1965*

Sir,

How on earth can any ordinary rational layman be expected to make head or tail of what he is currently being told about the economic situation?

First Mr George Brown is reported to have said that bad timekeeping and excessive holidays are damaging to the economy; and *The Times* discusses the degree of gloom that will be induced by a fall in the index of productivity.

Then on the very same day a survey by the National Institute of Economic and Social Research apparently concludes that the most promising cure for our economic troubles is one which will prevent anything up to half a million people from working at all.

What ought we to do? Should we all try to work harder? Or would it be better if half a million of us gave up work straight away? Or should we perhaps organize large-scale strikes so as to save our employers the embarrassment of putting us on short-time?

If contemporary economics makes any sense at all, somebody somewhere ought to be doing a very big job of interpretation.

Yours, &c.,
WOOTTON OF ABINGER

What Ought We To Do?
1965-1975

THE question was asked frequently throughout the period. After juvenile delinquency, Rhodesia, drug addiction, and the incompetence of shop assistants had bothered 1965, correspondents argued reform of the abortion laws. (By the late summer of 1974 they were considering discipline in universities, and the dissolution of the United Kingdom.) The 1967 New Year Honours, which bestowed the CBE on a famous woman novelist, drew a snort from Dame Rebecca West. There were objections to a proposed gasometer in the centre of Abingdon, and explanations of de Gaulle's decision to exclude Britain from Europe. The psychology of the hooligan who wrecked railway carriages was examined, the idea of Stansted as an airport frowned upon. The most profound question concerned dress: if a page could wear military uniform at a fashionable wedding, why was it improper when the same uniform (presumably with some lengthening of the trouser legs) was worn by a pop singer? In 1968 the Government urged the nation to 'Back Britain', the section which wrote to *The Times* reacting cynically. The paper's cookery editor was sternly rebuked for giving advice: 'to make asparagus soup, first open a tin . . .' Small wonder the French President did not trust the British. Meanwhile commuters objected to the over-crowding of trains, a motorist complained of a two-and-a-half-hour journey from Fulham to London airport. Student protests produced counter-protests, pop concerts in St Paul's despair. However, gaiety overcame correspondents when a member of the Government attributed our economic ills to the 'gnomes of Zurich'. Before long gnomes were discovered in London.

Reaction to revolting students at LSE gave 1969 a brisk start. Euthanasia was discussed. Lord Snow and Mr Edward Short disagreed when the former insisted the Jewish performance in every walk of life was ridiculously disproportionate. Abortions in Britain were seen as the only way of undermining the world population boom, though a Church of England parson did call for a 'Holy War' in Rhodesia. Sympathetic support was given to London squatters who refused to budge, Oxford's railway station was likened to a drain. Sex education for children was felt by some to be less important than sex education for adults. Violence in Northern Ireland evoked a sense of bewilderment. The assertion that legal language is designed for illiterate lawyers pleased 1970, but an omission in the Birthday Honours appalled. The actresses who had played Irene and Winifred in the BBC's *Forsyte Saga* received the OBE, he who had touched countless hearts as Soames nothing. Two instances of tragic absurdity were noted – Roedean's appointment of a headmaster which prompted the suggestion of a headmistress for Winchester, and the unloading of Belgian coal in South Wales.

Proposed art gallery admission charges were regretted by 1971 when cries of outrage or relief greeted the Industrial Relations Bill. A gurgle of delight was reserved for an advertisement in *The Times,* one page being occupied by a nude. Northern Ireland dominated 1972, the reaction to innumerable strikes and stoppages 1973. A simpler crossword was requested, the pronunciation of Milton Keynes shown to have nothing to do with the economist. Victoria station was declared a shoddy slum, adult illiteracy depressed. The Arab oil embargo shattered whatever complacency remained, then interest shifted to north-east England and strange happenings in local government. Two general elections, during which no one remarked on the presence of gnomes, occupied 1974. Doctors assumed their best bedside manner when expounding the merits of private practice, the virtual disappearance of Greek from the school syllabus was accepted with a sigh. Not long before the Conservative Party chose its new leader in 1975, a few correspondents had taken heart by chanting the names of English villages and hamlets. As these constitute a link between the end and the beginning of this book, they shall be noted:

Piddletrenthide

Wyke Champflower

Huish Episcopi   Shellow Bowells

Plush   Helions Bumpstead   Folly

Mucking

As She is Announced

[Correspondents now became increasingly anxious concerning the BBC]

From Mr L. D. Remmett-Peay   *3 December 1965*

Sir,

Before the War the BBC rendered a great service by disseminating, through its announcers and commentators, 'received pronunciation'.

The standard it set was respected throughout the country and indeed the world, and was safeguarded by its distinguished Advisory Committee on Spoken English. (Incidentally, they also published an invaluable series of books containing recommendations to announcers on the pronunciation of doubtful words, family names, British and foreign place-names, &c.)

Now the BBC lends its still considerable authority to 'provincial' and even 'colonial' speech.

A characteristic of 'received pronunciation' is that it is non-regional. If, however, in the future the speech of the various regions becomes 'accepted' and ubiquitous, the revolution will owe much to this apparent change of policy on the part of the BBC.

I am, Sir, yours faithfully,
L. D. REMMETT-PEAY

[The BBC later informed the public (*Children as Viewers and Listeners,* 1974) that many children, especially those retarded by living in a home where communication is usually in monosyllables, are helped to communicate by listening to Radio 1 disc jockeys]

The Forsytes

From Mr Henry Williamson   *25 March 1966*

Sir,

I wonder if the producer of the proposed serial on television would consider the pronunciation of the name *Jolyon* as Galsworthy once told me it should be pronounced: the name being a variant (in spelling) of *Julian.*

Yours faithfully,
HENRY WILLIAMSON

[then Senior Producer, BBC Television Centre]

Sir,

I am indebted to Mr Henry Williamson for giving us Galsworthy's own pronunciation for Jolyon.

I have never been quite sure, myself, particularly in view of the abbreviations, Jo, Jolly, and Jon, given to Old Jolyon's son and two grandsons respectively. Perhaps something midway between Joelyon and Julian would be appropriate in dialogue.

Could Mr Williamson now please confirm for me Galsworthy's pronunciation of the surname? I incline towards emphasis on the first syllable, but should it perhaps be on the second?

Yours faithfully,
DONALD WILSON

From Mr Rex Roberts 31 *March 1966*

Sir,

While we are finding out how to pronounce their name could we decide how to pronounce their author's name?

The late Horace Vachell told me that when he knew John Galsworthy the first syllable rhymed with pals. Now most people think it rhymes with palls. Can we have a ruling, please?

Yours faithfully,
REX ROBERTS

From Mr Henry Williamson 4 *April 1966*

Sir,

John Galsworthy said to me: 'The Galsworthys come from Galsworthy moor near Torrington in North Devon. When one left and became a builder in London, and went up in the world, he pronounced his name Galsworthy' – to rhyme with pals. 'I, in reaction, reverted to the original Devon pronunciation' – Galls-worthy.

Now, Sir, I understand, the greater uplift from having a famous author (and OM) in the family has restored the *status quo.*

Yours faithfully,
HENRY WILLIAMSON

Interviews on Television

[A correspondent had complained that television interviewers were a law unto themselves and did not show proper respect to statesmen]

From Mr Malcolm Muggeridge   *9 April 1966*

Sir,

Professor H. D. Lewis's attitude to television interviewing is surely rather heavy handed.

At least so it seems to me, who have been engaged, admittedly in a desultory sort of way, in this bizarre activity for some 12 years past, beginning with Billy Graham, taking in Salvador Dali and the late Brendan Behan (both highly successful interviews, which I attribute to the fact that the former's English was totally incomprehensible, and the latter – God rest his soul – too drunk to utter), and including a fair proportion of those set in authority over us. Professor Lewis equates the television interview with questions in Parliament and at public meetings; a truer comparison, it seems to me, would be with newspaper interviewing, whether in the frivolous gossip-column style, or with a view to seriously probing political views and intentions.

Politicians, in my experience, began by taking far too lordly an attitude towards being interviewed on television. I name no names, but there were. I assure you, those who confidently expected one (in my case always in vain, I am happy to say) to go over in advance what one proposed to ask, and to provide assurances that this or that topic would not be touched on. They gave one the feeling that coming to the studio at all was a great act of condescension on their part. Now the tendency is to go to the other extreme, and have so feverish a sense of the importance of television in building up their public image that some politicians, I really believe, would walk barefoot from John o' Groat's to Shepherd's Bush if they were assured of a peak-viewing time appearance on arrival there.

Of course television is important to politicians, as the press has been and to a great extent still is; but not as important as all that. They should take it easy. No one is going to make them appear if they don't want to, and they are under no obligation to answer a question which seems to them impertinent or irrelevant. By refusing to answer it, and giving their reasons for so doing in as emphatic terms as possible, they may rest assured that all the viewers' sympathies will swing to them and away from the interviewer. Mr Hogg – an excellent performer with whom it's always a pleasure to appear – has demonstrated that this is so again and again.

In general, however, men-of-letters and other non-politicians, who are less desperately concerned about how they are going to appear on the screen than politicians are, find it easier to fend off the too obdurate interviewer. Mr Robert Graves, the other day, fended off some questions of mine very skilfully and amusingly, making me, as we say in the Centre, look a proper charlie. Mr Evelyn Waugh, likewise, easily and adroitly turned aside Mr John Freeman's expert assaults in their superb Face to Face interview.

De Gaulle is one of the few politicians who has grasped the point that the balance of advantage is always with the man being interviewed if he cares to seize it. I saw him on French television being asked why he had delayed releasing the Ben Barka story till after the presidential election. Instead of getting hot under the collar, sending for the French equivalent of Sir Hugh Greene, transferring his favours to Radio Monte Carlo, or otherwise manifesting his displeasure, he just hung his old, battered head sheepishly, and muttered in a woeful, strangled voice: *'C'était mon inexpérience!'*

It really might be a good idea if in Downing Street they had a look at these Graves and Waugh interviews, and at the General's press conference, instead of fretting about well-informed and courteous interviewers like Robert Mackenzie.

Yours, &c.,
MALCOLM MUGGERIDGE

[Hogg (now once again Hailsham), Graves, Waugh, de Gaulle: add Lady Violet Bonham Carter, Sir Compton Mackenzie, Harold Macmillan and Sir Mortimer Wheeler, and it would seem that the best television performers are no longer young]

Rhodesian Legality

From Mrs Elspeth Huxley　　　　　　　*9 December 1966*

Sir,

Until last Monday most of us thought our quarrel with Rhodesia was about Mr Wilson's Six Principles, which in turn were about the political advancement of the Africans. Now it seems that we were wrong. What the quarrel is about, apparently, is something quite different, and called a Return to Legality.

Has not the time come to be quite honest with ourselves? Does anyone care tuppence about this? Really mind whether Mr Smith doffs his cap, kneels humbly in the dust and offers his submission to the Great White Queen, not to mention her chief Minister, like one of those dusky potentates in the nineteenth-century paintings paying homage to our former Queen?

Meanwhile Rhodesia's constitution is to be scrapped, the Government with its armed forces handed over complete, without reservations, to the British Governor, and in four months' time (whatever makes Mr Wilson think that any Royal Commission will report in four months?) a new constitution, in which the present elected government will have no say, will be imposed. All this in a country that has never been directly ruled by Britain, but has managed with *de facto* self-rule for over 40 years.

Wicked Mr Smith to turn down this generous concession. We sent a gunboat: a paper gunboat whose guns did not fire. So now we are sending for other people's gunboats whose guns may fire – but in what directions? We may get a nasty surprise.

All this to retrieve a lost legality. Rhodesia is fortunate: the only African country to have this treasure restored. Of the dozen or so former British territories in Africa on whom independence has recently been conferred, there is scarcely one whose legally bequeathed constitution survives. No doubt the military regimes of Nigeria, Ghana, and Sudan are as fully legal as a justice's wig. Nothing could be more legal than, as in Nigeria, to assassinate first a Prime Minister, then his successor, and seize power by military might.

It is perfectly legal to establish by decree single-party states, as in Tanzania and Uganda. Zanzibar disappears in a welter of bloodshed, floggings and forced labour, and does not lose its legality. But we cannot have this sort of thing with Mr Smith.

So now the fight is on for a Return to Legality – for Rhodesia only. Mr Smith must come to heel. If we lack a gunboat, we can at least have a gundog. Should we not pause long enough to understand that this, and not the constitutional rights of Africans, is our aim? Isn't this really Operation Face-Save? Helen's face launched a thousand ships: Mr Wilson's is to stop them. His must be the most expensive face since the sack of Troy.

I am, &c.,
ELSPETH HUXLEY

Progress Lost in All-day Pop

From Mr S. Gorley Putt   *23 December 1966*

[now Senior Tutor of Christ's College, Cambridge]

Sir,
In the heroic days of English liberal reform, the fight against poverty and the fight against ignorance were complementary. Good men sought to establish a subsistence level beneath which no countryman should be allowed to fall. Educators sought to create, through Acts of Parliament, a floor through which no countryman should crash into the brute miseries of ignorance.

In our own lifetime the BBC has played a superlative role on coaxing, satisfying and sustaining a national appetite for music, drama, literature and even the political skills. All this has been the wonder and the envy of foreign visitors.

At the very moment when a Labour Government may contemplate in the welfare state the victory in one great humanitarian campaign, it proposes to concede defeat on the other battlefront by deliberately deluging its educational paupers in a ceaseless stream of contemptuous rubbish. Having risen above the reactionary parrot-cries of 'Give them a bath and they'll only keep coal in it', we are now to shrug shoulders and say: 'Give them a wireless set and all they want is drivel'.

The worst effect of this craven and abhorrently snobbish decision will surely be a hardening of intellectual class-barriers far more rigorous than that brought about by the well-intentioned but now rightly repudiated shibboleth of the 'eleven-plus' examination. No rich man now living would dare to say: 'They are paupers, and must for ever remain so'. But our educated masters (for such we must suppose them to be) are now saying: 'They are fools and must for ever be treated so'.

A century of hard-won educational progress could be lost in one decade by an official disbelief that any goat should ever have a hankering to become a sheep. This, at least, the Light Programme never conceded. The vilest consequence of all-day pop will not be so much that the goats grow more goatish but that the sheep will feel finally and socially justified in nibbling away even more complacently at their Third Programme lawn.

O John Burns, O Albert Mansbridge, O Masterman and Hogg, O John Reith and every village schoolmistress, *what* are your successors trying to do to us?

Yours faithfully,
S. GORLEY PUTT

Saluting the Auschwitz Dead

From Group Captain Leonard Cheshire, VC   24 April 1967

[the official British observer at the dropping of the Atomic Bomb on Nagasaki, 1945; later founded the Cheshire Foundation Homes for the Sick; Order of Merit, 1981]

Sir,

To many in this country the absence of an official British representative at the unveiling of the memorial dedicated to the four million people of 23 nationalities exterminated at Auschwitz – and so movingly described in your issue of 17 April – is an occasion of the utmost regret.

Japan came, Italy came, India came, practically the entire Western Alliance came; alone Britain did not. Our dead who lie there were saluted by the Union Jack and by a handful of private pilgrims, not by our Government.

Whether political considerations, not apparently applicable to the rest of Europe, necessitated this decision, or whether in the official mind the occasion was not of sufficient significance there is no means of telling. Either way we have failed to measure up to the occasion and have lost in stature, not least because we have withheld an honour due to the dead.

It is sometimes thought, I know, that ceremonies like this are occasions for beating the drum and reviving old hatreds. Such is very far from the truth. One finds among the survivors, a hundred thousand of whom were present that day, not only a remarkable absence of bitterness but a solidarity and affection which transcends every frontier of race and political allegiance, and from which we have good reason to draw inspiration and hope. Out of evil God knows how to draw forth good.

I am, Sir, yours, &c.,
LEONARD CHESHIRE

The Secret of England's Fame

From Mr Colin MacInnes   *20 April 1967*

Sir,

The Times, in its new dispensation, has already published excellent articles and letters which all ask, basically, the same question, namely: what is the matter with England, and how can we extricate ourselves from our present predicaments?

May I suggest that the answer can be found if we all take five minutes off from our pressing worries and ask ourselves the following simple, basic question: which Englishmen, in our history, have *really* influenced not only England, but the world?

It seems to me that any short list will eventually reduce itself to three names: and these are Shakespeare, Newton and Darwin. The one a poet who helped to give shape and meaning to one of the most extraordinary languages the world has ever known. The next a young scientist of genius who, however much his theories have later been disproved, was one of the prime inventors of the modern world. And the third another scientist-philosopher who, more even than Karl Marx, has utterly altered almost everyone's ideas about everything.

If this diagnosis is correct, what might we have the intelligence to conclude? Surely this. When we pause to consider what our *real* genius is, is it not that of our artists and our scientists? And if we look around, even today, at who is really bringing credit to our country, will we not find that it is precisely these same people whom the world listens to, and respects, and admires?

Then what of that great procession of kings, generals, politicians and viceroys who have so much adorned our history? Have they contributed nothing?

They belong, it would seem to me, to our accidental period of imperial grandeur: which had certainly great will and courage in it, and earned us a lot of money, but also the unforgiving hatred of millions of human beings throughout the globe.

To the honourable list of our real heroes, Shakespeare, Newton, and Darwin, I would like to add the name of the eternal, anonymous Mr Smith. Mr Smith is a trader. Realizing, with his admirable common sense, that a basically poor island cannot live without commerce, and that these extraordinary poets and scientists would starve without him, he buys, and manufactures, and then sells.

And is that not, Sir, exactly what we really are: a people of artists and empirical thinkers and exporters? Are these not the people who have made our name respected, who have saved us a hundred times before, and who will do so again if we have the wits to recognize that they are what, at our best, we are?

Yours faithfully,
C. MacInnes

Thoughts from Roget

From Mr A. J. Woodman 　　　　　　　　　　*6 October 1967*

Sir,

Dr Roget included the following interesting entry in his *Thesaurus*: 'Inaction, passiveness, abstinence from action; non-interference; conservative policy.'

Can there be a moral somewhere in this?

Yours, &c.,
A. J. Woodman

From Mr M. F. Strachan 　　　　　　　　　　*7 October 1967*

Sir,

Another evocative entry in the *Thesaurus*: 'Socialism, collectivism; communism, bolshevism, syndicalism; mob law . . .'

Yours faithfully,
M. F. Strachan

A Matter of Address

[Mr Edward Bernays, an adviser to presidents and governments, offered $5,000 for the best ideas to improve transatlantic understanding]

From Mr Robert Graves   *24 April 1967*

Sir,

I am not angling for Mr Edward Bernays' $5,000 prize (18 April) when I suggest that one of the principal causes of Anglo-American misunderstanding, and one simple enough to remove by wide publicity, is a current American habit (in all except business correspondence) of putting the letter-writer's address on the back of the envelope only and not at the head of the letter. It has been explained to me that this is a national rule of epistolary etiquette, as taught in schools and colleges.

Few of us English, however, keep the envelopes in which letters reach us, nor do we as a rule answer our friends in the States until at least three or four days have elapsed; by which time the contents of our wastepaper baskets or refuse-bins are likely to have been collected by the municipal authorities for incineration. On finally getting down to the job and writing two or three affectionate pages to dear Bob, Hank, Chuck, Lambie, or Kiki, we can seldom find his or her address – even at the close of the letter where, I admit, it does sometimes half-apologetically appear. We are left only with our correspondent's boldly printed name at the head of the letter, unsupplied even by a telephone number.

(United States papers, please copy!)

On the other hand, we English have such faith in the infallibility of all post offices that we seldom put our addresses on the backs of our envelopes: so that if a letter goes astray we cannot hope to get it back, and are left without any means of knowing whether or not it has reached Bob, Hank, Chuck, Lambie, or Kiki.

(English papers, please copy!)

Yours faithfully,
ROBERT GRAVES

After Snow

From Mrs F. A. Pullinger   *15 January 1968*

Sir,

As a Frenchwoman who has lived for a short time in England I am astonished at your passivity when faced with a not very large snow fall. Would it lower your self-esteem so much to use a shovel? Is our expression 'roll up your sleeves and things will improve' untranslatable?

Three days after the blizzard the little town where I live is a veritable bog and even the pavements in London are still snow covered. In France everyone is responsible for clearing the pavement in front of his house or shop – and doing so at once. The lazy incur the liability to a fine.

Yours faithfully,
JACQUELINE PULLINGER

Reasons for Decline in National Morale

From Mr George Gretton   *12 December 1968*

Sir,

Your leading article The Danger to Britain makes an un-answerable case – at least to all those who care primarily for the well-being of this country and community. I meet a great many people in different walks of life, and it is some time since I spoke to anyone who is not disturbed or even disgusted at the present mismanagement and low morale.

Among the most sensitive points are:

(1) The enless inflation in which a minority is maintaining or improving its standard of living at the expense of the rest of the community;

(2) The growing indiscipline which enables small, selfish minorities to hold the majority to ransom in industry, to disrupt education and damage property and amenities with impunity;

(3) The failure of the Government to communicate clearly with the people;

(4) The wasteful element in public spending which often does not relieve genuine hardship but transfers money to categories of people who neither need nor deserve it; and

(5) The manner in which political debate is debased from serious discussion to a kind of fourth-form defence of frozen attitudes.

In 1948 I had the privilege of being a member of the small Allied team which introduced the German currency reform, which created the conditions for the German economic miracle. This was done quite simply by making it worth while for an honest man to do an honest job of work. Things had reached a point at which a skilled worker earned less in a month than his teenage son could make in a couple of hours by black market deals on street corners. We have not yet reached that point, but we are overdue for a mental or moral currency reform.

I believe there would be very wide support in the country for a Government of the kind you envisage, drawn from any or every party which would undertake to tackle our malaise in a practical way and re-infuse a spirit of purpose and a climate of responsibility. I also believe there are enough Members of the present Parliament willing to call a truce to the party vendetta and provide support for a Government pledged to a programme of sane, practical and humane administration. Such a move would do more than anything to restore confidence in this country and its currency, pending the negotiation of a more rational international monetary system.

Yours faithfully,
GEORGE GRETTON

From Mr George Mikes   *12 December 1968*

Sir,

You said (in effect) in your brilliant leading article that the Germans had no secret formula for success; that there is no reason why they should succeed where we fail.

I think there is a very good reason. At the moment I am (or up to the last minute I was) engaged in three transactions with British firms.

Case No. 1: I am hiring a television set which went out of order. The firm – a large and well known one – from whom I am renting is trying to get new customers with its promise of '24 hours service' and immediate repairs. I was given three definite dates for their man to appear, all broken. I rang up the manager, told them that if their repairer did not come within a few hours I would get in touch with the managing director of the firm. The repairer came.

Case No. 2: The under-floor heating of my house is also out of order. The London Electricity Board couples extreme courtesy with extreme inefficiency. Instead of not sending anyone, they have sent two men in quick succession – but they do not know who the first man is. He is lost and now – I am told – memos are being sent around in 154 Uxbridge Road, trying to find him. Before this is 'sorted out' nothing can be done to have my heating repaired. In the meantime I freeze.

Case No. 3: I wanted some plants for my patio so I went to a nearby gardening shop to make inquiries. The person who received me said that he knew nothing about anything but took my name and telephone number and promised that the firm would contact me. That was 10 days ago but no one phoned.

I have very little dealings with German commercial firms. The only one I remembered occurred in Ibiza last summer. I wanted a special German wheat product and I wrote to the German makers and asked them where I could obtain it on the island. I received a letter by returning post, thanking me for my appreciation of their product and giving me the names of the suppliers.

This is the secret formula, Sir, the Germans possess and we don't. Courtesy coupled with efficiency.

I remain, Sir, yours faithfully,

GEORGE MIKES

'Oh, Mr Porter . . .'

From Mr Richard Harvey   *18 October 1968*

Sir,

This afternoon I caught the 15.05 train from the recently modernized Euston Station.

According to the new electronic departure indicator, its destination was Rugby; according to the ticket collector and a notice on the platform it was Coventry; according to the destination blind on the train it was Wolverhampton. I got off at Watford, to hear the station announcer declare it was Wolverhampton; and walked home to look it up in my copy of the timetable and discover it was Birmingham.

Perhaps now that their modernization scheme is complete British Rail's executives will have enough time to decide where their trains are going to?

Yours faithfully,
RICHARD HARVEY

Brain Versus Computer

From Sir James Pitman   *28 January 1969*

[Conservative MP for Bath 1945–64]

Sir,

Those of us who complete (very occasionally) your crossword puzzle have our occasional 'leaps of imaginative insight'. They are not of course comparable with the 'great leaps' to which Professor Thorpe referred (article, 25 January) but those experiences make very easy of acceptance his contention that 'the brain is more than a mere computer'.

Will someone kindly tell us the number of possible ways, using all 26 characters, of filling the empty squares of today's puzzle? It will greatly cheer us to learn how many millions of other possibilities the brain needs to reject in order to select the one correct one which gives us lesser mortals such intense satisfaction.

How, too, does it happen that sometimes we have but to look at the characters – how blessed to some of us that bracketed 'anag' – to know at once the correct order in which to rearrange up to 15 characters? Moreover, we can do this without help from characters in crossing lines.

Such instantaneity seems to have been achieved not by any process of exhaustion of rejects but rather by a flash of light upon the one correct rearrangement.

Your faithfully,
JAMES PITMAN

From Sir John Carroll   *3 February 1969*

Sir,

The answer to Sir James Pitman's question is 26^{120} which is, approximately, 24873 followed by 222 noughts (0s).

Should anyone cavil because this includes solutions in which every letter is the same, here is a puzzle with just such a solution

All Across: Gently to annoy.
All Down: Used in golf.
The solution consists entirely of the letter T, viz.
Across: Tease.
Down: Tees.

Yours faithfully,
JOHN CARROLL

Stopwatch Dons

[Dons had reacted indignantly when asked to record their half-hourly activities, 8.00 a.m. to midnight, Monday to Sunday, including 'unallocable internal time']

From Mr P. G. Henderson   *2 December 1969*

Sir,

Dons in doubt as to how to answer their questionnaire may be helped by the reply reputed to have been given by the late Professor Dawkins, Bywater and Sotheby Professor of Byzantine and Modern Greek Language and Literature in the University of Oxford, to a former inquisition as to how he spent his time: 'I give an annual lecture – but not every year, mark you!'

Yours faithfully,
P. G. HENDERSON

The Hedge's Worth and Age

From Dr D. E. Coombe and others   *6 April 1970*

[writing from the University of Cambridge]

Sir,

My hon. Friend must know that all the hedges in our countryside have been man-made in the last 200 or 300 years (Hansard, Commons, 11 March). Thus Mr Mackie, Parliamentary Secretary to the Ministry of Agriculture, perpetuates the official myth that all our hedges are a recent addition to the landscape: a myth which generally carries the supposed corollary that the public ought not to object on aesthetic, scientific, or historical grounds to their destruction. Before we discuss this doctrine more seriously, may we ask what Mr Mackie imagines hedgehogs (word used in 1450) or hedge-sparrows (word used in 1530) did before 1670?

Officialdom would have us believe that hedges were intro-duced only by the parliamentary enclosures and 'improving' landlords of the eighteenth and nineteenth centuries. But a great body of documentary, archaeological, and ecological evidence, of which we can here give but a small sample, shows that many are Tudor, medieval, or even Anglo-Saxon. Even in the East Midlands, where enclosure acts covered half the land area, there is a large minority of ancient hedges. Many other districts, such as central Suffolk and much of Devon and Cornwall, were hardly touched by enclosure acts; enclosure had taken place much earlier, and many of the hedges or walls are medieval or older.

Many 16th and early 17th century drawings and large-scale maps depict hedges accurately and distinguish them carefully from other types of boundary. The history of individual hedges can be followed in later maps. Near Huntingdon, for example, the maps of Great Gidding (1541), Conington (1595), Gamlin-gay (1601), and Glatton (1613) all show several miles of hedges, many of which still exist, or did until recently. Even in the heart of enclosure-act country, ancient hedges are thus not rare. At Conington, no less than 62 per cent of the modern hedges existed in the 16th century. Even higher proportions of ancient hedges occur in the heavy lands of Suffolk, less than 5 per cent of which came under enclosure acts. The maps of Hintlesham (1595) and Hawstead (1616), among others, depict almost the same hedge-patterns as existed recently.

Such hedges were by no means all recent in Tudor times. In medieval documents there is often confusion between hedges and fences, but we can produce records of the planting and maintenance of *live* hedges back to 1330, of which some are still identifiable today. The evidence for pre-Conquest hedges is less direct, but although hedges and fences are not always distinguished in Anglo-Saxon charters there are many refer-ences which definitely imply the former. Some hedges are not directly man-made at all, but represent the edges of ancient woods long since cleared.

The hedges of our countryside have arisen over as long a span of years as its buildings, and like buildings are not all the same or all equally worthy of preservation. A medieval hedge with its great richness in plants and animals accumulated over the centuries is far more important biologically than the pure hawthorn hedge typical of 19th-century plantings. Ancient hedges are irreplaceable; the planting of new shelterbelts and groups of trees, often advocated (but too seldom performed) to offset their loss, is not an adequate biological or historical substitute.

Old hedges are ancient monuments and should be respected both on historical and biological grounds. It is usually possible to recognize them in the field. We urge that conservationists should not be indiscriminate in deploring the destruction of hedges, but should support farm reorganizations in which the less interesting hedges are sacrificed and the more interesting ones distinguished and retained as far as possible.

Yours faithfully,
D. E. COOMBE
D. P. DYMOND
M. D. HOOPER
O. RACKHAM

Kindly Forward

From the Dean of Canterbury   *5 February 1970*

Sir,
A few days ago I received a communication addressed to T. A. Becket, Esq., care of The Dean of Canterbury. This surely must be a record in postal delays.

Yours truly,
IAN H. WHITE-THOMSON

New Gothic Age

From Dr Carl Bode   *2 February 1970*

[now Professor of English in the University of Maryland]

Sir,
As the sainted McLuhan has said more than once, No fish ever defined water. So I hope I may be allowed as an American to define London, on the basis of a week's return visit, to Londoners. It is clear to me that London is in the middle of a New Gothic Age.

The clothes, especially of the young, are superbly weird;

their principle is the principle of exaggeration. The mini-skirts are heaven-pointing. The maxi-skirts drag the ground. The male's once sedate suit has been transformed into a thing of peaks, ridges, rough textures, and flying buttresses. I saw one young man march through Grosvenor Square in blue, belled trousers, a sleeveless lambswool jacket, a kerchief around his waist, and on his head a hat saved from some Victorian funeral. His face of course was furred.

The manners, again especially of the young, have grown Gothic also. They are elaborate in their rituals of touching, no longer as direct as when they used to clutch one another promptly. Even their speech now seems to me to have a Gothic way. Either they talk in high, astounding terms – I have heard them in Kings Road – or they speak obliquely. Then they use the passive more than the active mode. It reminds me of the speech of some of the black American militants, not the Panther type but the soul brother. Similarly: 'Turn me on', they say; 'Light my fire', they sing.

Lastly, the tone is Gothic. Once more, it is found in its extreme in the young but is manifest even in the old: note the lengthening sideburns of the City clerk. It is a tone of certainty; it is what we call in America the moral arrogance of the young. They stand convinced that their religion is the true one. They will no more listen to the pronouncements of their elders than would the medieval workman, chipping stone for a cathedral, to the seductions of the Arian.

Is London, today's London, Gothic in everything? Of course not. I do not want to force my thesis. I have only to scan, for example, the scores of new office buildings. In their bare brutality they seem even starker, even worse, than the latest skyscrapers in New York.

Anyway, I hail the New Gothic Age. May it be long and full, leaving many monuments behind it.

And I wonder what those monuments will be?

CARL BODE

South African Cricket Tour: Threat of Hooliganism

From Mr E. F. G. Haig   *5 February 1970*

Sir,

In your third leader today you suggest that the South African cricket tour may be cancelled. If it is, should we not clear our minds of cant and realize the true reason?

It will not be because the British public want to sever sporting connections with South Africa – there's no evidence that they do. It will not be because a minority of conscientious folk feel strongly enough about apartheid to gather in peaceful demonstrations. No: it will be, overwhelmingly, because we cannot control thugs and hooligans who attach themselves to any cause which gives them an excuse for vandalism. It will be because public and police together cannot protect such national institutions as Lord's and Old Trafford against young louts who don't shrink from scattering broken glass on Rugby grounds or digging up cricket pitches.

Unfortunately the vandals have been encouraged, during the Springboks tour, by the patronage of muddle-headed clerics and MPs who seem to have accepted two principles usually associated with Hitler and Stalin: (i) if you oppose a political system, persecute and insult any individuals in any way connected with it, even if they are quite unrepresentative, even if they may be its critics; (ii) use any means, whatever, towards an end which you imagine to be good.

So, if the cricket tour is cancelled, we shall have signalled to the world that Britain cannot keep order at home, and cannot prevent hundreds of thousands of her citizens from being deprived of an innocent summer pursuit by a small minority of barbarians. Such an admission would be a natural sequel to our recent failure to protect our Springbok guests from repeated insult and persecution by the uncivilized: but surely it is an admission we should do our utmost to avoid?

Yours sincerely,

E. F. G. HAIG

From Mr Laurence Meynell   *11 February 1970*

Sir,

The art of true government is the realization of what is possible.

It is not possible to protect a game of cricket from disastrous interruption. No number of uniformed police or plainclothes detectives can see the 'banger' in the young protester's pocket, nor prevent him from exploding it just as the batsman is about to receive a ball.

The only people who will benefit from the proposed tour – if MCC are stupid enough to let it happen – are the anarchists and the communists to whom it will be one more heaven-sent opportunity to 'have a go' at authority; to discredit the police (we shall hear a lot about 'brutality'); and at the end of a long, trying summer to bring about considerable disenchantment in the police force itself.

Yours sincerely,
LAURENCE MEYNELL

From the Canon S. W. Wilson   *30 April 1970*

Sir,

The Bishop of Gloucester asks for prayers that the South African Test matches may be rained off. This is a bit unfair, not least on the farmers in his diocese, for, as the bishop will recollect, the rain falls on the just and unjust.

Has the bishop considered the more dramatic and effective calling-down of fire and brimstone? Or he might make little wax images of the touring team and stick pins in them the night before each test match is due to start.

Yours faithfully,
SPENCER W. WILSON

[The Labour Home Secretary suggested the tour be called off. It was. 2 June, which should have seen the start of the Lord's Test, was instead the occasion of a general election. Labour lost]

Bertrand Russell

[The philosopher died on 2 February 1970, aged 97]

From Mrs T. S. Eliot   *10 February 1970*

Sir,

My husband, T. S. Eliot, loved to recount how late one evening he stopped a taxi. As he got in, the driver said: 'You're T. S. Eliot.' When asked how he knew, he replied: 'Ah, I've got an eye for a celebrity. Only the other evening I picked up Bertrand Russell, and I said to him: "Well, Lord Russell, what's it all about," and, do you know, he couldn't tell me.'

Yours faithfully,
VALERIE ELIOT

Without Letters

From Mr Richard Hughes   *10 February 1971*

Sir,

We have now tasted a total absence of postal services without finding it half so unpalatable as we had expected. Letter-writing is no longer our only or even principal means of communication beyond shouting-distance. We have already outgrown the Railway Age: are we now outgrowing the Postal Age too?

In the past, state letter-carrying has served many purposes. Queen Elizabeth first made it a royal monopoly to facilitate postal censorship. In the 17th century its monopoly profits were the attraction, for pensioning royal mistresses; and in the 18th, for financing French wars. Not till the 19th was it envisaged as primarily a service to the community (while still paying its way). If in the 20th it can no longer even pay reasonable wages out of reasonable charges, how can we avoid a suspicion that it is beginning to outgrow its usefulness?

Were letter-post suddenly abolished the inconvenience to business, the social injustices and hardships are obvious. No letters in hospital, no letters from boarding-school – and of course, no bills. The poor would suffer worse than the rich. But it may well be that we shall have to adopt in the future a deliberately discouraging policy of rundown (as with the railways) till only a minimal, essential skeleton-service remains. If we want to keep our friendly village postman we must pay him properly – or else do without him, collecting our own letters or setting our mail-boxes on the nearest mail-route (as in America) to be filled from passing vans.

The one thing that will not be affected is the *art* of letter-writing: for that is stone-dead already.

I am, Sir, &c.,
RICHARD HUGHES

From Mr John J. Smith   *22 March 1971*

Sir,

I have just been told by the manager of the local sorting office to collect today's mail by hand. The reason is that our postman is sitting as a J.P. *Tempora mutantur.*

Yours faithfully,
JOHN J. SMITH

Keep the Country in London

From Mr Yehudi Menuhin   *17 February 1971*

Sir,

London is still livable, lovable and sane. Today we can no longer take these essentials for granted. We must ask ourselves the questions 'why' and 'how' and implement the answers.

London is a city penetrated by the English countryside, by the trees and hedges, the flowers and shrubs, the animals which love and breathe the English air. They belong together and to us, as we belong to them. We thus remain sane by remaining lovable to and livable with each other. There is no other way. After all we cannot embrace a slab of poured concrete, but we can embrace a tree, and we can feel tender about a flower, the deer grazing in Richmond Park, the sheep in Hyde Park, or the return of the nightingale to Hampstead Heath.

It is time that we stringently defend the perimeters of and the approach to our heaths and parks as an essential measure of protecting our balance of mind. If we allow these irreplaceable rural incursions to shrivel, to be nibbled by greedy teeth at their circumference, London – perhaps the only city in the world to be accepted by her countryside – will no longer be penetrated by it.

It was only a few years ago that Parliament Fields including the Highgate ponds were saved for the nation from a similar fate. The owner fancied himself equally the owner of the grass, the birds, the trees, the air and the light of these beneficent spaces, just because his legal title to the land presupposed his right to sell and to build, or, as we euphemistically say, to develop. Public monies and private collections were mobilized and the spaces were saved for our own joy and for that of future generations.

This year is the 100th anniversary of the declaration of Hampstead Heath as an open space, representing as it does the accumulation of acts of public and private farsightedness and generosity. Witanhurst is the last great property belonging to this same green expanse; it belongs in concept to the Heath, as do the various green spaces adjoining it. These frontier spaces cannot be interpreted as empty and useless so long as they remain in their natural state, but rather as the property of that threatened Goddess of Nature, whose death humanity will never survive. This year must see our recurrent act of reverence renewed. More than ever today must we make amends for human follies and depredations; for only by defending our heritage of air, space, grass and earthworms can we or our children hope to avoid spiritual and physical suffocation and degradation.

Yours sincerely,
YEHUDI MENUHIN

Long-Haired Boys

From Sir Bernard Miles   *10 February 1971*
[life peer 1979]

Sir,
Hearing on the 'Today' programme on 5 February that Mr Temple, Headmaster of Bede School, Sunderland, has banned one of his pupils, Paul Kucharski, from future attendance until he gets his hair cut, I was reminded of the many representations of Our Lord Jesus Christ in European painting – Giotto, Piero della Francesa, Michelangelo, Leonardo, Titian, Rembrandt, the Van Eyck Bros., et alia, a First Division team if ever there was one – all of whom portray Him with shoulder-length hair.

Where does Mr Temple stand doctrinally? And where does the Local Education Authority stand?

Yours,
BERNARD MILES

PS. I believe there are also grave doubts about the Venerable Bede.

From Mr T. Y. Darling   *17 February 1971*

Sir,
If Sir Bernard Miles will refer to I Corinthians xi, 14, he will see that St. Paul asks: 'Doth not even nature itself teach you that, if a man have long hair, it is a shame unto him?'

It has always seemed to me unlikely that St Paul would have made this remark if Christ himself wore long hair. Is it not far more likely that the great painters, hundreds of years later, were quite mistaken on this point and were merely reflecting the fashion of their own times?

Yours truly,
T. Y. DARLING

Fashions in Words

From Mr J. R. Barnes   *2 December 1971*

Sir,

What comes across vis-à-vis the non-ambulent linguistic confrontation is a getting together of defensible media people at
this moment in time. I am personally oriented towards helpless
laughter at the postures of these bizarre communicators.

Yours ecologically,

J. R. BARNES

[But what of the writer's image?]

'Little Black Sambo'

From Miss Dorothy Kuya   *1 May 1972*

Sir,

The existence of *Little Black Sambo* for 73 years leads one
to think that it might well have contributed (along with other
things) to the prejudice that many white British have against
non-whites, rather than detracted from it.

Mr Laycock no doubt found him lovable but then most
white people find black babies also lovable, as one white lady
said to me recently, when admiring a black baby, 'It's a pity
they have to grow up'. It is a pity that we have to grow up
because the love and admiration is not transferred to us when
we are black adults, particularly when seeking employment,
accommodation and leisure facilities.

It is doubtful if the story of *Little White Squibba* gave any
British child a feeling of inferiority; after all the British were,
until recently, ruling nearly a quarter of the earth's land mass
and a quarter of its population, most of them black. The
white child might of course have felt different if *Little White
Squibba* had been presented to him/her in a class in which he
was the only white pupil, or one of a few, and in a country
which, according to Rose in *Colour and Citizenship* (1969),
only 17 per cent of the population were not racially prejudiced.

The days have gone when the British could talk of Sambos,
greasers, wogs, niggers and Chinks, and not find one of them
behind him, refusing to accept his description and demanding
to be treated with dignity.

We now have to take note that we live in a multiracial
society, and need to consider not whether the white children

find *LBS* lovable, or the white teachers think it 'a good repetitive tale', but whether the black child and teacher feel the same way.

As a black Briton, born and educated in this country, I detested *LBS* as much as I did the other textbooks which presented non-white people as living entirely in primitive conditions and having no culture. I did not relate to him, but the white children in my class identified me with him.

Helen Bannerman was a typical product of the age in which she lived: then the blacks were treated with at the most contempt and at the least paternalism. She may not have been malicious but she certainly was condescending.

Little Black Sambo along with many other such books must be removed from the classrooms if *all* our children, black and white, are to grow up with an understanding and respect for each other regardless of differences of colour, creed or religion. I would not suggest we burn the books, but rather put them in a permanent exhibition along with some of the jokes of *The Comedians*, the exhibition could be titled 'Echoes of Britannia's Rule' – subtitled – 'Information that made the British think they were great'.

Yours faithfully,
DOROTHY KUYA

From Mr Michael Flanders   *May 2 1972*

Sir,

All lovers of the tiger and conservationists in general must deplore a work (*Little Black Sambo*) in which a great number of man's noblest and rarest eaters is wantonly oleaginated without rebuke.

Nor, as parents, should we tolerate the encouragement it gives our children, at an age when eating patterns are established for a life time, to over-indulgence in pancakes (obesity forming carbohydrate), cooked in saturated fat (cholesterol – prime suspect in the fight against heart disease).

In the face of these arguments for the book's suppression the racist aspect must pale into insignificance. At the time when I was first exposed to it (*circa* 1927), my personal reaction was one of interest that the Blackamoor could figure in literature as a heroic child like myself and not solely as the bloodthirsty cannibal I had previously supposed him to be.

Yours faithfully,
MICHAEL FLANDERS

Palindromic Dates

From Mr Matthew Norgate   *1 August 1972*

Sir,

The sole point of this letter is the date at its foot. Apart from the three rather less pleasing palindromes arising on the 27th of the 8th, 9th and 11th months of this year, today's is the last palindromic date until 18.1.81, when I shall of course write to you again, unless I wait until the even more pleasing 18.8.81, and unless I am by then no longer in a position to be

Your obedient servant,

MATTHEW NORGATE

27.7.72

The Perfect Palindrome

From Mr Stelio Hourmouzios   *10 August 1972*

Sir,

Palindromic dates are chronologically predictable and mathematically calculable besides being coldly impersonal. Alphabetical palindromes on the other hand are an intellectual exercise, as they have to make grammatical sense and should ideally express some wise precept or axiom – I am referring, of course, to real palindromes and not catchphrase ones like the classic but ridiculous MADAM I'M ADAM.

In this connexion one may recall what is probably the perfect palindrome of all time:

NIPSON ANOMIMATA MI MONAN OPSIN

which was carved over a fountain outside St. Sophia's Cathedral in Constantinople. It means 'Wash thy sins not only thy face' and is in Greek, which is most appropriate since the word 'Palindrome' itself is pure Greek.

Let me anticipate inquiries by mentioning that 'PS' in Greek is written as one letter, ψ.

Yours very truly,

STELIO HOURMOUZIOS

Theatre's Fashion for Despair

From Mr J. D. Brown   *5 February 1972*

Sir,

Having read your correspondent's review of the play (if that is the right word) *Insulting the Audience* at the 'Almost Free Theatre' I am forced to ponder on the likely future direction of the theatre. As I understand it, this play (evidently written for masochists) consists of four actors (again, if that is the right word) who shout miscellaneous insults at the audience until they have run through their script. This is, by all accounts, the sum total of the performance.

Various critics seem to have taken the playwright, Mr Peter Handke, to task for writing a play which 'goes too far'; which transcends the bounds of what is normally regarded as theatre. I would suggest from reading these reviews of the play that this is a false argument. It seems to me that the fault of such a play is that it does not go far enough.

For a truly revolutionary theatre, the audience should hurl insults at the actors using scripts provided as they enter the auditorium. The actors should then show their contempt of the whole proceeding by performing some task which totally ignores the audience, such as eating a meal or playing bridge. The audience would leave when they became bored or felt they had had their money's worth.

As an extension of this, every now and again, the actors could break off from their activity and join the audience to shout insults at the empty stage. This would produce the unsettling effect which is a hallmark of all true masterpieces.

Perhaps a more perfect system would consist of having the audience and actors mingle together throughout the performance. They would then hurl insults at one another, taken at random from the script provided. Two refinements would of course, be important: the actors would not identify themselves so that nobody would know whether he was insulting an actor or a member of the audience and the shouters could make up their own insults if they did not like the scripts provided.

This leads to a still more perfect concept. That is, handing out scripts to random members of the population at some central point, such as Oxford Circus underground station (charging a nominal fee of course) and leaving people to insult their fellow travellers all the way home.

In contrast to the various critics concerned, I do not feel the slightest despondency for the future of the theatre. Indeed, I am full of optimism for it. I would even go so far as to say that should any theatrical management wish to take me up on any of the creative suggestions given over, I would be only too happy to provide them with full scripts.

Yours faithfully,
J. D. Brown

Causes of Violence

From Mr N. F. Simpson   *14 August 1973*

Sir,

During the course of some researches into the causes of violence in our modern society, I have had my attention drawn to what would appear to be yet another instance of the sort of mindless thuggery with which in recent times we have become, alas, all too familiar.

In this case, a young man, pleasant, likeable and totally inoffensive, known to those around him simply as Abel, is attacked in a field by a psychopathic elder brother by the name of Cain, and receives injuries from which he subsequently dies.

One is loath indeed to draw overhasty conclusions from insufficient data, but one cannot but be forcibly reminded of scenes in *A Clockwork Orange*, where I believe similar muggings result, likewise, in the deaths of the victims concerned.

It is, of course, a matter for speculation whether it was this or some other film or television programme that in fact triggered off this abominable crime, but, bearing in mind that it had the effect of reducing the total world population at that time by no less than 25 per cent at a single stroke, it seems to me that the makers of films and television programmes, together with the writers of the books on which films and television programmes seem so often to be based, have a good deal to answer for.

Even though, as my assistant now somewhat belatedly tells me, the crime was committed some time before a good many of them were made, the principle remains the same, and the lesson is crystal clear to those not too wilfully blind to see it.

Yours in anger,
N. F. Simpson

Sending a Clergyman to War

From The Bishop of Croydon   *7 September 1973*

[the Rt Rev. John Taylor Hughes]

Sir,

Mr Paul Oestreicher's article calls into question the role, the purpose and indeed the integrity of all chaplains who serve in HM Forces. A good deal of what he has to say is peripheral and generalized and is probably both true and untrue of almost every vocation and profession.

But the main gravamen of his criticism is contained in these words: 'What role is there in that situation (sc. as a commissioned officer under military discipline) for a priest determined to wrestle with the ethics of nuclear warfare? Can he possibly do other than raise disturbing thoughts if he is not to evade the real issues?'

First, the 'ethics of nuclear warfare'. Can he wrestle with them, and having wrestled with them remain a chaplain? The implication seems to be that he cannot. The fact is that many (how many I do not know) can and do, because I know that they do. Mr Oestreicher has raised the most difficult question of our time which besets not only the clergy but all people, especially Service people. He does not supply us with an answer. I cannot answer it. I can only set out an approach to the painful subject which helps me to believe that a serving chaplain can both wrestle with the ethics of nuclear warfare and without selling his soul find an authentic place and ministry among the men and women he seeks to serve.

John Ruskin, I believe, once wrote that a shoemaker may be said to be a person who not only mends shoes but keeps Christendom shod. That is to say his work is not only a livelihood or a career but a service. I believe that the Army, the Royal Navy, and the Royal Air Force are here to be what their designation tells us they intend to be – services, and that theirs is the service of our protection and security. In any debate we had better begin here.

Whatever they may have to inflict they have also to be willing to take. Serving men therefore put some of the best that human beings can give, even life itself, into their service, and for our sakes. I have recently visited a military hospital and seen in the men there some of the results of service in Northern Ireland and I doubt whether anyone can see what I have seen and remain unmoved and not be filled with respect and gratitude.

But the heart of the problem is well known. Can we kill – can we go on to engage in nuclear warfare in the service of protection and security?

Many years ago when Dietrich Bonhoeffer's *Ethics* was first published in English I came across for the first time in my life a contention which both startled and illuminated me. We have, he says, at times *to be willing to be guilty* and to take the consequences of our guilt. In the privacy of my study I have on more than one occasion had to be willing to be guilty – to condone sin in another, even to agree that it shall continue, lest the one bright light in a dark and otherwise hopeless situation be completely extinguished. To have said that I could do nothing because it was all so sinful would have been the most appalling failure. And had I so acted I should have been guilty for a different reason. I should have been guilty of passing by on the other side for the sake of my own salvation.

I do not write articles in the papers about such situations and the counsel I have ventured to give, or preach sermons in public about it. It would be largely misunderstood if I did. Yet I have been guilty of allowing a sinful situation to continue because in order ultimately to preserve and increase the good in it, there seemed to me no other responsible way.

The second point has to do with being a commissioned officer under military discipline. There are those who, knowing all the limitations that this imposes on a priest, would also acknowledge that only by living under the same restraints and under the same command as his men could a chaplain serve them with any sense of reality. Why should he fare better than they? But this also might be added. One serving chaplain once said to me that he crosses swords with his Commanding Officer at least once a week, and it is foolish to suppose that such free exchange is exluded from life in the three Services.

All this can be debated. But what I am concerned to argue is that there are serving chaplains who choose to continue as serving chaplains in the situation of nuclear warfare knowing what they are doing and knowing how they would seek humbly and 'with fear and trembling' to justify to themselves and to others what they are doing and that in so doing they have wrestled with the terrible subject of the Christian and nuclear war, and have come to a responsible conclusion. And they will know that having arrived at that conclusion, they will then need to be forgiven. They may be wrong and I may be wrong and if so it will not be through lack of responsibility and painful thought and decision.

Yours faithfully,

✠John Croydon
Bishop to Her Majesty's Forces

Inspiration

[Britain's oil stocks were down to a supply of sixty-five days]

From Mr. Albert M. Gomes   *8 December 1973*

Sir,

Can't an Arab princess be found for the Prince of Wales?

Yours, etc.,

ALBERT M. GOMES

The Art of Giving Hell

From Mr Roderick Colyer   *21 December 1973*

Sir,

This is the first time I have ever written to a newspaper, but what I feel must out.

I am a working class engineering employee.

Dictator Heath and his £10,000 plus a year henchmen have imposed a three-day working week. Why? Because this yacht owner claims the miners/electricians are causing such severe damage to the nation that it is essential.

Until now I believed the miners to be wrong not to accept the £44m offered, but then minister after industrialist hammered them for what irresponsible men they are. Why are they irresponsible? Because they are not doing overtime? I don't like working overtime, so why should the miners/electricians be forced to. It is not illegal. If by refusing overtime they are causing such disruption let those people who know the industry get their heads together and devise a system fair to all which will get all work needed to be done within working hours.

Why a three-day week? According to Peter Jay in the ITV programme *Weekend World* if industry repaired its draughty factories, broken windows and insulated their buildings this alone would save 17 per cent on fuel – besides improving, immeasurably, the working conditions of millions of workers.

Why hit the workers' pay packets? Will that unite us? Will it hell!

What about switching off all advertisements (and don't say this is already being done – walk down many high streets); street lighting from midnight; instruct industry to cease all overtime, and weekend working, and to absorb all night workers into day shifts until further notice, with the exception of continuous process workers. Initiate immediate petrol rationing and ban Sunday driving. Instruct industry to operate from 9 am to 4 pm. Institute Wilson's 12-point programme; especial attention to rents, property speculators, and pensions.

I was once referred to as a floating voter. I do not want Communism, but I do want a Britain where no one man forces another to be his slave to earn a survival wage.

If I sound bitter, it is because I am. I am bitter because I have to work continuous nights to earn a gross wage of £35, and a take home pay of £29. I am bitter because I can no longer meet mortgage payments, and other financial expenses. I am bitter because my marriage has broken under financial strain. I am bitter because of the fortunes being made and lost by the upper and middle classes over the backs of the workers. I am bitter because the same people – the so-called industrialists and ruling classes – stop a worker having a couple of pounds extra whilst they line their pockets with rises of £315 a week plus, or the Government give them salaries of £10,000 to £20,000 a year. What on earth do they do with that type of money? I am bitter because pensioners, like my Mum and Dad, cannot get £480 a year, yet it was they that brought us through the last two world wars that the Government and others keep referring to.

Unite us, Heath? Not me – and not millions like me. All I want you to do is resign and get out of politics and let Roy Jenkins, or Willie Whitelaw do the job.

Yours faithfully,
R. C. Colyer

Streakers and Quakers

From Mr Ben Vincent   *13 March 1974*

Sir,

   May I, a Quaker Elder and 'publick Friend' protest against
the attitude of the authorities to 'streaking'? In the seventeenth
century young Friends, male and female, were often moved to
parade naked 'as a sign' (I'm not sure of what, except high
spirits). They were hounded by the Justices but I should have
expected modern governments to be less interfering.

   Solomon Eccles, alias Eagle, destroying his musical instruments, not only went nude through the City but bore on his
long locks a burning brazier and cried 'Woe unto the bloody
city,' James Nayler rode into Bristol while Friends cast their
clothes before him shouting 'Hosanna' for which he suffered a
punishment so atrocious that even the grim parliamentarians
were ashamed of themselves afterwards.

   Such punishments proved of no avail. The Society proli-
ferated. But it began to shrink when the eighteenth-century
descendants of these young enthusiasts, now no longer ferociously penalized, became so staid that their shovel hats and
bonnets attracted more derision than their grandparents'
nudity. Early the following century they became a bourgeois
coterie of bankers, brewers and cocoa-growers.

   If you leave the streakers alone the same fate will befall
them. Meanwhile I think we should be grateful to a set who,
at great inconvenience to themselves, provide us without
charge such innocent entertainment. I'm a bit fed up with
The Times for denying us pictures of them.

                              Yours faithfully,
                              BEN VINCENT

[A good week for streaking: in Calgary, Alberta, despite
a temperature of − 4°F, and in St Louis, Missouri, where
two students entered the front door and left by the back
of the Penrose district police station]

Christian Names in 1973

From Mr J. W. Leaver   *10 January 1974*

Sir,

In accordance with past practice I send you my annual statement of the most frequently chosen Christian names given to children whose birth or adoption was announced on the back page of *The Times*. The figures for 1973:

BOYS			GIRLS		
James (1)	...	... 214	Jane (1)	...	... 125
John (2)	...	... 152	Elizabeth (3) ...		... 123
Alexander (3) ...		... 124	Louise (2)	...	... 109
Edward (4)	...	... 124	Mary (4)	...	... 101
William (5)	...	... 112	Sarah (5)	...	... 71
Charles (6)	...	... 103	Emma (9)	...	... 67
Richard (9)	...	... 98	Catherine (11) ...		... 65
Thomas (8)	...	... 92	Caroline (14) ...		... 61
Robert (14)	...	... 87	Lucy (7)	...	... 61
David (7)	...	... 87	Charlotte (8) ...		... 55

(The figures in parentheses indicate the place occupied in the list for 1972.)

Among the boys James occupies the first position for the tenth consecutive year, while 'the team' includes Robert to the exclusion of Nicholas (now 11th with a score of 82). During 1973 Benjamin displayed considerable increase in popularity, as did Francis and Hugh to a lesser degree. On the other hand, Christopher, Dominic, George and Stephen failed to maintain the favour they had received from parents in 1972.

The leading place in the top ten for the girls is yet again filled by Jane as has now been the case for 17 successive years. Caroline and Catherine take the places of Clare and Victoria who are now 14th and 11th respectively. Camilla, Fiona, Helen, Kate and Sophie have returned higher totals, whereas Anne, Charlotte, Jane, Louise and Lucy are among the names that showed lower scores than in the previous year.

It may be of interest to mention that while during 1973 many Biblical Christian names (of both sexes) continued to be consistent in appeal, there were two further instances of increase in popularity, viz. Joshua and Hannah.

The 'first names only' table again shows James and Emma at the head of their respective sections:

BOYS		GIRLS	
James (1)	93	Emma (1)	57
Nicholas (3)	70	Lucy (4)	44
Thomas (5)	69	Charlotte (5)	43
Alexander (2)	66	Sarah (3)	43
Richard (7)	62	Caroline (11)	40
Edward (6)	53	Rebecca (10)	36
Robert (23)	53	Victoria (2)	35
Andrew (4)	51	Catherine (7)	35
William (8)	51	Sophie (16)	32
Jonathan (11)	44	Alexandra (11) ...	31
Matthew (13)	44	Katherine (6)	31

The further analysis of 'happy events' that occurred in 1973, as announced on the back page of your paper up to and including today's issue, reveals 5,173 births, of which 2,646 were boys, 2,526 girls and one instance where the sex was not stated. The following summary gives the number of Christian names announced:

	One	Two	Three	Four	No Names	Total
Boys ...	396	913	427	13	897	2,646
Girls ...	415	1,105	176	6	824	2,526

The number of occasions when three Christian names were given is 603 compared with 649 in the previous year. The figure for twins born in 1973 is 62 (63 in 1972) made up of 19 boys, 21 girls and 22 mixed. There were two announcements of the birth of triplets (3 girls: 1 boy and 2 girls).

The adoptions totalled 53 and related to 27 boys and 26 girls as against 61 (21 boys and 40 girls) in 1972.

> Yours faithfully,
> JOHN W. LEAVER

[J. W. Leaver, who died on 11 February 1974, chronicled Christian names for twenty-seven years. It is worth noting that before the Second World War a child's given names were only very rarely included in the births column of *The Times*. However, the lot of women had improved. Compare an imaginary announcement for 1938:

SMITH. – On Nov. 10 at The Paddock, Warmington-on-Sea, to GLADYS (*neé* Boggs), wife of EDWARD SMITH – a daughter.

with one for 1913:

SMYTHE. – On the 10th November, in Jubbulpore, the wife of CAPTAIN HECTOR SMYTHE, 23rd Dragoon Guards, of a son. Colonial papers, please copy]

Half a Skeleton in the Cupboard

From Mrs Joan Tucker   *13 June 1974*

Sir,

When my elder son began his medical training seven years ago he paid £10 for half a human skeleton. Three years later my younger son entered medical school, and the value of these bones had risen to £20. My daughter is soon to train as a physiotherapist, and one of her requirements is half a human skeleton. And the cost now? £40 to £50.

What better investment than a skeleton in the cupboard?

Yours faithfully,
JOAN TUCKER

What the Economic Future Holds?

From Professor I. F. Pearce   *17 January 1974*

[Professor of Economics, University of Southampton]

Sir,

Many of our current economic difficulties, not to mention those which evidently lie ahead, arise directly out of widespread beliefs which are in fact mistaken.

It could do nothing but good if during the present crisis, on each and every day *The Times* and all other newspapers, together with all three television channels, exhibited the figures quoted below in such a way that the simple truth they embody cannot be missed. Let it be explained also that for technical reasons which anyone is quite free to investigate it is logically impossible that the numbers given could be so far wrong as to make any appreciable difference to the conclusions we are bound to draw from them.

1. In 1972, which is the most recent year for which we have the full figures, the value of all goods and services produced in the UK and sold amounted to about £62 thousand million. This includes government goods and services as well as those purchased by persons out of profits, wages, rent and income from capital of all kinds however obtained.

2. Of this approximately 20 per cent is taken in direct taxation for essential government expenditure. A further 18 per cent must go to maintain or renew the 'means of production' whether or not these are owned by 'capitalists' or 'workers'. This leaves a total of £39 thousand million of goods and services available at 172 prices to workers, management, capitalists, children and others.

3. The total population in 1972 was not far from 55 million.

4. If therefore total income available were equally divided, each man, woman and child would receive £700 per annum. The take-home pay of a worker with a wife and two children would be £54 per week. An old age pensioner and his wife would receive £27 per week and an unmarried worker would earn £14 per week. There is nothing else left in the barrel unless production is increased above the 1972 level.

Those who rely for their evidence on casual observation of the behaviour and apparent consumption of the very rich will find these figures hard to believe; but they are roughly correct and if they are not, in the near future, universally accepted as correct and widely understood, their truth will be made apparent the hard way.

Unrealistic aspirations will not be met. Inflation will continue at an ever-increasing rate with consequential horrors which only a student of economic history can begin to understand. Economic justice cannot be pursued by pretending that there exists a pot of gold which has only to be tapped to provide affluence for all. Those who ask for more should be required to say who should get less and why and to demonstrate that the books can be balanced at the national level.

Yours faithfully,

IVOR PEARCE

The First Picket?

[The General Election of 28 February 1974 saw the return of a minority Labour government]

From Mr J. G. Mavrogordato   *28 March 1974*

Sir,

Mr Michael Foot's proposal to give pickets power to insist that drivers, etc, stop and listen to their case has a precedent in the case of the Ancient Mariner (the first recorded picket?).

True, he stopped. only one of three; but he was of course single-handed. He at first held the Wedding Guest with his skinny hands, but, realizing that this might amount to intimidation, eftsoons his hand dropt he; being content thereafter to hold him with his glittering eye.

The Wedding Guest could not choose but hear; though he evidenced his reluctance by beating his breast, not once but twice.

The Ancient Mariner, no doubt deliberately, took so inordinately long a time to put his case that he forced the Wedding Guest to miss the wedding – presumably the real objective of the picketing.

Yours faithfully,
J. G. Mavrogordato

Aid to Gun-Running

From Mr N. D. J. Lane   3 May 1974

Sir,

I once purchased, in the Grand Bazaar of Istanbul, and at ruinous expense, an elderly musket about five feet long and with a stock riddled with woodworm. I wrapped it most carefully in copies of the airmail edition of *The Times* and drove home with it.

Of course, it arrived in one piece. But I was even more impressed by the fact that at the innumerable border posts on the journey, from a Turkish Nissen hut to a wet and crowded Dover at four in the morning, *The Times* seemed to insulate it completely from more than a cursory glance from a comprehensive selection of Europe's customs officers. I cannot say, Sir, what might have happened had I sought the protection of a lesser journal.

Yours faithfully,
N. D. J. Lane

Ruination of Lord's—2

From Sir Brian Batsford   *14 June 1974*

Sir,

Much of the enjoyment of watching cricket, especially on television, is now marred by advertising.

The batsman's stroke, the bowler's run up or the catch in the slips is no longer seen against the traditional green of the cricket field or the white rails of the pavilion, but instead against the incongruous and garish board of an advertisement.

Is there no authority in the world of cricket, of advertising or of government which can halt this steady deterioration in our standards?

Yours faithfully,
BRIAN BATSFORD

[There is also a betting shop at Lord's]

Mr Prentice and Mr Foot

[Mr Michael Foot (Secretary of State for Employment), seeking to solve the nation's problems by application of a 'social contract', had not received full support from Mr Reginald Prentice (Secretary of State for Education)]

From Professor Joel Hurstfield   *4 March 1975*

[member of the War Cabinet Offices 1942–6; later Astor Professor of History, University College, London]

Sir,

I have no wish to intervene in the exchange of pleasantries between Mr Prentice and Mr Foot save to protest that, on the eve of St David's Day, Mr Prentice directed a gratuitous insult at the Land of my Fathers-in-Law whence (I trust) before long a bardic thunderbolt will descend upon him.

I do, however, sympathize with the Prime Minister who apparently feels that Mr Prentice's speech should first have been passed through the Department of Employment. I was myself a Civil Servant during five instructive years so I think that I know the kind of speech which would have emerged. Instead of warning the trade unions about 'welshing' the passage would have read:

299

With the very greatest respect, might I suggest to the miners' leaders that the recent award while, on the one hand, it clearly falls within the social contract; could on the other hand be regarded, by those unfamiliar with contemporary industrial techniques, as perhaps falling marginally outside the contract.

Mr Foot's observation about 'economic illiteracy' would have emerged if he had submitted it to the Ministry of Education, as follows:

In so far as my colleague Mr Prentice has made certain observations about contemporary industrial developments which, it would appear to some of us, must be received a little sceptically, it is to be hoped that, when the Ministry of Education has finally pressed forward with its goal of mass comprehensivization, some of this tremendous success will be reflected in the Minister of Education who will emerge as better equipped to understand the economy and more literate to comment upon it.

If Mr Prentice and Mr Foot remain members of Mr Wilson's Cabinet I shall be happy as a former Civil Servant to place my services at their disposal.

Your obedient servant,
JOEL HURSTFIELD

[A former employer of Professor Hurstfield might have reacted with a memorandum: 'This is English up with which I will not put.']

Why French?

[On 5 March 1975 Rolls-Royce announced the Carmargue]

From Mr Ralph Sheldon   *8 March 1975*

Sir,
Why, Oh why does Rolls-Royce, brightest diamond in the crown of British technological achievement, supported as it is by British taxpayers' money, in a time when British prestige is at its lowest ebb since the Hundred Years War, have to name its latest product after an area of French marshland?
Have we no British bogs to commemorate? Surely Dun Fell,

Char Moss, Baldersdale, Wastwater, Swinside or Muckish would more aptly evoke the antics of our present masters and the state of the nation or, if it is thought that these British names lack commercial appeal how about Abadan, Dallas, Frankfurt, Zurich or Cayman, to give us a silver ghost of a chance in the golden markets of the world.

Yours sincerely,
RALPH SHELDON

Surprises in Churches

From the Reverend H. Benson   *14 March 1975*

Sir,

Sometimes the truth is more surprising than the myth. I quote from Wordsworth: 'Our churches, invariably perhaps, stand east and west, but *why* is by few persons *exactly* known; nor, that the degree of deviation from *due* east often noticeable in the ancient ones was determined, in each particular case, by the point in the horizon, at which the sun rose upon the day of the saint to whom the church was dedicated.'

I have made a study of this over a number of years and have examined nearly a thousand churches. I am convinced that Wordsworth has been dismissed too soon. Careful calculations show that a considerable number of churches do face sunrise precisely on their patronal festivals – or did when they were built. The rest are equally surprising, with only half a dozen exceptions they all faced sunrise on some other important saints day. Who can say that this was not their original dedication?

Now it follows that a church built in honour of St Mary, for example, and facing sunrise on 25 March, would after a century or so, owing to the Julian calendar, be found to be facing too far south. If then a new chancel was built, it would be set out to face the new sunrise position. Hence the crooked chancel. There are 81 crooked churches in Oxfordshire alone and every one of them supports this thesis. The crookedness of the chancel, far from being due to carelessness, is due to a most scrupulous care.

Yours faithfully,
HUGH BENSON

Valentine Senders

From Mr Jeremy Mortimer   *19 February 1975*

Sir,

I was interested to see from your St Valentine's Day message column on 14 February that what appears to be a substantial proportion of *The Times* readership are named after rabbits, birds, mice and fictional characters. Are these the people who are announced at birth as being plain James or Anthony, Mary or Elizabeth? If so have they found with romantic attachment the temporary solace of disappearing into a world of innocence populated by no one harsher than Piglet and no one more exciting than Tinkabell? Or is there actually a section of society, unknown to many of us, communicating with each other through a soft series of 'miaous' and sentimental 'coos' and only surfacing once a year in the columns of *The Times*?

Yours,
JEREMY MORTIMER

Towards Armageddon

1975-1980

LIFE continued after the hymns to Piddletrenthide and Mucking, a correspondent reporting that he had picked mushrooms near St Paul's. More common was bitterness expressed in questions. Why wasn't a dog licence at least £5? Why did an experienced solicitor get offered only £400 a year more than inexperienced typist? What was this nonsense about workers in the board room when there were already many such workers – *directors*? Would the Master of the Rolls kindly refrain from changing any more laws until a student had taken her examination? And while it was all very well for a bishop to judge a Miss Great Britain beauty contest, what if the strutting pulchritude should insist on appointing bishops? Letters were signed by gentlemen whose given names were Nick (a headmaster), Mike and Steve. Trade union power threatened apoplexy, a correspondent suffered a seizure on buying a tin of sardines only to find its contents were physically retarded and four in number.

1975 reacted strongly to index-linked pensions.

The perfect summer of 1976 prompted the view that 'God loves England. Ladybirds abounded, an eyebrow was raised at the creation of Lady Falkender. The Chancellor of the Exchequer, Mr Healey, was rebuked for speaking of 'tiny Chinese minds', Mr Michael Foot for making May Day a public holiday. The idea of televising the House of Commons appalled, threatening – as it did – the livelihood of professional comedians. The father of three daughters asked why the cost of weddings should fall on him and his like. He was advised to organize elopements or double weddings; his eldest daughter intervened with 'Auction me!' The sight of private helicopters at Glyndebourne irked some; others pointed to the number of employed admirals – four times as many, relative to the strength of the Royal Navy, as in 1913. The way to write to parsons was debated: to a stranger 'Reverend Sir', although British India had sometimes preferred 'Reverend and Bombastic Sir'. A Rabbi was resigned to the Inland Revenue addressing him 'Dear Rabbit'.

1976 reacted strongly to index-linked pensions.

Divorce by post worried 1977, a disillusioned husband stating categorically that 'women can't boil eggs'. When a television company followed *Jesus of Nazareth* with a book of the film, a gentle voice intervened with 'But surely this already exists?' Two questions went unanswered: if a picket was entitled to put his case to a Grunwick worker, why was it inappropriate for a worker to put his case to pickets? And why do bishops always laugh when caught by the camera? Perhaps something to do with judging beauty contests.

1977 reacted strongly to index-linked pensions.

Football hooliganism and the quality of British Rail food occupied 1978. Sociologists were held to bore millions, striking hospital porters seen as a sign of the times. The outcome of a national study by the Institute of Mathematics disconcerted, only $6 \cdot 5$ per cent of school leavers achieving full marks when asked to solve problems like

$$35 + 14 = ? \qquad 13 \cdot 5 \div 5 = ? \qquad \text{What is } \tfrac{2}{3} \text{ of nine?}$$

Correspondents were indignant when it was suggested they themselves could not do such sums. Herr Axel Springer hailed *The Times* as 'the London queen of all newspapers'. Whereupon, on 30 November, the paper closed down, so preventing 1978 from continuing to react strongly to index-linked pensions.

Almost a year later New Printing House Square returned to business, just in time for 1979 to say what it thought of the word 'sheepmeat'. Before long, 'cowmeat'. Early in 1980 it was clear that everyone's pay was falling behind, the question 'Then whose is in front?' confounding correspondents. Riots in Bristol encouraged wisdom after the event. The BBC had a bad year, its desire to purge several orchestras being criticized by Sir Adrian Boult in London, and by Maestro Giulini from Los Angeles. A television programme on Brain Death united the medical profession. Then suddenly a notice was affixed to *The Times* – FOR SALE. Colchester's equivalent of John Wayne and the Fifth Cavalry prepared to gallop to the rescue (see letter, 31 October 1980).

The year reacted strongly to index-linked pensions.

Personally Speaking

From the Public Orator, Oxford University   *5 April 1975*

Sir,

Our legislators are regrettably no longer distinguished for verbal felicity, but since far-reaching powers are, it seems, to be vested in the Equal Opportunities Commission, the once-great British Public must exercise its inalienable right, before it relinquishes the last shreds of personal freedom left to it, to be consulted by the new-fangled device of a referendum on the choice of words it will be allowed to use. The suggested —*person* suffixes to replace the unacceptable termination in —*man* produce some curious additions to the dictionary, so that the claims of rivals, such as —*body* (eg *pigbody, cowbody,* and *ploughbody*, which have an attractively agricultural ring) should be seriously considered.

Unfortunately our legislators' proposals show that they have not the vision to finish the job off. They have failed to consult vested interests: the crossword industry will have strong views. Here *signalperson* will commend itself since it is made up of *sign + Alp + Norse* (anag) whence ready-made clues suggest themselves: signalbody lacks this virtue.

Song-writers are vitally affected: 'My old person's a dustperson' makes a casualty of a catchy tune. The Church is not exempt: the Rt Rev the Bishop of Sodor and Man must submit either to embodiment or impersonation. Geographers in particular are in serious legal jeopardy: the Tasman Sea must in future be the Tasbody (or Tasperson) Sea, while Manchester must resign itself to becoming Personchester or Bodychester, with grievous consequences for the postcodes of the surrounding countryside, while the residents of Godmanchester deserve special sympathy.

Further afield the Sultanate of Oman must recognize itself as Operson or Obody. Academe too is threatened: holders of degrees in social anthropology will be suspect, to say the least, but will justly complain if they have to enter the employment market with a DPhil (PhD) in social gynandrology, with its unsavoury ambiguity.

For my part I shall cheerfully go to the stake or the concentration camp for my contumacious determination to admire and even worship women for their charm, skill in housewifery and other distinctive virtues, while turning my blind masculine eye to any countervailing characteristics which, as one of the few survivors of the nearly extinct breed of gentlepersons (gentlebodies), I have, like the ancient Greek historian, 'forgotten on purpose'.

Believe me to be, Sir, in deadly earnest,

Your obedient servant,
JOHN G. GRIFFITH

Common or Garden Gnome

From Mr Hanno Koppel   *21 May 1975*

Sir,

I have been reading the recent correspondence in your columns, on wildlife in London with the greatest of interest. I am, however, sorry that no mention has been made of one of this country's most fascinating beasts – the common, or garden gnome. Though prevalent in the lusher suburbs, this retiring creature appears to be most scarce in the city. I am happy to report that there is a mating pair of gnomes in our garden, and I have hopes that a brood of young will be reared before the autumn. I wonder whether other London dwellers have made similar sightings.

Yours faithfully,
HANNO KOPPEL

Navigating the Greek Trireme

From the President of Wolfson College, Cambridge
4 October 1975

Sir,

Thank you for giving space to such a fascinating and instructive correspondence. May I try to cast the account? All good men seem to agree to the following:

1. That oared ships did not go into battle under sail;
2. That the Greek trireme used full oar power, to produce up to $11\frac{1}{2}$ knots in short bursts, only in battle or in emergency;
3. That oared ships did not put to sea when the wind was unfavourable, rowed out of harbour and then either hoisted sail or continued rowing according to the state of the wind;
4. That a trireme's speed in still water under oar can be

credibly calculated to have been five to six knots with one division rowing, a little more with two;

5. And that this calculation does not conflict with Xenophon's '120 nautical miles under oar in a long day.' The word he uses can only mean the hours of daylight. So, with 15 hours of daylight plus one hour of twilight at latitude 42° on midsummer day, the speed works out at seven knots and a half, but there would have been little help from the current for the last 103½ miles. According to the Navigation Department of the National Maritime Museum, Black Sea currents run counterclockwise, but through the Bosphorus there is a north-south current because of the 17in difference of levels at each end. The later MSS of Xenophon have a variant reading 'a *very* long day', which suggests that the scribe shared your correspondents' feeling that Xenophon was exaggerating a bit. Etesian winds blowing with the current through the Bosphorus would have kept a galley in port.

Lord St David's galleys were the *a scaloccio* type of the second half of the sixteenth century with gangs of men pulling and in some cases also pushing, very long sweeps. A contemporary admiral reported them slower, in spite of greater manpower, than the earlier *a zenzile* galleys in which three or four men sat at benches set herringbone fashion, each rowing an oar of 30ft or so. Dr Tarn was rightly impatient of the theory then current that the ships of high numerical denominator in the Hellenistic navies had many banks of oars; and suggested instead that the Greeks must have had an *a zenzile* system for triremes and *a scaloccio* systems for the rest. The first part of this suggestion has been rejected because:

1. The Greek trireme's oars were 12⅔ or 13⅓ft long (the longer oars amidships and, surprisingly, no difference between the levels);

2. an *a zenzile* galley rowing 170 men would have been far too long to fit into the known length of the Piraeus trireme sheds, the three-level system being (obviously) more economical of space.

There are other more detailed, equally cogent, reasons but these two are conclusive. Tarn was quite right about the ships of numerical denominator higher than three. They must have rowed more than one man to an oar at no more than three levels, usually, to judge from the monuments, at two. And the numerical denominator has nothing to do with levels, as people still tend to think; but indicates the power to which the original rowing unit had been raised by the various developments (i.e.

3, 4, 5, 6, etc. men to the oar-room, the space between the row-locks, irrespective of level). A three-level trireme does not imply a four-level quadrireme.

Two final points:

1. The men who rowed the Athenian galleys in the fifth century were not slaves, indeed the slaves who rowed exceptionally at Arginusae were given their freedom for it.

2. If the hashish-carrying Punic warship reported in your columns is the one about which Miss Honor Frost has recently published excavation reports, it is too small to be a trireme.

Yours faithfully,
JOHN MORRISON

Nocturnal Bells

[Mr Antony Gasson appeared at Marlborough Street Magistrates' Court on 29 July 1975 charged with having kicked a burglar-alarm from the wall outside his bedsitting room. He was conditionally discharged for a year – no order being made for compensation]

From Mr Patrick Napper   *4 August 1978*

Sir,

The recent case of Mr Gasson, who silenced a burglar-alarm in Chelsea, prompts me to write regarding this much unpublicized invasion of one's peace.

My top-floor maisonette in Chelsea's King's Road lies in the heart of 'boutique-land'. During my 17 years stay the alarm-bell situation has become impossible to live with. Bells go off during the night approximately one night in every three. Our bedroom overlooks the King's Road, our children sleep in relative peace at the back.

When I telephone the police they say they can only attempt to contact the key-holder, who is frequently uncontactable and who, even if contacted can merely return to sleep, leaving the bell to ring all night. These nocturnal bells continue for at least $1\frac{1}{2}$ hours during which our sleep is totally ruined: many continue throughout the night. My wife and I are becoming nervous wrecks.

Surely an alarm-bell should alert people of a break-in? No one, however, seems to take any notice. A good time, it seems, to do a burglary!

I pay high rates and I am desperate, probably as was Mr Gasson, to find out what I can do to minimize this Chinese torture we have suffered for so long.

Yours faithfully,
PATRICK NAPPER

Dogs by Motorail

From Mr Gerald Williams   *14 July 1975*

Sir,

I am taking my wife and two dogs to Scotland and back by British Railways Motorail. My wife gets one side of a compartment to herself plus blankets and pillow. The dogs sleep on the floor, but they cost me five pence more than my wife.

Yours faithfully,
GERALD WILLIAMS

From Mr Max Lightwood   *8 August 1975*

Sir,

If Mr Williams in taking his wife and two dogs to Scotland by train gives the dogs one side of the compartment plus blankets and pillow, and puts his wife to sleep on the floor – as plainly British Rail intends and right thinking people would consider reasonable and proper – then can he not say with some satisfaction that to take his wife cost him 5p less than the dogs?

Yours faithfully,
MAX LIGHTWOOD

[Mr Lightwood is clearly a disciple of Sir Almroth Wright – see page 25]

Design of Modern Postage Stamps

From Mr A. B. Innes Dick   *1 June 1976*

Sir,

Concern must be felt in philatelic circles, as well as by those of the public who care, about the design of the postage stamps which will commemorate next year's Silver Jubilee of Her Majesty's Accession.

Ever since the introduction of commemorative stamps the designs have been getting increasingly unsuitable to provide the dignity and good taste so essential for British postage stamps. The frequency of the issues of new stamps is, no doubt, for the benefit of the New Issue Department; perhaps the Post Office's only profit earner?

It is a sad thought that a nation which, for so many years in the nineteenth century, produced such works of art as the 'Penny Black' and other classic issues for Empire countries should have sunk to postcard-like pictures of, amongst other things, the modern restaurant of a provincial university.

In his recent autobiography Lord Clark tells of the earnest wish expressed to him by King George V that British stamps should always retain their traditional design, containing only the Sovereign's head, the word 'Postage' and the value, these being all that was necessary for good design. Events have proved him to have been only too right.

In later years, after Lord Clark had become Chairman of the Stamp Design Committee, he resigned from it rather than accept the idea of illustrative stamps. But could he not be persuaded to take up this responsibility again, with the Jubilee issue in mind, and let public opinion pass judgment on the result?

Yours etc.,
A. B. INNES DICK

Times Past

From Mr Patrick Ide　　　　　　　　　　　　*17 June 1976*

Sir,

For a newspaper titled *The Times* you seem singularly rash about your timepieces. I read in today's Diary (15 June) that the Henry Moore sundial intended for the courtyard of your last new building was sold to *The Observer* and is now in Brussels.

I can testify that when your original building was pulled down the clock, centrepiece of your masthead was sold for £50 because I bought it and your readers may like to know that I turned the cast-iron face into a sundial in a courtyard that I built specially at my home in Sussex where the clock enjoys a peaceful retirement surrounded at its base by, what else (?), several varieties of thyme.

I remain, Sir, yours faithfully,
PATRICK IDE

The British Malaise

From Mr Merlin Minshall   *25 June 1976*

Sir,

Admiral Clutterbuck (23 June) suggests that British industrial management needs, to cure its current malaise, the administrative efficiency of the fighting services, which the Admiral assures us has never since World War I 'been accused of deficiency in good management'. Surely Admiral Clutterbuck must be joking.

During the whole of the five years that I spent in the wartime RNVR (1939–45) I witnessed an inefficiency of management that would have run any industrial concern out of business in a matter of weeks.

Was the passage of the Scharnhorst and Gneisenau through the Straits of Dover an example of good management? *The Times* described it by saying: 'Nothing more mortifying to the pride of our sea power has happened since the seventeenth century.' Was it good management for the Royal Navy to need (I quote Churchill) 'forty-seven ships to sink the Bismark.' Were Dunkirk, Arnhem and the quite unnecessary destruction of Dresden examples of good management? And what about the cod war?

The present malaise of Britain stems not from managerial inefficiency but from our self-satisfied refusal to admit that the malaise exists.

Yours sincerely,
MERLIN MINSHALL

A Window Tax

From Mr Brian Sterry Ashby   *4 June 1976*

Sir,

May I suggest the reintroduction of a Window Tax? First

311

levied in this country in 1696 under William III and finally re-
pealed in 1851, it may again be relevant today.

Consider the glass-walled prestige office block, and the
picture windows of the modern executive mansion, compared
with the small sparse windows of the workingman's council
house, and the slit and mullioned windows of the impoverished
nobleman's castle. Is this the simple and fair method of assess-
ing local taxes for which we are searching?

Yours faithfully,
BRIAN STERRY ASHBY

An Awkward Shortage

From Dr Alec Vidler   *6 May 1976*

Sir,

I shall be grateful if you will allow me to draw public attention to the hardship that is increasingly experienced by septua-
genarian men when they are away from home, and *a fortiori*
by octogenarians and nonagenarians. I refer to the disappearance of the chamber pot as an article of bedroom furniture, or
rather of guest room furniture. Of course some bedrooms have
a bathroom directly attached to them and in that case I make
no complaint. But, like many of my contemporaries, I am often
invited to spend the night in a room that has no such convenience. We do not like to disturb our hosts by wandering
about dark passages in quest of light switches and uncertain
doors and at last by the noise of flushing.

We plead for the restoration of the traditional chamber pot
to its rightful place either under the bed or in a bedside cabinet.
It is true that most of them now seem to have found their
way into antique shops and thence to the United States. But
various sizes in plastic are obtainable and, for my part, I am
ready to settle for one of those as a substitute for an elegant
piece of china.

I would add that I entirely agree with the late Dick Sheppard
that the recipients of such relief should always be responsible
in the morning for emptying and cleansing any receptacle
which they have used, and not leave that operation as a chore
for their hostess or any minion of hers.

Yours faithfully,
ALEC VIDLER

Sir,
   Dr Vidler should take his own chamber pot when visiting.
Packed in the ordinary suitcase in a neat plastic cover, it
makes a useful receptacle for sponge bags, socks, collar studs,
draft sermons and so on.

Yours faithfully,
A. V. COTTAM

Sir,
   Canon Vidler's problem is, by all accounts, not new. Was
there not a clergyman who complained of Lambeth Palace that
there were 40 bedrooms and only 39 articles?

I have the honour to be your obedient servant,
TOBY ROBERTSON

Sir,
   Those of your readers who have recently been deploring the
decline in the use of the chamber pot may like to know that a
personal chamber pot is still supplied by British Rail to passengers travelling by first-class sleeper between Edinburgh and
London. It is a light and elegant model, and is contained in a
specially designed rack under the wash-basin. It is clear that
British Rail planners have given considerable thought to its
provision, and a carefully worded notice gives guidance in its
use. This facility is not, I understand, available for second-class
passengers.
   It is a disturbing thought that the chamber pot – once a
classless and functional object in the days of Victorian utilitar-
ianism – is becoming our newest status symbol.

Yours faithfully,
ALAN THOMPSON

[The professor wrongs British Rail. Second-class passengers
are likewise served]

From Mr John Herbert   *22 May 1976*

Sir,
  Far from using it, well-mannered people do not even remark on it.

      Yours sincerely,
      JOHN HERBERT

No Sunday Post Collection

From Sir Robert Lusty   *17 March 1977*

Sir,
  The actions and reactions of the Post Office render coherent thought almost impossible. So besotted are they with their own inefficiencies that they spare no effort to impose these on others.
  Their casual refusal to reinstate Sunday collections must be against the wishes of virtually every one of their customers. Were they not a monopoly such a decision would put them rapidly out of business. It is not simply the loss of a Sunday collection. It confounds almost the entire week. In this area (and I think in most others) there is virtually no collection between Friday afternoon and Monday morning. The one on Saturday is made at 9.30 am which is practically useless.
  The Post Office seems obsessed with the passion to invest hundreds of millions of pounds in telephonic enterprises. Their business is communication and the posting of a letter is as important a part of it as making a telephone call. I do not know, but my guess is that the majority of their captive customers would prefer the ability to post a letter on Sunday than to dial a call to Afghanistan.

      Yours faithfully,
      ROBERT LUSTY

Slow Post

From Mr John Turner   *4 October 1976*

Sir,
  A letter was delivered this week to a busy doctor's surgery in a scarred and perforated envelope. In explanation a Post

314

Office official had added the legend 'Found adhering to a snail.'
Comment would be superfluous.

Yours faithfully,
JOHN M. TURNER

Trade Union Immunity under the Law

From Professor F. A. Hayek, FBA   *21 July 1977*

[Nobel prize in Economic Science 1974]

Sir,

When will the British public at last learn to understand that
there is no salvation for Britain until the special privileges
granted to the trade unions by the Trades Disputes Act of 1906
are revoked? Mr Robert Moss is probably right when in his
recent book he writes that 'the Liberals who blithely passed a
Bill drawn up by the first generation of Labour MPs in keeping of an electoral promise quite literally had no idea what
they were doing'.

But they were soon unmistakably told. A. V. Dicey presently
spoke of the Act of 1906 as having conferred 'upon a trade
union a freedom from civil liability for the commission of even
the most heinous wrong by the union or its servant, and in
short conferred upon every trade union a privilege and protection not possessed by any other person or body of persons,
whether corporate or incorporate. The law makes a trade union
a privileged body exempted from the ordinary law of the land.'

And in 1925 another great jurist, Sir Paul Vinogradoff,
again emphasized that 'the Trades Disputes Act of 1906 conferred upon the unions an immunity from prosecution on the
ground of tortious acts of their agents; the immunity stands in
flagrant disagreement with the law of agency and the law as
to companies represented by their officers in accordance with
the Statutory Order of 1883.'

In 1942 a foreign economist intimately familiar with British
affairs, the late Professor Joseph Schumpeter, looking back on
developments, wrote that 'it is difficult, at the present time,
to realize how this measure must have struck people who still
believed in a state and in a legal system that centred in the institution of private property. For in relaxing the law of con-
spiracy in respect to peaceful picketing – which practically
amounted to legalization of trade union action implying the
threat of force – and in exempting trade union funds from

liability in action for damages *for torts* – which practically amounted to enacting that trade unions could do no wrong – this measure in fact resigned to the trade unions part of the authority of the state and granted to them a position of privilege which the formal extension of the exemption to employers' unions was powerless to affect.'

And only twenty years ago Lord MacDermott reiterated that, in short, the act 'put trade unionism in the same privileged position which the Crown enjoyed until ten years ago in respect to wrongful acts committed on its behalf'.

Yet still, when the fatal effects of this are before everybody's eyes, nobody dares to consider removing the source of all that misfortune.

There can indeed be little doubt to a detached observer that the privileges then granted to the trade unions have become the chief source of Britain's economic decline. It is an illusion to believe that a Labour government is in a better position to deal with the unions. It is no use suggesting to them moderation when they do all that harm by exercising their chartered rights.

A Labour government cannot touch the sacred charter which is the authorization of all this licence. The public hardly yet understands that the power of the trade unions to destroy the economy has been conferred on them as a special privilege by an irresponsible government buying a few more years of power. That fatal mistake must be undone if Britain is to recover. No government can pull the country out of the mire unless it obtains at the elections an explicit mandate to revoke the unique privileges which the trade unions have enjoyed too long. Only such a power can enable a Conservative government to reverse the trend towards abject poverty.

I am, etc.,

F. A. HAYEK

Their First Cuckoo?

From Mr David Mallon   *25 June 1977*

[writing from the Mongolian State University at Ulan Bator]

Sir,

I heard today the first cuckoo of this year. Is this a record for Outer Mongolia?

Yours faithfully,

DAVID MALLON

[Mr Mallon's letter was written on 4 June, its means of transit presumably by slow camel]

Elderly Travellers

From Lord Clark, OM, CH, FBA   *15 April 1977*

Sir,

Contrary to a widely held view, elderly people are human. They want to visit their friends and relations, go to concerts and exhibitions and even do a few days' shopping in the metropolis. Many of them drive a car but would dread taking it to London owing to the difficulties of parking and their unfamiliarity with the London traffic. They therefore take a train.

Once in one's seat there is no pleasanter form of travelling, but if an elderly man or woman arrives at a London station with a heavy suitcase what is he or she to do? There are no porters and very few trolleys.

Worse still when a train gets in to London if his compartment is at the back, for he will find himself marooned at the far end of a long platform. All he can do is sit down on his baggage and hope that some member of the station staff, perhaps a kindly cleaner, will come his way.

I have mentioned London, but there are many other examples, of which the worst is Oxford, where the arrival exit has been closed, and the traveller has to carry his baggage down and up two flights of steep stairs in order to reach the ticket barrier. Yet Oxford must contain an exceptionally large number of distinguished elderly people whose visits to London, Cambridge and other places of learning would be a benefit to the community.

The philosophy of social service has closed for the idea that after 75 or even 70, people should settle down, live on their pensions and not move about. This may be true of a majority; but the reputation of a country depends on a minority of outstanding people, and a good many of these (I need not give examples) are over 70. I may add that the predicament is equally serious for a young mother with children.

I asked a railwayman whom I have known for many years what he thought of the situation. He said it was a source of shame to him and his colleagues.

I am, yours faithfully,
KENNETH CLARK

317

On the Bread Line

From Mr Eric King   *14 September 1977*

Sir,

What superb timing by Mr Peter Jay to reveal to the world that his father-in-law, Prime Minister James Callaghan, sees himself in the role of Moses just as the bread strike was about to take effect.

When, in Exodus 34, the people complained to Moses of a lack of bread, you will recall that the Lord said unto Moses: 'Behold I will rain bread from Heaven upon you: and the people shall go out and gather a certain rate each day, that I may prove them whether they will walk in my law or no.'

We can but wonder now whether any word from on high has reached Downing Street.

Yours faithfully,
ERIC KING

[Mr Peter Jay was Ambassador to the United States of America 1977–9]

An Author's Earnings

From Mr David Holbrook   *5 September 1977*

Sir,

I am glad to see that some *Mirror* Group printers are considering the offer of a weekly payment of £174 for a 34-hour week. I am one of those whose words they print, an independent author.

Last year, my accountant tells me, I earned something like £53 a week gross for a 70-hour week. But by the time I deducted postage, telephone, typing costs, and stationery (£1,025) from £2,790, this left only just enough to pay for my rent, insurance, heat, light, cleaning, transport and auditor etc – leaving me nothing to *live* on. I should perhaps add that expenses for post, telephone, and such items rose by £400 in the period above the previous year, largely because of trade union achievements. I was saved by an Arts Council grant of £40 a week, but this year I do not have any such assistance and wonder how I am going to survive.

There was a time when, as a professional in adult education,

I used to give my services at reduced rates to trade unions, to help promote understanding of social issues. Perhaps now the tables are turned, so to speak, the earners of high wages should pay a levy to help subsidize such people as authors?

It seems clear that, however successful a serious writer, he can no longer survive in a time of inflation and high wages rises. A visit to the public library confirms that one's work is useful: the only question remains – how is it to be rewarded?

Yours, etc.,

DAVID HOLBROOK

National Front Manifesto: Effect on the Young

From Mrs J. Fearne   *1 September 1977*

Sir,

With reference to the appeal that the National Front appears to have for teenagers, particularly boys, I think perhaps I can throw a glimmer of light.

My son, now 22, felt at the age of 16 and 17 that the NF was the only party holding out some hope for England and the English. He was disenchanted with the policies of the Left, who he felt soft-bedded those with no desire to work and the coloured people – brought up to disagree with colour prejudice, working in close quarters with a certain section of the coloured community changed his outlook completely. The Conservatives held no appeal as he felt they were ineffective, trying to please all voters.

He desperately wanted to be proud of England and identify with a party that was 100 per cent for the English, he felt 'The Front' could weld the English people together again and bring back law and order. Having fallen for some of the media propaganda, he considered that returning all coloureds home to their land of origin would ameliorate our economic and labour problems. He also believed the NF when they stated in their literature that the economic problems of the world were caused by high financiers who wished to make countries indebted to them, and would then dictate their terms, thus controlling the world.

When NF literature and members started coming to the door and he expressed his intention to join the party I became alarmed. I argued that all their literature bore a resemblance to the propaganda put out by the Nazis before the war. Eventually he agreed that we should obtain the party manifestos of all the parties, NF, Labour, Conservative and Communist, not forgetting Liberal. We went through them word for word together, comparing where possible with past and present performance.

It was an enlightening experience, but one of the things that became forcibly clear was that the colour problem was being used by the NF to gain a platform, that anyone disagreeing with their policies and ideas would receive the same rough treatment, and although not directly stated, the underlying current was that once in, it would be extremely difficult to get them out because they would take over everything, including the banks, as this was the only way to ensure their policies were carried out.

We asked for the party membership rules on many occasions; there were always excuses, but we never received a copy. (The natural conclusion was 'what have they to hide?'.) I instilled in my son that to join the party without knowing to what he was committing himself was utter folly. They wanted him to enter a local talent contest in a coloured area, so that when he lost, which was almost a foregone conclusion, they could start a hoo-hah about colour prejudice against the whites.

He no longer supports the NF but is still looking for a party that can act with firmness, that says 'work or starve' to all but the old and sick, and can give him a country and people of which he can feel proud.

There is a new breed of voter coming up, they are fed up with being taxed to the hilt to pay for those they consider a load of layabouts; they hear their country denigrated at home and abroad and having seen permissive politics and morals at work they are turning against this very permissiveness, and demanding a return to a country and people of whom they can be proud to be a part and a new party with the guts to do it.

As a rider, I would add that my son is hourly paid, state educated, and a product of post-war education and thinking – one of many who are looking in their teens to the extreme Right or Left.

Yours faithfully,
J. FEARNE

Violence at the Notting Hill Carnival

From Mrs M. Nelson-Payne   *1 September 1977*

Sir,

It was deeply upsetting to read and hear the reaction of the media to the two day Notting Hill carnival.

Why was it that the only pictures put out of the festivities were the violent ones taken on the last day, during a one hour period when a minority of rioting youths caused an affray which was quickly dealt with by the police.

I have lived here for 10 years, and as do most other members of the community, get on very well with my black neighbours and we live in peaceful harmony – perhaps with the exception of a certain 'element'.

The youth of today are all going through a violent time with so little work to be had for white or black, and I do not see the issue as a racialist one, but one based on our economic situation.

I have a grandstand view of the carnival which passes underneath my first floor windows, and with nearly a quarter of a million people dancing past to the music of the steel bands, it was very apparent that everyone of them was having a very good time, and there was no thought of agro or violence.

For the sake of the majority I would ask it to be stressed that this was a 95 per cent peaceful and happy carnival, and as a resident of the area to beg that the Notting Hill carnival be allowed to continue.

I think the police and the stewards deserve our thanks too for helping to make the occasion as peaceful as it could be with such a multitude of people.

Don't stop the carnival.

Yours faithfully,
M. NELSON-PAYNE

A Wife's Worth

From Canon A. C. A. Smith   *1 March 1978*

Sir,

'She's worth her weight in gold!' I would say: and many of your readers sharing the sentiment would echo the saying, thinking of their own wives. But, Sir, I wonder how many of those who give their wives that worth have ever paused to work it out.

Estimating, and without sparing her blushes, my wife at, say 9 stone, gives the following interesting calculation:

9 stone = 126lb = 2,016oz.

Gold, according to your financial column, was (February 20 pm) fixed at $182.25 per oz. Converting $ to £ at a rate of 2; and oz avoirdupois to troy at an approximate rate of 16:15 gives my wife a worth of some £172,226·20 . . . and if I may say so, worth every pennyweight of it.

Yours sincerely,
A. C. A. SMITH

[Should any cleric admire the contours of Empress of Blandings, and persuade his wife to increase her weight to 15 stone, he will find her worth about £287,000]

Silent Knit

From Miss Madeau Stewart   *6 March 1978*

Sir,

After a pause of 30 years I have taken up knitting again. What was my horror when I discovered that needles are now made noiseless. Miss Marples would not approve. I regret that the opinions of the women at the Bastille are no longer available.

The varying tempo and volume of the clicketee of needles once provided an interesting and expressive accompaniment to conversation, and also introduced a form of friendly music into the solitary silence of the industrious spinster.

The technology that produced this particular suppression of sound would have been better applied to road drills. Where have all the tuneful needles gone?

Yours faithfully,
MADEAU STEWART, Spinster

Yesterday's Sounds

From Mr B. G. Guy   *18 March 1978*

Sir,

Tragic to think that the modern child can never again hear

and see the 'puffer-train', perhaps particularly the occasional joyous scream in ascending arpeggios as the big wheels skidded under the heavy load, followed by the slow, dignified crescendo as the train finally moved off. Dear old 'puffer-train'.

Yours nostalgically,
B. G. GUY

From Mrs Prudence Murray   *18 March 1978*

Sir,

My favourite song of yesterday was the portable piano, wheeled on a hand-cart by a courtly old gentleman in the Harley Street neighbourhood 20 years ago. We became friends, he played Chopin waltzes for me and he used to raise his hat with such elegant sweep and dignity that it was not easy to drop a coin into his tray without appearing condescending.

Yours faithfully,
PRUDENCE MURRAY

The Repatriation of Russian Prisoners

From Sir Bernard Braine   *3 March 1978*

[MP for Essex, South-East (Conservative)]

Sir,

All who care about the honour of our country must remain grateful for your moving article (20 February) concerning the forcible repatriation of millions of Russian prisoners and displaced persons in 1944–47, the cruelty with which the policy was enforced, and the way in which the nation was kept in complete ignorance of what was being done.

What was done was unforgivable. It is not a question of being wise after the event over mistakes made at a time when Britain was war weary and anxious to speed the return of our prisoners of war in Soviet hands; for the policy was continued after the last British prisoner came home.

It was not only that great numbers of terrified Russians were ready to take their own lives rather than to return to death, torture and the living hell of Stalin's prison camps, but that the policy resulted in thousands being handed over who were not even Soviet citizens. Well might an emigré Cossack general, our comrade in the First World War, who had lived in the

West since the 1920s, tell his NKVD interrogators at the Lubianka before his execution that he reproached himself only for having trusted the British.

In my view it would be of little use holding a tribunal of inquiry now. Some of those responsible are dead: those who live can best be left to their consciences. Certainly the vast majority of their victims are dead and those who survived the Soviet executioners are old and broken.

Equally, it would be of little use to introduce Lord Greenhill's novel suggestion (1 March) for a contemporary and confidential record of controversial events to be kept by officials. History can be and has been falsified by the destruction of documents. The truth is that in a democracy there is no substitute in government or anywhere else for integrity. After all, the plea that those who issued orders in 1944–47 were obeying higher authority was the defence of every Nazi war criminal.

There is, however, one gesture that could be made that might atone for what was done. Just as Chancellor Brandt, who of all men was totally innocent of any complicity in Nazi deeds, went down on his knees publicly at the memorial to the dead of the Warsaw ghetto, and did penance for the crimes committed in the name of the German people, so someone in our own Government, all honourable men and women who have no responsibility for what was done in the name of all of us in 1944–47, could say publicly, even now 'We are sorry – the British people did not know. We pledge ourselves to see that nothing like this happens again.'

Yours faithfully,
BERNARD BRAINE

Don't Blame the Toad

From Mrs M. E. Parsons   *17 March 1978*

Sir,

I must protest at the untrue remarks (copied from a disgraceful article in the *Daily Mirror* last year?) concerning the behaviour of toads towards gold fish which you have printed today (15 March). This is how myths are propagated and for such a paper as yours to persist in this fallacy to the detriment of the much maligned and ill treated toad is disgraceful.

I have many gold fish in two ponds. For years each spring hundreds of toads visit these little ponds engaging in eager song and dance in competition for the more rare female toads that chance their way. Frequently in warmer weather they form the extraordinary Knot of Toads which can become so heavy that it sinks to the bottom of the pond and writhes there for a time.

Never, in the closest watch upon these amazing activities of these enchanting little creatures, have I ever seen one reach out to a goldfish who stand about rather nonplussed during these goings on, or keep to a lower level of water.

Toads may clutch at other male toads in their games among the weeds, but almost immediately let go again – sensing their error of course. Should any deranged toad clutch in a most unlikely incident at a fleeting goldfish (I do not believe this tale) he would obviously let go again as he does with other male toads. If goldfish die in consequence of the invasion of toads to the ponds, let the owners consider the oxygen content of the water, and ask if it is not *that* which causes goldfish to die and give up this ridiculous notion that the fish are 'strangled'.

Please will you correct this wrong information.

Yours sincerely,
M. E. PARSONS

Nearly a Blue

From David R. Johnston-Jones   *8 April 1978*

[Rector, Morrison's Academy Boys' School, Crieff, Perthshire]

Sir,

When I taught at the Edinburgh Academy I had as colleague a fellow-linguist who was universally liked for his high scholarship, cordial disposition and absence of mind. He had actually achieved a blue at Oxford, for throwing the javelin, although his real non-academic interest was in wild flowers. He used to explain that on going up he had thought that games or athletics were compulsory and had won his blue before realizing his mistake.

Yours faithfully,
DAVID R. JOHNSTON-JONES

Is this a Rekord?

From Mr Graham Greene, CH   *24 May 1978*

Sir,

May I suggest that the number of misprints per page in an English daily newspaper would be a worthy candidate for the *Guinness Book of Records*? Just to establish a claim I nominate page 4 of *The Times* of 12 May which contains 37 misprints. They include two well worth preserving: 'entertoinment' has a fine Cockney ring and 'rampaign' combining in one word the ideas of campaign and rampage in an article on vandalism, deserves to find a permanent place in the Oxford Dictionary. I was glad to note too the firm attitude taken to juvenile delinquency – two defendents aged 3 and aged 0 were committed for trial at the Central Criminal Court.

Yours truly,
GRAHAM GREENE

['Defendents' (*sic*) – was this the compositors' revenge?]

Production Troubles at 'The Times'

From Mr David Wilson   *9 September 1977*

Sir,

The Times, Tuesday 6 September. Typesetting errors 18, spelling mistakes 35.

Is this a record?

Daily Mirror, spelling mistakes 1.

Yours faithfully,
DAVID WILSON

Exclusion from a VIP Lounge

[On 11 August 1978 Lord Ramsey of Canterbury and the Bishop of London arrived at London Airport en route to Rome where they were to attend the funeral of Pope Paul VI]

Sir,

I was astonished to read that Lord Ramsey of Canterbury, who until four years ago was Archbishop of Canterbury and Primate of All England, is not enough of a VIP to be granted the facilities of one of the five lounges set aside for distinguished visitors at Heathrow Airport. This treatment was also given to the Bishop of London, the foremost Diocesan Bishop of the Church of England, and two foreign Archbishops.

It is remarkable that one who is a Peer of the Realm, a Bishop, a Privy Councillor, and until recently came immediately after the Royal Family in precedence should be so regarded by the British Airports Authority, who recently extended this courtesy to the guerrilla leader Joshua Nkomo.

One would like to know who does qualify for VIP lounges: presumably some television 'personalities' and some entertainers? Are former Prime Ministers turned away, despite the fact that this office comes three places lower than the Primate in the Official Table of Precedence?

The British Airports Authority immediately should apologise to the Archbishops and Bishops, and overhaul their list of categories who qualify for VIP treatment.

Yours faithfully,
PATRICK W. MONTAGUE-SMITH

From Miss Anthea Lahr   *18 August 1978*

Sir,

Pontius Pilate, Herod and Caraphas would be in the VIP lounge. Jesus Christ would have been talking to the people who were waiting.

Yours faithfully,
ANTHEA LAHR

[*Debrett*'s query concerning television 'personalities' and entertainers – and, of course, pop singers – is relevant. If such persons were obliged to mix with the common rabble, they would at once be kissed, debagged and lynched by their fans. The fans of primates and bishops are more circumspect]

Notable Figures

From Mr C. E. C. Dickens   *17 June 1978*

[a more expert navigator than Mr Hastings C. Dent – see letter for 5 January 1900]

Sir,
It is not only dates that make nice patterns of numbers. Some years ago I was bringing a Destroyer home from the Far East and was required to report my position twice a day.

One evening, I saw that we would be passing close to where the Greenwich Meridian cuts the Equator so arranged to arrive there dead on midnight. Once there I altered course to due North and stopped engines so my position signal read:

At 0000 my position Latitude 00°00′N, Longitude 00°00′E. Course 000°. Speed 0.

I had considered saying I was Nowhere but thought (probably correctly) that Their Lordships would not be amused.

Yours faithfully,
CLAUD DICKENS

['Speed 0' – Their Lordships, dismissing the idea of Commander Dickens's crew being on strike, would surely have despatched a tug]

The Issues at 'The Times'

From Dr Leslie A. Hill   *29 November 1978*

Sir,
I began subscribing to *The Times* in 1936, when I was 18 years old. I chose *The Times* because I thought it gave the news with the least amount of slanting.

Since that time, I have subscribed to your paper whenever I have been able (eg not when I was a POW, nor when I was in a Gestapo gaol), and I have continued to find its presentation of the news impartial, except for a period in 1968 when a new young team of reporters allowed their enthusiasm for the student riots in Paris to lead them astray.

If now you either have to close down or submit to interference in your editorial work, I for one will not change to another British paper, but shall subscribe to the Paris edition of the *New York Herald Tribune*. I shall do this because I do not believe that the printing unions in Britain should receive any support from *Times* readers. I hope others will follow suit.

> I remain, Sir, your obedient servant,
> L. A. HILL

Brief Silence

[*The Times* begins its long day's journey into night]

From Mr Hamish McLellan   *30 November 1978*

Sir,
  The last cuckoo?

> Yours faithfully,
> HAMISH McLELLAN

❖ Spring always returns.

[The Letters Editor appropriately had the last word. As spring returned later than anticipated, a less familiar sound was heard]

Up and Away

From Mr D. J. Connolly   *13 November 1979*

Sir,
  Last Monday I believe I heard the sound of the first phoenix of the year. Who said it was extinct?
  Welcome back.

> Yours faithfully,
> D. J. CONNOLLY

The Language of Common Prayer

From the Principal of St Hugh's College, Oxford, and others
14 November 1979

Sir,
  Some of the signatories of this letter also signed the petition which was presented last week to the General Synod. But we

thought it right to address our arguments to a wider public as well.

It is becoming increasingly hard to find a church where the Authorized Version of the Bible and the Book of Common Prayer are used in main services. This, we think, is a matter for concern, whatever the merits of experimental services, since there is a manifest danger of new generations of clergy, laity, and those who profess no religious belief, being cut off from the vital linguistic sources which have animated and enriched our common culture.

The undersigned, some professing Christians, some not, are united in the belief that this is not a simple issue between a beautiful archaic language and its accessibility to present day hearers. The full meaning of the Bible cannot be conveyed in a strictly non-poetic language, and by offering it in such terms the Church inevitably deprives believers and the community at large of a spiritual dimension in which society has existed for four centuries.

We acknowledge that there is no deliberate intention on the part of the Church to destroy this linguistic heritage. We recognize the views of those who support innovations for doctrinal reasons. We know that there are some who approve changes because they believe (we think mistakenly) that the language of the age is the only language of belief available to that age.

We feel that the Church may not sufficiently appreciate that these two works are part of a literary and imaginative heritage which can only decay if they are not used as they were intended to be used. The Book of Common Prayer cannot, like Shakespeare's plays, become a set text for every school and university; it cannot be performed except as it was meant to be performed – as liturgy. The Authorized Version of the Bible, the idioms of which have passed into common speech, unless it is read as scripture in our churches, will become inaccessible, and those many vital metaphors and figurative expressions with which it has enriched the language must inevitably decay with its disuse.

No one, Christian or non-Christian, who cares for language and its ethical and imaginative function in society, can view this position with equanimity. We are not persuaded by arguments against continuity, for it seems to us that it cannot be good to cut people off from a living consciousness of their past. Such consciousness is most innocently and immediately served by the traditional usage in ceremonies which the whole

330

community requires – baptism, marriage and burial – of a liturgy and scripture with which over four centuries everyone has become familiar.

It is absurd to contend that these liturgies are less meaningfull today than when they were linguistically contemporary, if only because, from their inception, subsequent generations have kept them alive and understandable simply by usage. They can be rendered meaningless only by disuse.

Such disuse, then, will inevitably destroy far more than the doctrinal attitude from which the Prayer Book derived. We think that this is not widely enough understood. The Book of Common Prayer was composed at a peculiarly happy moment in the development of the English language. The translators of the Authorized Version of the Bible felt this themselves, and used a conservative and sometimes archaic language in order to demonstrate the importance of continuity.

We are concerned about the effect of recent innovations among all sections of the community, most of whom had their first, and sometimes only, experience of imaginative prose and its wider implications in the context of ordinary life, through their acquaintance, however cursory, with the Prayer Book and the Authorized Version of the Bible. Because we believe in the primary importance of language as a means of communication, we urge the Church to look seriously at its responsibility in this matter.

It seems to us complacent and futile to suppose that either of these two works will survive as more than antiquities outside their traditional place in church worship. We believe it would be irresponsible wholly to sacrifice their traditional influence on language and thus on society for ecumenical, sectarian, or any other reasons.

Yours faithfully,
RACHEL TRICKETT,
BLAKE,
TREND,
BASIL MITCHELL,
JOHN CAREY,
PETER STRAWSON,
JOHN BAYLEY,
IRIS MURDOCH,
MICHAEL GEARIN-TOSH,
BRIAN WILSON,
MARY WARNOCK.

Those who Write to 'The Times'

From Mr R. J. E. Taylor   *14 November 1979*

Sir,

The following information about letters to the Editor published on the centre page of *The Times* in 1978 may be of interest.

The total number of letters published in the year was 4,197, of which 3,762 were written by men and 435 by women. Just under half the total (2,090) came from London, and of these 1,618 were from addresses in London postal districts, and 116 from outer districts of Greater London. 356 letters came from the Palace of Westminster – the largest single source – 248 from the House of Commons and 108 from the House of Lords. Of letters written by Members of Parliament (from any address) 166 were from Conservative members, 76½ from Labour, seven from Liberal, two from Ulster Unionist and one Plaid Cymru. (All half units stem from letters with two joint signatories.)

Outside London, sources were classified by country, counties and leading cities – 49 in all. 140 letters were received from 40 overseas countries, of which the USA (22), France (20), the Republic of Ireland (11) and the Federal Republic of Germany (10) were the leading contributors. The top ten sources, excluding London, were as follows:

Overseas	140	Yorkshire	95
Sussex	137	Wales	93
Oxford	125	Scotland	90
Cambridge ...	103½	Kent	89
Surrey	101	Lancashire	71

In over half of the letters it was possible to identify, within broad groupings, the occupation of the sender. 49 such groups were distinguished. Easily dominant among them were academics (477) and politicians (460½), followed by administrators (325) and ecclesiastics (218). The twelve leading occupations were:

Academic	477	Medicine	91
Politics	460½	Law	90
Administration ...	325	Armed services ...	89
Ecclesiastic	218	Journalism	71
Arts	128	Local government ...	69
Trade and industry ...	119	Teaching	52

The subjects of the letters could also be classified into broad categories, of which 88 in all were recorded. Their relative positions were reckoned both by number of letters and by their length. First on both counts came international affairs (including foreign and commonwealth affairs, but not EEC), the only subject to evoke over 300 letters. The order of the rest varied somewhat according to whether the count is by numbers or by length; but in the following table of the first fifteen positions by number, the only omissions necessary if length were the criterion would be press and conservation (equal 15th), which would be replaced by nuclear policy.

The table shows the number of letters, and in brackets the number of column inches.

International affairs	...	311	(1,660)	Economic ...	133	(739)
Arts ...	...	283	(1,097)	Pay policy ...	127	(628)
Politics	...	278	(1,226)	Radical questions ...	120	(694)
Church affairs		254	(1,107)	Human rights	116	(595)
Legal matters		191	(993)	Medical ...	112	(605)
Environmental planning	...	179	(847)	EEC	85	(460)
Education	...	142	(634)	Conservation	79	(381)
Transport	...	137	(538)	Press	79	(299)

The longest letter published in the year occupied 27.3 column inches, and the shortest, 0.1 column inches.

Yours faithfully,
R. J. E. TAYLOR

An Arab's View of London

From Mr Ali Mousha Tarabassi   *19 May 1980*

Sir,

I am an Arab from Sharjah. I write to you very angry and upset about my treatment by some people here. I do not know why! Is it because of the Iran embassy siege or of the film?

The story is that I used to like to come to Britain with all my family. We love the parks and flowers, green places we don't have in Sharjah. Every year I work hard to have some money and come for holiday here with my wife and two sons, but this year I come with my wife only because she is ill.

We decided immediately to come to Britain to see a doctor. We would never spend our holiday money anywhere but Britain.

No wonder we were upset when we met the immigration officer at the airport. He was bad to us, he keep asking us questions for more than 30 minutes. We were very tired, the long flight, the waiting and my wife ill but he must to know how much money we have and where we come and where we go. My English is not quick, when I did not understand he talk quick. He said to me, and I swear it, 'we have enough ill people here to see, you go back and stay with your camel'. He never use thank you or please. British are very famous for please and thank you.

On Tuesday 6 May me and my wife standing on Baker Street waiting to go to the hotel. We cannot find taxi we wait for a bus and at 3.30 afternoon bus No 30 came. We were in queue and as we were going in the bus the conductor said no to us. He said you are rich Arabs take taxi and the people behind us went on the bus. Two people saw this, I was upset, we walk and my wife ill. Why, what happened to the British we never treat people like in home?

I am going home to be with my camel but we leave depressed and upset, my wife never come out from the hotel since Tuesday. Why, we never hate you, why hate us?

Please excuse my English, thank you.

ALI MOUSHA TARABASSI

From Sir Patrick Macrory   *22 May 1980*

[writing from The Athenaeum]

Sir,

Mr Ali Mousha Tarabassi's sad letter reporting the hostility that he has met with in this country calls not only for sympathy but for an explanation of our boorish behaviour. I can think of several reasons: –

(a) rightly or wrongly, the British believe that the Arabs in general have in recent years become immensely rich, not because of any special virtue or hard work on their part but simply because they have the good fortune to live in lands beneath whose surface there is oil in abundance; in the extraction of that oil the entrepreneurial risk-taking and all the technological skill has come from the West; the Arabs have done nothing, except jack up the price, thereby fuelling our inflation, and the richest of them are now over here buying up hotels, country houses, etc, at ludicrous prices; the idle rich, as the Arabs now seem to us, will always arouse envy;

(b) rightly or wrongly, the British have got the impression, perhaps from selective reporting, that much of the shoplifting in this country (which puts up the price to honest customers) is perpetrated by ladies from Near and Middle East countries who, when arrested, invariably turn out to have hundreds and sometimes thousands of pounds in their handbags;

(c) rightly or wrongly, the British believe that much of the infamous traffic in drugs originates in the countries of the Near and Middle East;

(d) rightly or wrongly, the British object to their country being made a battlefield for the bloodthirsty feuds of the followers of Islam, which endanger the lives of peaceful citizens as well as of our hard-stretched police and soldiers.

Let the Arabs put their house in order in these respects and I am sure that Mr Tarabassi will again find in this country the welcome which, from his letter, he so obviously deserves.

> Yours sincerely,
> PATRICK MACRORY

Horse Sense

From the Reverend I. H. G. Graham-Orlebar   26 April 1980

Sir,

Some years ago, I had a horse called Ministry so that if the Bishop called when I was out riding, he could truthfully be told: 'The Rector is out exercising his ministry.' I now have a new horse to be named. Could your readers make any suggestions along similar lines?

> Yours faithfully,
> I. H. G. GRAHAM-ORLEBAR

From Mrs J. G. Cliff Hodges   1 May 1980

Sir,

'I'm afraid the Rector is unable to see you – he's just fallen from Grace.'

> Yours faithfully,
> LINNEA CLIFF HODGES

Sir,

Considering the supposedly low level of stipends may not the Rector have gone to collect 'Social Security'?

Yours faithfully,
FRANCIS HOPKINS

From Canon George Austin   *5 May 1980*

Sir,

May I suggest that the Reverend Ian Graham-Orlebar calls his horse Praxis? Thus when the Bishop telephones he may be told that the Rector 'is developing Praxis in an on-going interface situation'. Such a use of current liberal ecclesiastical jargon will surely, by its very incomprehensibility, convince the diocesan hierarchy that here indeed is one parochial clergyman attempting to meet with contemporary society in relevant and meaningful confrontation.

Yours,
GEORGE AUSTIN

From Mrs P. C. Stephens   *9 May 1980*

Sir,

When the Rector of Barton-le-Cley is out on Parish Business (or away on Retreat), are Tact and Great Discretion exercised by his staff?

Yours faithfully,
PATSY STEPHENS

From the Reverend I. H. G. Graham-Orlebar   *13 May 1980*

Sir,

The horse is to be named Sabbatical at the suggestion of Canon Eric James of St Alban's Abbey, who thinks I need one, having been in the same parish ten years on the trot.

Yours faithfully,
I. H. G. GRAHAM-ORLEBAR

From Mr R. J. Paine   *9 May 1980*

Sir,

If the gentleman gave his correct name and address and his Bishop reads *The Times*, whatever he calls his horse the game is up.

Yours faithfully,
R. J. PAINE

Fear of Debasement

From Mr Milton Shulman   *26 September 1980*

Sir,

In your leader commending the Government for acceding to Welsh nationalist demands for a Welsh dominated fourth television channel (18 September), and in Bernard Levin's pungent disagreement with that decision (23 September), there is an implied assumption that the Welsh language would be enhanced and the Welsh heritage preserved by the wider dissemination of Welsh on television. What concrete evidence is there to support that assumption? All the available evidence points in exactly the opposite direction.

In every highly industrialized country where television has been free to act primarily as a source of entertainment for the masses its impact on language, culture and logic has been more deleterious than beneficial. Let me list some of the consequences of this type of television.

1. Reading skills amongst the young, in spite of massive increases in spending on education, have remained static or deteriorated.

2. Serious novels and poetry have become even more of a minority art form than they were before the advent of television. The standard of novels has seriously deteriorated and fewer publishers are interested in financing them.

3. Conversation between members of a family, and particularly between parents and children, has diminished. Every survey that has assessed the activities of individuals when they are deprived of television reveals that there has been an immediate rise in the volume of conversation between parents and children.

4. Language through the infiltration of expletives, obscenities and cliches has become vulgarized.

5. Television has been positively and scientifically identified

as a major contributor to the increase of violence in society, particularly amongst the young.

6. To many, television has become a daily fix or habit, deterring them from engaging in the other multiple leisure activities available in a civilized society. It encourages a spectator, rather than a participant, population.

In totalitarian societies, or in countries where television has been used primarily as an information or educative medium, it has tended to become a bureaucratic arm of governments, to be deployed as a means of propaganda or a weapon of state control.

Why do Mr Gwynfor Evans and his supporters believe that the Welsh heritage and language will escape the fate of so many other 'telly' societies? Is there a patriotic Welshman prepared to starve to death in protest against a Welsh-dominated television channel and the potential debasement of all he holds dear?

Yours faithfully,
MILTON SHULMAN

The Nervous Strain of Being a Tea-Boy

From Mr Beverley Nichols   *19 August 1980*

Sir,

My acquaintance with tea-boys, alas, is not extensive, but I have long admired their expertise, and the dedication with which they perform their vital services. Where would British industry be without them?

Imagine, therefore, my shock on learning from a successful industrialist, the shameful conditions under which they are employed and the ludicrous pittance they are asked to accept.

Their hours of work – though not legally 'unsocial' – are arduous. Two hours *every* morning from 10 to 12, two hours *every* afternoon, from three to five.

They are subjected to great nervous strain. Placing the tea-bags in the pots, bringing the water to the boil, pouring the water on the bags, arranging the cups on the tray (in the case of my industrialist friend no less than 11 cups), calculating the amount of sugar needed and the correct quantity of milk.

Finally – as if all this were not enough – carrying the tray with the 11 cups for a distance of nearly 20 yards along an uncarpeted corridor, with no assistance, in all weathers.

And how much are these gallant young people being offered for their efforts? A paltry £80 a week! This is of course slave labour, and I am happy to report that up till now it has been scornfully rejected. A recent advertisement attracted only four applicants. Two, having no English, walked out as soon as the terms were translated. The others, obviously rendered speechless by the insult, shrugged their shoulders and returned to the dole queue.

This, Sir, is a true story. I can supply the name and address of my informant but he has warned me that if the facts were published his entire work-force would go on strike.

Yours faithfully,
BEVERLEY NICHOLS

P.S. As a step in the right direction, may I suggest that the phrase 'tea-boy', which has its distinctly racialist undertones, should be banned by law. They should be described as 'infusion experts' and suitably remunerated.

Heart-warming

[William Howard Russell of *The Times* was war correspondent in the Crimea when, in the words of Shaw's General Burgoyne, 'the British soldier can stand up to anything except the British War Office]

From Lieutenant-Colonel J. F. W. Wilsey   31 October 1980

Sir,

We remember that your correspondent in the Crimean Peninsula was kind enough to supply all members of our Regiment (the 39th of Foot) with winter underwear at a time of crisis during that campaign.

It has been brought to our notice that it is now you that face crisis and are concerned that winter might catch you unprotected. Please inform us if we can be of assistance.

Yours faithfully,
J. F. W. WILSEY,
Commanding 1st Bn The Devonshire
and Dorset Regiment (Her Majesty's
11th, 39th and 54th of Foot),
Roman Barracks,
Colchester, Essex

HOW TO GET A LETTER IN *THE TIMES*

[Readers now inspired to write a letter to *The Times* with some future anthology in mind (perhaps *The Second Cuckoo*?) may be grateful for advice]

From Mr J. Armour-Milne   *26 January 1970*

Sir,

You're joking. You must be. 'Who will be writing to *The Times* tonight?' is printed on the face of an envelope containing a letter to me from *The Times*. The letter 'assures you that your remarks were read with interest'. But not sufficient interest to warrant publication. I wonder why when one considers the amount of drivel that is to be found in the Letters to the Editor.

Three times in my life I have written a letter to the Editor. Three times he has found my letter interesting, but not sufficiently so to warrant publication.

The first was on the subject of east Germany, on which I have had a book published. Probably I was not considered an expert on east Germany.

The second was a protest, and an invitation to others to do so, against the victimization of Lieutenant-Colonel Emil Zátopek, the Czechoslovak Olympic athlete. Presumably I was not considered an expert, although, in Prague itself, at the height of his career and for seven years, I advised Zátopek on his training. And wrote two books on sport in Czechoslovakia under the communists.

The third, recently, was a reply to Sir Peter Mursell, a member of the Royal Commission on Local Government, on the implications of the Maud Report. Again, I assume, I was not regarded as an authority on the subject, although the Guardian has given a pen picture of my work against Maud spread over four columns and I have been invited to debate Maud with Lord Redcliffe-Maud at University College, Oxford, of which he is Master.

What does one have to do in order to be recognized by the Editor of *The Times*? Bring about a counter-revolution in communist east Germany? Run faster than Zátopek? Become chairman of a new Royal Commission on Local Government in England?

Yours faithfully,
J. ARMOUR-MILNE

First and Foremost

From Miss Sylvia Margolis   *28 January 1970*

Sir,

The answer to Mr J. Armour-Milne's question is simple.

Last year I had two letters published in *The Times* and I've been dining out on them ever since. They involved me in an exchange of letters of ever-increasing lunacy with other correspondents. I can bear witness that the prime qualification you need to get letters published in *The Times* is eccentricity.

Yours faithfully,
SYLVIA MARGOLIS

Closed Shop?

From Mr W. P. Courtauld   *28 January 1970*

Sir,

Mr J. Armour-Milne asks what does one have to do in order to be recognized by the Editor.

The short answer would seem to be either a Member of Parliament or of the Athenaeum. Needless to say I am neither one myself.

Yours faithfully,
W. P COURTAULD

[Correspondents writing from the House of Commons or the Athenaeum are outnumbered three to one in these pages by academics and clerics. This may of course indicate that the latter are underemployed]

Deterrent

From Mr P. H. H. Moore   *28 January 1970*

Sir,

Mr J. Armour-Milne refers to 'the amount of drivel that is to be found in the Letters to the Editor'.

Whether or not you, in fact, publish drivel is not for me to decide, but a sure method of raising the standard of letters that you receive would be not only to publish your usual selection of letters, but also to print, each day, a complete list of the names of those correspondents whose letters you have rejected.

The thought of possibly being included in your Rejects List, and then to have one's acquaintances saying, 'I see that you have had yet another letter refused by *The Times*', would be too much of a risk for most people.

Yours faithfully,
P. H. H. MOORE

Homage

From Mr J. S. Hocknell   *29 January 1970*

Sir,

In his letter Mr J. Armour-Milne asks 'What does one have to do to be recognized by the Editor of *The Times*?'

I hope nothing will move you to answer such a presumptuous question.

The criteria by which you recognize your correspondents are no more to be bandied about by ordinary people than those governing the nomination of bishops, Royal Commissioners, Presidents of MCC or even newspaper editors.

I had not intended to reveal that I have been making a study of what I like to imagine is your epistolary policy. But Mr Armour-Milne has forced my hand.

Until it can be published (perhaps in your pages?), I ask him to ponder his fortune. To have received your invariably courteous but *private* acknowledgement of 'interest' is to have moved in the foothills of immortality. Only grosser spirits would seek public proof of your editorial regard.

Yours faithfully,
JOHN HOCKNELL

The Penalty

From Mr Thomas Frankland   *3 January 1970*

Sir,

   Aspirant contributors to your correspondence column should beware. My last letter, on conserving British butterflies, a rather esoteric matter, produced 63 replies – from as far afield as Iran, Kenya and St Helena. It took me a fortnight to write suitable replies. I vowed never again to subject myself to such possibilities; the vow is broken only to protect, dissuade and enlighten.

Yours faithfully,
THOMAS FRANKLAND

Animal, Vegetable or Mineral

From Mr Hockley Clarke   *31 January 1970*

   [editor, *Birds and Country Magazine*]

Sir,

   It may be of interest to state that I have been privileged to have had over 40 letters published in *The Times*, and to indicate some of the subjects to which they referred: birds, animals, tomato plants, bats, caterpillars, hotels, the Christmas post, chemical sprays, railway closures, wintering in England, &c.

I am, Sir, yours faithfully,
HOCKLEY CLARKE

An Outcome

From Mrs Mary Powell   *31 January 1970*

Sir,

   If my husband had not written to *The Times* on 16 January 1930, there might never have been a Crossword Puzzle to intrigue your readers.

Yours faithfully,
MARY E. POWELL

[The *Times* Crossword Puzzle dates from 1 February 1930]

Definition

From Gimpel Fils   *31 January 1970*

Sir,

René Gimpel (1881–1945) – French art dealer, collector and diarist – was a noted Anglophile.

His sons remember his definition of an English gentleman: 'A man with a passion for horses, playing with a ball, probably one broken bone in his body and in his pocket a letter to *The Times*.'

Yours faithfully,
GIMPEL FILS

Royal Nod

From Mrs Helen Reid   *4 February 1970*

Sir,

King George V, approached by a friend who hoped that a word from His Majesty in the right quarter would solve a difficulty, said 'My dear fellow, I can't help you! You'd better write to *The Times*.'

I have the honour to be, Sir,

Your obedient servant,
HELEN REID

THE FUTURE

From Mr G. E. Christ   *12 December 1968*

Sir,

The situation is of course serious. But we need not despair.

You say 'We are picnicking on Vesuvius'; and that we have 'pitched our tents on thin ice'. Surely any nation able to perform such a remarkable feat is capable of anything.

Yours, &c.,
GEORGE E. CHRIST

INDEX OF SUBJECTS

experimental theatre 278–8

353

INDEX OF CORRESPONDENTS

AMAZING TIMES!
A selection of the most amusing and amazing articles from *The Times*

Chosen by Stephen Winkworth
Illustrated by ffolkes

The kangaroo which stole a five pound note, the soldier who stowed his girlfriend in his kitbag, artificial icebergs, the penicillin black market in Berlin, the golden eagle which travelled in a laundry basket, how the Vatican was invaded by white ants, the elephant that water-skied, the couple who lived in a tree, the 101 year old lady who slid down banisters, the curry which turned a girl pink . . . Add to that Lucky Luciano's funeral, the last days of Nijinsky, Casanova's autobiography, Picasso's painting machine, the curse of the Hope diamond and the founding of the Order of the Mosquito . . . and you have Amazing Times!

'wry effectiveness . . . the human interest is rich'
The Observer

'fascinating stuff'
Manchester Evening News

NEW WORDS FOR OLD
Philip Howard

In this witty and elegant survey of new vogue words which assail the eyes and the ears, Philip Howard examines the changing English language. That it continually renews itself is admirable. But do we need, let alone enjoy, such horrific words as 'prestigious', 'hopefully', 'ambience', 'perameter' and 'syndrome' in their new, bastardised senses?

Philip Howard raises other questions. What, for instance, is a student? What pitfalls gape before the casual advertiser, applying for the services of a duke (or, for that matter, a duchess)? What about 'gay' and 'camp'? What is 'obscene'? What constitutes 'hysteria'? Would the world of the sports writer crumble to dust if he were no longer allowed to exaggerate (for instance, would our lives be the poorer if we were denied a sentence like 'Irish can give underdogs added bite in their heroism of despair')? As Mr Howard discovered, when he began to air his doubts about certain linguistic trends in the columns of *The Times*, people do care about the misuse of words. Now he has revised and rewritten his ironic and sometimes savage pieces to form an essential primer – essential and entertaining.

HIGH LIFE, LOW LIFE
Taki and Jeffrey Bernard

Taki and Jeffrey Bernard observe contemporary society with a sharp eye and a sharper wit. Their columns, which appear together in the *Spectator*, and various other publications in Britain and America, range over fact and gossip, private victories and public disasters. Taki moves among the rich and famous and between New York, London and Gstaad. Jeff records one trip to Barbados, but normally he can be found in Soho or the racing village of Lambourn. But their worlds overlap: gambling, sport and sex figure prominently in both − and in these pages − and they are equally concerned with the dramatic changes in English life and society. It is above all an uproariously funny book.